Narrating Human Rights in Africa

Narrating Human Rights in Africa claims human rights from the perspective of artists from the African continent and situates the key theoretical concepts in African perspectives, undercutting the stereotypes of victimhood and voicelessness.

Instead of positioning literary texts as illustrative of points already theorized elsewhere, the author foregrounds the literature itself to show the concepts it offers, the ideas and responses stemming from complex historical circumstances in Africa and expressed by African writers. The book focuses on how narrative creates new categories of thought challenging human rights dogma, whereas the sum of the literary voices evoked also stands by the values of social justice and protection of human rights. The chapters take up key challenges to the narration of human rights in which the contribution of African writers is particularly important. This includes human dignity in the resistance to apartheid, the figure of the child soldier, how humanitarianism affects representational strategies of contemporary African writers, the challenge of testifying about rape in war, how to evoke the disappeared body of the torture victim, the centrality of flight in the refugee and migrant experiences, and finally the long shadow of the "heart of darkness" motif.

Offering a sustained examination of the narrative treatment of key human rights concerns as expressed by African writers, this book will be of interest to scholars of African literature, postcolonial studies, African studies, and human rights

Eleni Coundouriotis is a professor in the Department of English at the University of Connecticut, USA.

Routledge Contemporary Africa Series

Greening Industrialization in Sub-Saharan Africa
Ralph Luken and Edward Clarence-Smith

Health and Care in Old Age in Africa
Edited by Pranitha Maharaj

Rethinking African Agriculture
How Non-Agrarian Factors Shape Peasant Livelihoods
Edited by Goran Hyden, Kazuhiko Sugimura and Tadasu Tsuruta

Toward an Animist Reading of Postcolonial Trauma Literature
Reading Beyond the Single Subject
Jay Rajiva

Development-induced Displacement and Human Rights in Africa
The Kampala Convention
Romola Adeola

Death and the Textile Industry in Nigeria
Elisha P. Renne

Modern Representations of Sub-Saharan Africa
Edited by Lori Maguire, Susan Ball and Sébastien Lefait

Narrating Human Rights in Africa
Eleni Coundouriotis

Higher Education and Policy for Creative Economies in Africa
Developing Creative Economies
Edited by Roberta Comunian, Brian J. Hracs and Lauren England

For more information about this series, please visit: https://www.routledge.com/
Routledge-Contemporary-Africa/book-series/RCAFR

Narrating Human Rights in Africa

Eleni Coundouriotis

Routledge
Taylor & Francis Group

LONDON AND NEW YORK

First published 2021
by Routledge
2 Park Square, Milton Park, Abingdon, Oxon OX14 4RN

and by Routledge
52 Vanderbilt Avenue, New York, NY 10017

Routledge is an imprint of the Taylor & Francis Group, an informa business

© 2021 Eleni Coundouriotis

British Library Cataloguing-in-Publication Data
A catalogue record for this book is available from the British Library

Library of Congress Cataloging-in-Publication Data
A catalog record has been requested for this book

ISBN: 978-0-367-19466-6 (hbk)
ISBN: 978-0-429-20258-2 (ebk)

Typeset in Times New Roman
by MPS Limited, Dehradun

Contents

Acknowledgements

This book came together over an extended period. Its core material appeared first in the form of a series of essays that were published in a range of journals with different disciplinary homes in law and the humanities. Assembling and significantly revising the earlier essays into a book while also adding new material enabled me to define more clearly what my interventions as a scholar of comparative literature are in the field of human rights. Moreover, it brought into focus the engagement of these reflections with Africa and the intersection of my work as a scholar of postcolonial literature and history.

The work would have been impossible without the contributions of my colleagues at the Human Rights Institute at the University of Connecticut. The intellectual life at the institute has shaped every chapter in direct and indirect ways, and has been definitive in my formation as a scholar in the last 15 years. Some colleagues have moved on to other institutions, but I cherish what they taught me and, in some instances, my continued collaborations with them. I thank all these scholars for pushing me to think more clearly and for their inspiring engagement: Kerry Bystrom, Emma Gilligan, Shareen Hertel, Elizabeth Holzer, Molly Land, Kathryn Libal, Samuel Martinez, Glenn Mitoma, Serena Parekh, David L. Richards, Sara Silverstein, Katharina von Hammerstein, Sarah Willen, Richard A. Wilson, Sarah Winter, and Sebastian Wogenstein. The Research Program on Humanitarianism at the Human Rights Institute has been a particularly productive space, and I thank especially Kerry Bystrom and Sarah Winter for leading the program and supporting my turn as director. I also thank the Human Rights Institute for the research funds that enabled me to bring this book to completion.

Two professional organizations provided me with repeated occasions to test my ideas over this extended period: the American Comparative Literature Association and the African Literature Association. The panels and seminars that I organized and participated in are too numerous to mention, but I want to note these organizations' consistent support of original lines of inquiry. Their international and interdisciplinary scope have been crucial to developing a conversation about human rights that goes beyond the established discourse.

I owe special thanks to Bert Lockwood, editor of *Human Rights Quarterly*, for publishing my work over the years and for his openness to the humanities. Continued conversations with Joseph R. Slaughter have also meaningfully impacted this book and I am grateful for his careful shepherding of "Congo Cases" (now Chapter 2) to publication. Sophia A. McClennen and Alexandra Schultheis Moore supported my work on refugee narratives, and I greatly benefited from their feedback. An invitation from Crystal Parikh to speak at the "Symposium on Archives, Institutions, Imaginaries: Human Rights and Literature" at New York University in 2018 gave me a valuable opportunity to develop my ideas on Assia Djebar and human rights. My colleague Bhakti Shringarpure has been a valuable interlocutor and I am grateful for her spirited engagement. Thanks also to Michael Bronner for his comments on my work on *Guantánamo Diary*.

The anonymous readers for the press gave me very useful feedback and meaningful support, for which I am very appreciative. Marlene Eberhart's work on creating a stylistically uniform manuscript was invaluable. My editor at Routledge, Leanne Hinves, was instrumental in bringing this book to fruition and I thank her for the encouragement.

This book was completed during the 2020 COVID-19 crisis and the Black Lives Matter protests. I will always remember the long weeks at home with my spouse, Tom Recchio, and our son, Thomas, as a special time of togetherness when we kept each other going, but also as a time of deep angst and political distress. This was the backdrop that drove my effort to argue succinctly and honestly for human rights. Tom's readiness to read my never-ending drafts was especially meaningful and helped sustain my motivation. Thomas's perseverance in his studies, like that of so many college students in the Spring 2020 semester, was a constant reminder of why teaching and research go together, mutually reinforcing the goals of inquiry and learning.

***

I would like to thank the following presses for allowing me to reprint material published earlier. Each of these essays has been revised and updated for publication in this book.

Chapter 1, "The Dignity of the 'Unfittest:' Victims' Stories in South Africa," Copyright © 2006 by The Johns Hopkins University Press. This article was first published in *Human Rights Quarterly*, 28, no. 4 (2006): 842–867. Reprinted with permission by Johns Hopkins University Press.

Chapter 2, "Congo Cases: The Stories of Human Rights History" was first published in *Humanity: An International Journal of Human Rights, Humanitarianism, and Development* 3, no. 2 (2012): 133–153. Reprinted with permission by the University of Pennsylvania Press.

Chapter 3, "The Child Soldier Narrative and the Problem of Arrested Historicization—An Argument Revisited" is significantly revised from the earlier version, "The Child Soldier Narrative and the Problem of Arrested Historicization" which appeared in the *Journal of Human Rights* 9, no. 2: 191-206, Taylor & Francis Ltd, http://www.tandfonline.com. Reprinted with permission of the publisher.

Chapter 4, "Improbable Figures: Realist Fictions of Insecurity in Contemporary African Fiction" was originally published in *NOVEL* 49, no. 2: 236–261. Copyright, 2016, Novel, Inc. All rights reserved. Republished with permission of the copyright holder, and the present publisher, Duke University Press. www.dukeupress.edu.

Chapter 5, "The Refugee Experience and Human Rights Narrative" is expanded and revised from "In Flight: The Refugee Experience and Human Rights Narrative," which appeared in *The Routledge Companion to Literature and Human Rights*, edited by Sophia A. McClennen and Alexandra Schultheis Moore, 78–85. New York: Routledge, 2015. Reprinted with permission of the publisher, Taylor & Francis Informa, UK Limited-Books.

Chapter 6, "'You Only Have Your Word:' Rape and Testimony," Copyright © 2013 by The Johns Hopkins University Press. An earlier version of the chapter was first published in *Human Rights Quarterly,* 35, no. 2 (2013): 365–385. Reprinted with permission by Johns Hopkins University Press.

Chapter 7, "Torture and Textuality: *Guantánamo Diary* as Postcolonial Text" first appeared in *Textual Practice*, 15 February 2019: 1–20. Web. DOI: 10.1080/0950236X.2019.1580216, Taylor & Francis Ltd, http://www.tandfonline.com. Reprinted with permission of the publisher.

Introduction
Narrating human rights in Africa

> Over the three days, many people who had been the victims of torture came to Freedom Corner and began to tell their stories. "What you do not know," they said, pointing to Nyayo House, a government building opposite the Nyayo Monument in Uhuru Park and immediately across the road from Freedom Corner, "is that underneath that house are torture chambers ...."
> ... While some of us knew, or at least suspected, that such things were happening, it was nevertheless shocking to hear the details. However, some were hearing the information for the first time, and people could barely believe the horrific stories they were being told by fellow citizens.
>
> Wangari Maathai, *Unbowed*

In early 1992, Wangari Maathai, founder of The Greenbelt Movement and future Nobel Peace Prize laureate, threw her support behind the Release Political Prisoners campaign in Kenya, an effort initiated by mothers of detained democracy activists. Committed as ever to peaceful protest, Maathai accompanied five mothers to the Attorney General of Kenya, met with him, and then announced that the group would wait for the promised release of the prisoners at Uhuru Park. Equipped with bedding to spend the night, the women encamped in this important public space of Nairobi where Maathai erected a simple sign on a large board declaring the spot "Freedom Corner" (Maathai 2007, 219–220).

What followed was a spontaneous outpouring of testimony by passersby accusing the government of human rights abuses taking place literally across the street, in a basement hidden from view. The circumstance itself is extraordinary and displays signatures of Maathai's leadership: her principled solidarity responding to the protest rising from below, the simple declarative gesture, and patient persistence. However, the narrated account of this episode is also remarkable and exhibits many qualities that are the focus of this book concerned with narrating human rights in Africa. Maathai is an important witness and her documentation of this protest is certainly valuable as a record of what happened. Her narration,

however, goes further than documentation. She is the shaper of meaning on multiple levels.

Although a participant and leader of the event, Maathai never ceases also to be an observer and ultimately becomes the teller of its story, shaping the event's import. In the how of her narration, she illuminates a particular series of actions converging to expose truths that the full force of the state attempted to hide. Moreover, her story contains the stories of others: it narrates elements of the testimony of those who came forth, putting it in quotation marks and preserving those voices. Reflecting on what made this a significant moment, Maathai shows how the event cohered for her, and now possibly for us, into a scene conveying a collective stance against harm. Thus, she offers a narrative of intention and contingency shaping something new: standing across the way from the torture chambers was fortuitous, and the spontaneous up swell of witnesses to torture a surprise. In that convergence, something unexpected happened: an occasion of witnessing formed that brought a fluid cross-section of Nairobi's public into the orbit of truths unmasking state violence. More than the facts about torture, Maathai's narration stresses expression and connection, how people come together around a significant revelation. Retrospective narration that illuminates human action in this manner creates a powerful common reference point on which to build ongoing solidarity for the respect of a dignified life.

This book examines many such impactful texts that come from a range of voices: activists, memoirists, survivors, and, most of all, creative artists (novelists, in particular), all of whom engage with the meaning of human rights in the lived, historical experience on the African continent. Luminous narrative moments, such as Maathai's encapsulation of the Freedom Corner protest, stand apart as something added to the actual events they recount, offering retrospection and reflection. They operate by signaling that they are drawing the full meaning of an event after the fact and invite us to engage with that realization as a new encounter with what happened. Although sometimes instrumentalized for advocacy, such narratives do not collapse back into the events they talk about as coterminous with them. They exceed the occasion as discourse available long past the event and arrive to us in a new context. It is important to assert this integrity or distinctness to ward off received ideas that can potentially override these texts' meanings. Such pitfalls include the pattern of representing Africa as a place of extremes of violence, poverty, and disorder where little to no reason arises; the objectifying tendency of the discourse that categorizes subjects exclusively as victims, perpetrators, or saviors; and a persistent insistence on seeing human rights as entirely western, hence not fully owned, claimed, or shaped by Africans themselves.

By closely examining Africans' narration of human rights, we find a deep engagement with the meaning of rights and the fuller historicity of individuals, captured through their expression and thought. A human rights regime with rigid protocols of communication, however, frequently elides or

coopts these voices. Human rights activists tend to stress documentation and to be suspicious of narrative. This suspicion operates on several levels by determining what types of testimonies have value. It looks at story and fiction as coextensive and hence delegitimizes narrative as subjective, and it attributes affect and sentimentalism to narrative, further diminishing it (Dudai 2009, 253). In the realm of publishing, marketing drives what comes to be perceived as human rights inflected fiction, which results in troubling trends especially as regards the representations of gender.[1] Whether in an overly legalized dispensation or a widely implemented humanitarian governmentality that takes up speaking for others, such protocols of communication reinforce the pattern of seeing Africa as "a 'dark continent' against which the lightness and whiteness of 'Western civilization' can be pictured" (Ferguson 2006, 2).

This construal, moreover, has an almost infinite capacity to renew itself, especially in relation to human rights, and calls for our constant vigilance. Its tenacity drives an ascendant critique in response, which breaks with the unfulfilled progress narratives of modernization and development. As Joseph R. Slaughter notes, discursive structures centered in the West have corollaries in the "Enlightenment human rights progress narratives" and the "diffusionist model" from their origin in the Universal Declaration of Human Rights (UDHR) (2018, 737, 748). The critique of Eurocentrism, moreover, urges us to rethink the relationship between the real and representation. The objective of this study, then, is to show how African voices and viewpoints shape the way we think about human rights and are hence consequential in influencing their meaning. As a starting point, it heeds the critique that radically reorients us to the real in Africa and creates conditions for a greater receptivity to Africans' perspectives beyond the dominance of legalism and humanitarianism.

Moving away from description

How to dislodge from received ideas of the real in Africa entails developing a hesitance towards descriptive discourse. James Ferguson posits a post-empirical orientation, shifting away from paradigms of Africa as "empirical territory," or "culture region, or historical civilization." Instead, he suggests we think through Africa "as a category that (like all categories) is historically and socially constructed (indeed, in some sense arbitrary), but also a category that is 'real,' that is imposed with force, that has a mandatory quality; a category within which, and according to which, people must live." From this purview, Africa then is a "category through which a 'world' is structured" (2006, 5). What Ferguson means by "real" and "category" are of particular interest as human rights narration *makes real* to readers events and situations whose extremity often seems unreal and, hence, the worry is, easily denied or distanced. Ferguson stresses the formative impact that ideas about Africa end up having on African lives. If Africa is a category—a set of

historically constructed associations that shape it, then the "category" funnels the "real." In simpler terms, the category Africa mediates the "real" and, as a result, the realism of human rights narrative is a construct as well.

Furthermore, Ferguson calls for grappling with Africa's "place-in-the-world" where "world" stands for "a more encompassing categorical system [Ferguson purposefully eschews the term 'globe'] within which countries and geographical regions have their 'places,' with a 'place' understood as both a location in space and a rank in a system of social categories (as in the expression 'knowing your place') ..." (2006, 6). It follows that this place is not freely chosen but a "forcefully imposed position," and hence can be thought of as a historical constraint (6). At the level of the individual, an awareness of their "place-in-the-world" becomes a measure by which individual subjects orient their aspirations and make choices about how to live (6). Human rights, I suggest, offers one way to assess this measure. Moreover, the value of Ferguson's "place-in-the-world" is that it prioritizes the scholar's extreme attentiveness to situated points of view that take into account complex global vectors. It then breaks open the possibility for a reciprocal understanding that exposes disparity but also emphasizes recognition. If the foundation of a human rights practice is human dignity (a topic I return to below), Ferguson's proposal is a good springboard for its emphasis on reciprocity.

Achille Mbembe's trenchant diagnosis of Africa as an "absent object" (from which Ferguson draws extensively) offers more cautionary lessons (2001, 241). What V. Y. Mudimbe earlier called the "invention of Africa" through the "discourses of competence" of European anthropologists contributes to the "absent object." For Mudimbe, this is less a misdescription than an outright "invention," a fictive world (Mudimbe 1988, 175–176). Mbembe projects the consequences and compiling effects of this operation. Thus, how can we meaningfully grapple with Africa historically? Trying to discern the "self-determination" of Africans, Mbembe says "we find ourselves thrown back on the figures of the shadow, into those spaces where one perceives something, but where *this thing* is impossible to make out—as in a phantasm, at the exact point in the split between the visible and graspable, the perceived and the tangible" (2001, 241, italics in original). Africa as "absent object" draws attention to the disjunction between how we talk about Africa and the lived reality: they are permanently out of sync, which makes the possibility of the real recede from our grasp to such a degree that it can barely be apprehended as a shadow of itself, if that. Hence, we are always confronting a "chimera" (241). Offering this as a diagnosis of Africanist discourse at the end of the twentieth century, Mbembe concludes that "there is no description of Africa that does not involve destructive or mendacious functions" because it is impossible to maneuver around the problem of the "absent object" (242).

Importantly, however, this is a problem of lived experience, not of representation alone. Life is lived wavering between the "imaginary realized

and the real imagined … This interweaving takes place in life" (Mbembe 2001, 242). Mbembe's refusal of positivism is not antithetical to the mode of writing human rights that I explore. It is often adopted by writers who seek to capture the liminality created by extreme events that place one on a threshold or tipping point, the turn of catastrophe. Exploring this indeterminacy is a way to resist the erasure that catastrophe threatens.

Maathai's narration of the Freedom Corner protest foregrounds a moment where the demarcation of the quotidian from some parallel, hidden reality (the "dangerous dark" of the torture chamber posited by human rights [Marks 2013, 230]) is sharp, destabilizing the "real imagined" which appears as the quotidian. My focus, however, is on what Maathai does to take this scene beyond the formula of "shin[ing] a light into these hidden spaces" of secret detention and torture (Marks 2013, 230). The human rights "myth of the dangerous dark" operates from the presumption that there are two spheres, one open and the other hidden, and that human rights penetrates the secrecy of the state to expose its abuses. Whereas this type of shadow may bear a superficial resemblance to Mbembe's, its dualism is misleading. As Susan Marks argues, the worst abuses might be out in the open, escaping the scrutiny of those looking only for those dark spaces (2013, 230–231). Writing after torture became a widely recognized fact of the Daniel Arap Moi regime, Maathai is not exposing the "dangerous dark" in *Unbowed*. Instead, she is depicting a moment when the "real" breaks through and is discernible in the citizens' converging understanding. Fleeting and precarious (the state attacked the protesters and drove them out of the park), this moment does not describe the real that is hidden but a scene witnessed by Maathai. Avoiding instantiating another discourse about Africa that may "not necessarily [be] applicable to [its] object," another chimera, or fantasy (Mbembe 2001, 242), Maathai carefully delimits what claims she can make about the event even as she honors what is extraordinary about the spontaneous bursting into voice of the participants. A better way to read Maathai, then, is to drive a wedge between description and narration the way canonical theorists of realism have done, and thus to move with the dynamism of the action, the sense of an arc to a story, and in this case, to the moment of converging recognition. The coming together as event rather than the exposure of torture (as a "real" discovered) makes this a significant moment of human rights narration.

The wedge between description and narration separates the determinism of naturalist discourses from realism and historicism. A naturalist aesthetics is bound to description by hewing to the determinants of biological and social environments. According to Georg Lukács, description as manifested in naturalism inhibits a portrayal of characters as agents. "The dramatic element," which showcases characters in action in their particular setting and thus lends realism its historical dynamism, cannot develop in naturalism as the characters remain subordinated to that environment, one that is, moreover, prone to be viewed through the lens of "catastrophe," or crisis

(Lukács 1971, 118, 122). Narrative, by contrast, is "committed to action," which includes the mental processes of characters (Schmitt 2016, 104).[2] In this light, the environment of state terror, the torture cell, is the naturalist setting, wholly determined by the unchecked force of the state. The classic literary example is South African Alex La Guma's depiction of the torture chamber in *In the Fog of the Seasons' End*, which according to J. M. Coetzee, exposed the "inner sanctum of the terroristic state" (Coetzee 1992, 358). The determinism of such fiction precludes the characters' escape from their fate, but at the same time registers the author's resistance and protest to the regime by vividly portraying harm and human suffering.

Njabulo Ndebele's influential essay defining the post-apartheid literary project as the "rediscovery of the ordinary" demonstrates how the shift from naturalism to realism is also a shift to an increased narrativity.[3] Ndebele calls for the abandonment of documentary "protest fiction" such as La Guma's and outlines an aesthetic that aims to surprise with "rediscovery," putting us back in touch with the rhythms of daily life obscured by the protracted anti-apartheid struggle that had been insistently in the foreground (1994, 53). He places the arc of ordinary lives against a backdrop of persistent poverty and insecurity after the end of apartheid and urges the reader to look for how story emerges from the unspectacular.

This goal captures another key dimension of narrating human rights in Africa: the avoidance of spectacle. Narrative frequently, therefore, also checks a tendency to rely too much on images. Images should prompt us to ask for a story or context to explain them; they should not speak for themselves. Thus, urging that we read images historically rather than by classifying them as types, Ariella Azoulay warns against the "justifying photograph." Such images used by human rights organizations, for example, seem to distill the violation to an essence in order to legitimate the human rights intervention. The same image, however, might circulate elsewhere and for a different purpose, showing that "photographs do not speak, and justification of any sort is never present within a photograph" (Azoulay 2013, 675–676). By contrast, narrative effort declares its gestures of ownership over meaning, imbuing it with point of view and anchoring it in a historical perspective that invites us to define ours as readers in response and come into relation with it.

Narrative meanings of human rights

An obvious place to look for narrative meaning is the historiography of human rights. Debates within the field pit different histories of human rights against each other, vying for narrative authority. An effort to decolonize the narrative of human rights is most relevant to my concerns here as it tries to wrest back some authority over the meaning of rights by contesting the origin stories that locate human rights only in Europe and America. Who tells the history is part of the challenge, but not the only issue. Edward W. Said noted the problem of accessing the "permission to narrate" for subjects and constituencies marginalized by dominant discourses. Moreover, "[f]acts do not at all speak for themselves, but require a socially acceptable narrative to absorb, sustain, and circulate them" (1994, 254). It follows, therefore, that certain facts would have trouble adhering or attaching to those narratives that are able to circulate. This matching of fact to narrative exposes how story-telling convention structures meaning and hence exerts a constraint.

At a moment when there is valuable revisionism in the field casting doubt on the Eurocentric progress narrative of human rights, the field has also, according to Slaughter, collapsed within itself and become more exclu-sionary as a result. The problem stems from an inability or unwillingness to recognize the narrative authority of different points of view. By discrediting self-determination as a human right and executing a "rollback" that narrows the scope of human rights to the supranational individual rights held against states, recent historiography has accomplished nothing less than a "hi-jacking," a capture of the meaning of rights that renders the Global South mute and puts it in a position to receive once more the tutelage of the North (Slaughter 2018, 764–765). Echoing a broad sentiment among postcolonial scholars, Slaughter also explains that "accounts which treat human rights as a single coherent discourse or a clear canonical set of international legal texts inevitably oversimplify the immeasurable complicated interactions among innumerable historical agents that contribute to the various com-mitments that people call human rights" (737). To identify these "various commitments" is not a matter of defamiliarizing what we know as human rights, but of complicating their narrative so that it reflects common un-derstandings and the less precise terms of non-technical discourses.

In the effort to make Global South claims on the meaning of human rights more robust, African historians have moved beyond the relativism critique of rights to reclaim the universalism of rights in such a way that it does not exclude African meanings for the term (Zeleza 2007, 486; Ibhawoh 2004, 28–29). Warning of "a human rights language that is highly suscep-tible to perversion," especially when applied to Africa, Sean Hawkins urges that we heed "the worlds of people in Africa who strive to imagine, define, create, and defend their own ideas of rights" (2007, 394). The possible so-lution to the loss of meaning of human rights is the "reworking of existing language so that it is rendered mutually comprehensible" (400). Bonny Ibhawoh sees a "universal human rights regime" as a work in progress and thus as still emergent and in flux (2004, 38). Putting the emphasis on iden-tifying continuities in the long durée from the eighteenth century to the present, Ibhawoh offers a periodization approach that eschews the narrative structure of an origin story and foregrounds instead a history of ideas marked by progress and regression (2018, 12). In his comparative, global approach, Ibhawoh characterizes the history of human rights as a history of struggle: "how people challenged the everyday oppressions and injustices they experienced from antislavery through the anti-colonial and anti-apartheid movements, to pro-democracy movements and opposition to dictatorship and one-party rule in the era of independence" (27). Common foundational threads become visible: Ibhawoh speaks of struggles for "inclusion and recognition" (6) that come to blend traditional ideas about human dignity at play in pre-colonial times with the impact of the liberal rights regimes that came with colonialism (6).

Paul Tiyambe Zeleza sees the potential for a problematic developmentalist logic in an African idea of human dignity prior to human rights, but recognizes that human dignity is a powerful foundation for a global understanding of human rights: "The idea of 'human dignity'—ridiculed by some as characteristic of societies that have yet to develop a concept of 'human rights' is the only thread that connects the world's different religious, philosophical, and cultural traditions. And human dignity for the human person with his/her multiple dimensions must surely encompass multiple rights" (2007, 487). Thus, like Ibhawoh, who avoids a focus on "human rights in the limited sense of entitlements that individuals hold against the state" (2018, 17), Zeleza's Africanist approach is multidimensional without being relativist. This book focuses, moreover, on how narrative creates new meanings or complicates existing ideas to challenge human rights dogma. Because the history is marked by a toggle between refusal and embrace, it is important to understand the implications of human rights as betrayal in African history and consequently as a cause of the loss of dignity. This clarifies why we must then recast human rights in order to "rediscover" (to use Ndebele's formulation) their currency in African lives.

In Africa, human rights were invoked to accuse colonial regimes of hypocrisy. They name at once a betrayal and the demand for self-determination as the corrective of that betrayal. In their devastating comparative history of the anticolonial wars in Kenya and Algeria, Fabian Klose and Dona Geyer underscore the disregard of Britain and France for the standards of international law that they helped establish:

> As prosecuting parties in the Nuremberg Trials and as signatory states of the 1949 Geneva Conventions, Great Britain and France had significantly contributed to this development of international criminal law. However, as mentioned above, both countries rejected the validity of international humanitarian law in their colonial conflicts and thereby relieved their troops from the responsibility of upholding the principles that they had just agreed upon. In short, war crimes were nothing less than an essential characteristic of their colonial warfare .... Collective punishment, expulsion, forced resettlement, detention, torture, and mass executions created an outright 'system of war crimes' in Kenya and Algeria. (2013, 139)

The enduring problem at the root of this double standard is the "African exclusion from humanity by the Western World" (Hawkins 2007, 400).

Klose and Geyer provide a sharply delineated and thoroughly documented history that connects the sense of betrayal specifically to "crimes against humanity." The aspiration to self-determination to redress these wrongs resonates to the present day as weak countries and political subjects find themselves with less than the desired degree of autonomy and recognition.

Violent conflict features prominently in the intersection of human rights and African history and invariably becomes a flashpoint of betrayal and indignity. Most human rights and humanitarian interventions on the continent since Biafra have been in response to war. The imbrication of human rights with humanitarianism, moreover, is so extensive that they blend to the point of being hard to distinguish (Barnett 2011, 197–98). For some, the International Criminal Court (ICC) indictments and the UN tribunals are the face of human rights on the continent and, on the other hand, the activities of aid and relief organizations are humanitarian. Yet, this clarity does not hold for long, as, for example, when one considers the international refugee regime (also largely a product of violent conflict) which blends human rights and humanitarian appeals and practice. Stefan-Ludwig Hoffman (and others) have seen the convergence of humanitarianism and human rights as the "ethical turn" of the 1990s (Hoffman 2016, 308).[4] It resulted not only in international prosecutions with highly moral undertones but exposed how concern with distant suffering accentuated the narrowing of "human rights as individual, pre-state" and based on a "common humanity" (Hoffman 2016, 308). Moreover, for Hoffman, the focus on distant suffering amounts to a rendering of human rights "atemporal" veering from the "only good kind of human rights as 'internationalism, which were centered on group rights, sovereignty and social justice'" (Hunt 2017, 325).

This convergence of humanitarianism and human rights has its discontents, therefore. In fact, the narration of war in Africa has oscillated between the two discourses of human rights and humanitarianism. As I have shown elsewhere, war novels frequently call for political solutions to war (Coundouriotis 2019, 474). War fiction pulls away from humanitarianism because of its tendencies to get mired in a totalizing depiction of war. Moreover, the "emergency imaginary"—within which humanitarianism operates—naturalizes disaster, something which the historicizing orientation of the war novels tends to question (Calhoun 2004, 378, 392). It is instructive to remember that, before Biafra, the anticolonial wars did not invoke a humanitarian response to relieve suffering. As noted, the colonial powers' cruel treatment of resistant, colonized populations crystallized human rights claims against them. These, however, remained largely unresolved despite strides in fulfilling the right to self-determination. Independence did not wipe out the aftermath of these wars. The use of torture by the French in Algeria or forced detention by the British in Kenya have continuing repercussions on the political landscape of these nations to this day. Yet France and Britain retain what I would call greater narrative authority emanating from their stronger "place-in-the-world." In order to address such disparities, Ibhawoh prioritizes "discourse analysis" in his history of human rights in Africa. A component of this history is the inscription of power within the discourse that continues to demarcate strong and weak subjects despite the universalism of the language of human rights.

Legal anthropologists have also sought a more Afrocentric approach. The legacy of colonial violations on the standing of the ICC in Africa (tasked to prosecute crimes against humanity) concerns Kamari Maxine Clarke (2019, 8, 27, 261). In an effort to decolonize international law, she taps into lived ideas of justice that have broader currency because they look beyond a legal model where justice occupies a "stand-alone space" (10). What she calls "affective justice" works through processes of "reattribution" of guilt that perform a turn in the narrative of justice (20).[5] Clarke's use of narrative is specific to affect: affect is carried or conveyed in narrative (xxii). Affect is also the thread that runs through the "component parts" making her "assemblage" of "affective justice" legible. By drawing from assemblage theory's openness to what is emergent, to fluid concentrations and dispersals, Clarke's model gives more ownership to the communities affected and takes justice out of the legal discourse bubble (258).

In addition to the narrative mechanism of "reattributions," Clarke takes on the troubled figures of the perpetrator and the victim/survivor that undergird the international legal language of human rights. Her critique seeks to avoid "the production of a liberal and individuated moral universalism that disarticulates the conditions of its making" (2019, 15). Taking a different tack than Makau Mutua in his now classic critique of the "savages-victims-saviors" metaphor for human rights,[6] Clarke focuses specifically on the effects of individual high profile defendants in international trials on the larger body politic. She then examines the public's refusal of the authority of the ICC, which takes the form of a narrative recasting where those deemed perpetrators by the courts become popular heroes (140). The highly atomized construal of culpability and responsibility by the ICC indictments creates a simple story, too simple to handle the scope of the historical and structural problems with which the people live on an everyday level. The public's refusal of the court's construction of guilt gives it ownership of the story, creating a sense of justice that trumps the court. For Clarke, this affective dimension is crucial to a fuller understanding of the meanings of justice. Thus, it is clear that we need complex narratives, and that trials, tribunals, even truth and reconciliation processes, despite "relying on overarching narratives to organize individual facts, visual images, and other forms of evidence into a coherent whole" (Wilson 2011, 8), tend to hew to a linear unfolding and tight cause and effect structure that serves their purposes but are not capacious enough as history.

The ethical turn of the 1990s identified by Hoffman has as its corollary an increased interest in using trauma to understand suffering and make human rights claims (2016, 300). The turn to trauma theory is very pronounced in literary studies as well. Trauma provides a widely used paradigm for reading human rights narratives. Although its temporality yields nonlinear, interruptive, complex accounts of suffering, it is not the emphasis in this book. Trauma theory has undergone a thorough postcolonial critique, which has sought to recalibrate its method of reading so it does not rely as much on western assumptions of personhood (Craps 2013, 2). It has also been applied as a theory on the level of the collective, on nations, and ethnic communities (Kurtz 2014, 424). Overall, however, I tend to focus on its limits here, as in the case of child soldier recovery (Chapter 3) or the testimony of rape victims from the Rwanda genocide (Chapter 6). When used in the context of human rights, trauma too frequently becomes a way of making real the pain of others by funneling it through a familiar even if rejigged theoretical frame. It fails as a practice of "theory from the South," as John and Jean Comaroff argue.

More Afrocentric concerns are putting their mark on the narrative of human rights history—the response to the narratives produced by the ICC and the UN tribunals, as well as the wide diffusion of a trauma paradigm for casting the stories of human rights. A more systematic examination of individual narratives that together constitute a corpus of African narratives advances this effort some more. Working against the silencing of subjects of human rights, the effort in this book is to highlight voice and expression. The objective of *Narrating Human Rights in Africa* is to claim human rights from the perspective of artists and other writers from the continent and thus to situate the key theoretical concepts in African perspectives.

A disaggregated approach

Making something real is a problem of verisimilitude that human rights narration should struggle with. It should not come easily and, although this mode of writing will always be tasked with testimony and documentation, its narratives challenge us to apprehend points of view that are not easily legible. For literary scholars, the assumption that facts might lie safely ensconced outside narrative structures seems jarringly unsophisticated, but it behooves us to understand what boundaries are operating in these statements. Whereas I am suspicious of any claim to a pure form of documentation that does not present facts organized in some narrative fashion, I am also aware that scrutinizing narrative that purports to make events real leads us back to puzzling over practices of documentation. Thus, it is the synergy of narration and documentation that is of interest, rather than presuming that the terms stand independently of each other. A theoretically nuanced approach to the method of narration is important. History as a problematic is explicit in Said's "Permission to Narrate," and John and Jean Comaroff's return to the problem of situatedness and the degree of authority that emanates from it aims to break down the rigid dualism of North and

South. The place one theorizes from shapes the kinds of questions asked. It cannot, however, preempt the contingencies of the work's reception. Those will play out in the same "real" that the theory has distanced or estranged itself from to formulate its critique.

John and Jean Comaroff thus outline a "grounded theory" practice that is applicable to the reorientation of human rights narrative. "Grounded theory" is:

> the historically contextualized, problem-driven effort to account for the production of social and cultural 'facts' in the world by recourse to an imaginative methodological counterpoint between the inductive and the deductive, the concrete and the concept; also, in a different register, between the epic and the everyday, the meaningful and the material—and here in particular, between capitalism and modernity, the fitful dialectic at the core of our present concerns" (2012, 48).

According to this definition, theory involves imagination ("an imaginative methodological counterpoint") and aims to breakdown appearance as reality with "the problem-driven effort to account for the production of social and cultural 'facts.'" Both of these operations begin or are launched as expressions of the aspiration to authorship, or writing. Authorial ambition—the narrative beginning that Said theorized—casts the mold, sets the discussions, and places one vulnerably in the position of initiating a speculative conversation (Said 1975, 83). All of this takes place in a contingent circumstance, unavoidably in the context of our historical being. Therefore, instead of trauma theory and its restrictive frame, which tends to repeat and homogenize its material, I approach human rights narrative as ambitiously straddling history and theory. Human rights narration is hybrid: propositional like theory but engaged with history and actual events. These events are far from ordinary as anyone thinking about human rights knows, and their extreme nature cautions us to intellectualize them and maintain an observational distance. This is not a generalization that holds across the board but it delineates the types of texts that draw my attention.

The essays in this book disaggregate the topic of human rights narration into key areas of human rights concerns and examine the patterns distinguishable in their narrative treatment. The constraint of convention, the way fact must adhere to accepted narrative, is in the background of much of this analysis, whereas I pull to the fore what is surprising and non-intuitive, such as the individualized meanings that can give us fresh insight. Accordingly, I offer sustained readings of several topics: human dignity in the resistance to apartheid (Chapter 1), the figure of the child soldier in relation to history (Chapter 3), the improbable improvisers in places of insecurity (Chapter 4), the tension between flight and stasis in refugee and migrant narratives (Chapter 5), the challenge of testifying about rape in war (Chapter 6) and of evoking the disappeared to resist state oppression (Chapter 8). Two additional chapters situate African narratives in global trajectories: Chapter 2 looks at histories that use the international legal frame of crimes against humanity. These texts repeat the problematic motif of a "discovery" made by reading about Africa far from the continent. The penultimate chapter examines Mauritanian Mohamedou Slahi's *Guantánamo Diary* to resituate his testimony on the African continent and hold at bay the capture of his story by US-centric liberal concerns. In addition, the chapters cluster around concerns with children (Chapter 3 and 4) and torture (Chapters 7 and 8). Gender is an important concern in the discussion of dignity (Chapter 1) and, of course, as concerns rape as a war crime (Chapter 6). The through-line emphasizes the intersection of political struggle and human rights, undercutting the stereotypes of victimhood and voicelessness.

As stated, the objective of *Narrating Human Rights in Africa* is to claim human rights from the perspective of artists from the continent and consequently to situate the key theoretical concepts in African perspectives. The study's beginning premise is that it is necessary to flip the methodology around. Instead of positioning literary texts as illustrative of points already theorized elsewhere, we must foreground the literature to show the concepts it offers, the ideas and responses stemming from complex historical circumstances in Africa and expressed by African writers. Narrative is a means of engaging with historical events, giving a complex account of how truth and reality are entangled. It portrays but also potentially mobilizes historical actors. The book focuses consistently on how narrative creates new categories of thought challenging human rights dogma, whereas the sum of the literary voices heard here stand by the values of social justice and human dignity.

Notes

1 As James Dawes remarks, "it is startling to notice how many human rights fictions use an elaborately injured female body as the central narrative focus" (2007, 215). Furthermore, he extends the preoccupation with saviors to the role of the human rights novelist since central to the genre, popularly conceived, is "the idea that language has been ruined, that it must be rescued" (219).
2 Cannon Schmitt elucidates what is at stake in this Lukácsian distinction for novelists: "Novelists narrate when they present a world in flux, riven by forces of change—change, moreover, in which the novelist and her or his narrator have a vested interest. Of necessity, then, narration is committed to action (including inner action: epiphany or disillusionment, for example). It also links every detail in a novel to the fate of that novel's characters." Schmitt goes on to emphasize Lukács's negative assessment of description as "filler." "Description treats as mere backdrop or setting that which, in narration, would be freighted with consequentiality. As a result, description amounts to nothing more than a kind of 'still life'" (2016, 104).
3 Narratologist Marie-Laure Ryan focuses the definition of narrative on story, "independent of the distinction between fiction and nonfiction" and discusses it as a "scalar" concept (26, 28). She outlines five dimensions ("spatial," "temporal," "mental," "formal and pragmatic"), which she then delimits with six conditions, including a prohibition on "static description" (29).

4 In a challenging formulation, Jacques Rancière finds historical transformation instead of convergence. The meaning of rights changes from the rights of man to "humanitarian rights," and reflects a diminishment of the concept, an emptying out and narrowing of rights as they become defined through social consensus (2004, 306–307).

5 Clarke explains "[reattribution] relates to the affective dimension of justice making through the process of actively refusing, directing, and redirecting meanings of justice through sentimentalized discourses that, at times, shift how culpability is understood" (2019, 20).

6 A passionate defender of the "nobility and majesty that drive the human rights project," Mutua, however, critiques "the biased and arrogant rhetoric and history of the human rights enterprise" (2001, 202). He sees the "perpetrators-victims-saviors" metaphor structuring human rights morality as an extension of colonial mentalities that divide "actors into superior and subordinate positions" (204). Furthermore, the savior who promises "freedom" sets out to recreate the savage in his image: "the savior is ultimately a set of culturally based norms and practices that inhere in liberal thought" (204). Instead human rights should operate within a "genuine cross-contamination of cultures to create a new multicultural human rights corpus" that would have greater legitimacy and be more effective in fighting immunity (245).

Works cited

Azoulay, Ariella. "Photography Without Borders." In *The Handbook of Human Rights*, edited by Thomas Cushman, 669–682. Oxon, UK: Routledge, 2013. DOI: 10.4324/9780203887035.

Barnett, Michael. *Empire of Humanity: A History of Humanitarianism.* Ithaca, NY: Cornell University Press, 2011, www.jstor.org/stable/10.7591/j.ctt7z8ns.

Calhoun, Craig. "A World of Emergencies: Fear, Intervention, and the Limits of Cosmopolitan Order." *Canadian Review of Sociology and Anthropology* 41, no. 4 (2004): 373–395. DOI: 10.1111/j.1755-618X.2004.tb00783.x.

Clarke, Kamari Maxine. *Affective Justice: The International Criminal Court and the Pan-Africanist Pushback.* Durham, NC: Duke University Press, 2019.

Coetzee, J.M. *Doubling the Point: Essays and Interviews.* Cambridge: Harvard University Press, 1992.

Comaroff, John L., and Jean Comaroff. *Theory from the South or, How Euro-America is Evolving Towards Africa.* Oxon: Routledge, 2012.

Coundouriotis, Eleni. "The War Novel and Human Rights." *Journal of Human Rights* 18, no. 4 (2019): 474–483. DOI: 10.1080/14754835.2019.1644928.

Craps, Stef. *Postcolonial Witnessing: Trauma Out of Bounds.* New York: Palgrave Macmillan, 2013. DOI: 10.1057/9781137292117.

Dawes, James. *That the World May Know: Bearing Witness to Atrocity.* Cambridge, MA: Harvard University Press, 2007. www.jstor.org/stable/j.ctt13x0m08.

Dudai, Ron. "'Can You Describe This?' Human Rights Reports and What They Tell Us About the Human Rights Movement." In *Humanitarianism and Suffering: The Mobilization of Empathy*, edited by Richard Ashby Wilson and Richard D. Brown, 245–264. Cambridge, UK: Cambridge University Press, 2009.

Ferguson, James. *Global Shadows: Africa in the Neoliberal World Order.* Durham, NC: Duke University Press, 2006. DOI: 10.1215/9780822387640.

Hawkins, Sean. "Rethinking Rights in Africa: The Struggle for Meaning and the Meaning of the Struggle." *Canadian Journal of African Studies / Revue Canadienne Des Études Africaines* 41, no. 3 (2007): 393–401. www.jstor.org/stable/40380096.

Hoffmann, Stefan-Ludwig. "Human Rights and History." *Past and Present* 232, no. 1 (August 2016): 279–310. DOI: 10.1093/pastj/gtw013.

Hunt, Lynn. "The Long and Short of the History of Human Rights." *Past and Present* 233, no. 1 (2017): 323–331. DOI: 10.1093/pastj/gtw044.

Ibhawoh, Bonny. *Human Rights in Africa.* Cambridge, UK: Cambridge University Press, 2018. DOI: 10.1017/9781139060950.

Ibhawoh, Bonny. "Restraining Universalism: Africanist Perspectives on Cultural Relativism in the Human Rights Discourse." In *Human Rights, the Rule of Law, and Development in Africa,* edited by Paul Tiyambe Zeleza and Philip J. McConnaughay, 21–39. Philadelphia: University of Pennsylvania Press, 2004. www.jstor.org/stable/j.ctt3fhjj0.

Klose, Fabian and Dona Geyer. *Human Rights in the Shadow of Colonial Violence: The Wars of Independence in Kenya and Algeria.* Philadelphia: University of Pennsylvania Press, 2013.

Kurtz, J. Roger. "Literature, Trauma, and the African Moral Imagination." *Journal of Contemporary African Studies* 32, no. 4 (2014): 421–435. DOI: 10.1080/02589001.2014.979607.

La Guma, Alex. *In the Fog of the Seasons' End.* Oxford: Heinemann, 1992.

Lukács, Georg. "Narrate or Describe." In *Writer and Critic and Other Essays,* 110–148. New York: Grosset and Dunlap, 1971.

Maathai, Wangari. *Unbowed: A Memoir.* New York: Anchor, 2007.

Marks, Susan. "Four Human Rights Myths." In *Human Rights: Old Problems, New Possibilities,* edited by David Kinley, Wojciech Sadurski, and Kevin Walton, 217–235. Chelthenham, UK: Edward Elgar, 2013. DOI: 10.4337/9781781002759.

Mbembe, Achille. *On the Postcolony.* Berkeley, CA: University of California Press, 2001.

Mudimbe, V. Y. *The Invention of Africa: Gnosis, Philosophy, and the Order of Knowledge.* Bloomington: Indiana University Press, 1988.

Mutua, Makau. "Savages, Victims, and Saviors: The Metaphor of Human Rights." *Harvard International Law Journal* 42, no. 1 (Winter 2001): 201–245.

Ndebele, Njabulo S. *South African Literature and Culture: Rediscovery of the Ordinary.* Introduction by Graham Pechey. Manchester: Manchester University Press, 1994.

Rancière, Jacques. "Who is the Subject of the Rights of Man?" *South Atlantic Quarterly* 103, nos. 2-3 (2004): 297–310. DOI: 10.1215/00382876-103-2-3-297.

Ryan, Marie-Laure. "Toward a Definition of Narrative." In *The Cambridge Companion to Narrative,* edited by David Herman, 22–35. New York: Cambridge University Press, 2007.

Said, Edward W. *Beginnings: Intention and Method.* New York: Basic Books, 1975, 1994.

Said, Edward W. "Permission to Narrate." In *The Politics of Dispossession: The Struggle for Palestinian Self-Determination, 1969–1994,* 247–268. New York: Pantheon, 1994.

Schmitt, Cannon. "Interpret or Describe?" *Representations* 135, no. 1 (2016): 102–118. DOI: 10.1525/rep.2016.135.1.102.

Slaughter, Joseph R. "Hijacking Human Rights: Neoliberalism, the New Historiography, and the End of the Third World." *Human Rights Quarterly* 40, no. 4 (January 2018): 735–775. DOI: 10.1353/hrq.2018.0044.

Wilson, Richard Ashby. *Writing History in International Criminal Tribunals*. New York: Cambridge University Press, 2011. DOI: 10.1017/CBO9780511973505.

Zeleza, Paul Tiyambe. "The Struggle for Human Rights in Africa." *Canadian Journal of African Studies* 41, no. 3 (October 2007): 474–506. DOI: 10.1080/00083968. 2007.10751366 www.jstor.org/stable/40380100.

1 The dignity of the "unfittest"

Victims' stories in South Africa

Introduction

The word "unfittest" in my title is borrowed from Bessie Head's essay "A Personal View of the Survival of the Unfittest," where the "unfittest" refers to the victims of apartheid (1995, 125). What I propose is an exploration of the varied ways that the concept of dignity appears in anti-apartheid literature and an attempt to link these representations of dignity to the ways in which dignity is deployed in human rights discourse, especially by South Africa's Truth and Reconciliation Commission (TRC). The TRC connected dignity to the act of testimony. The Commission's role was partly to acknowledge the real suffering of individuals by elevating a notion of "personal or narrative truth" found in the testimony of individual victims (1999, 112). Dignity, truth, and narrative are thus linked by the Commission in a way rich with implications for the reading of anti-apartheid literature. Furthermore, the TRC struggled over its choice of the word "victims" (instead of survivors), acknowledging that victims are perceived as "acted upon rather than acting, suffering rather than surviving" (59). The TRC justified its use of the term victim by shifting the emphasis onto the perpetrators: "when dealing with gross human rights violations committed by perpetrators, the person against whom that violation is committed can only be described as a victim, regardless of whether he or she emerged as a survivor" (59). What matters, the Commission argued, is the "intention and action of the perpetrator" (59). How to represent victimization is the key aesthetic, moral, and political problem of apartheid-era literature. It is captured aptly by Head's polemical word unfittest, which, with its echoes of social Darwinism, addresses the way she was perceived by her society. The questions raised by the work of the Commission supply a rich context in which to recast the literature of the apartheid era that was so centrally concerned with dignity, truth, and the narratives of suffering.

Although dignity is a foundational concept of human rights, it has a peculiar position in the discourse because it rarely elicits critique. It is seen either as inherent to being human and hence a starting point for elaborating a theory of rights, or the illustration of the good that comes when rights are realized.

This later view is especially true when dignity is glossed as human equality. Occupying a place at the beginning or the end of the human rights narrative, dignity is rarely part of a discussion of process. A brief overview of how dignity figures into definitions of human rights makes this clearer.

The dignity of human beings is proclaimed in the preamble of the Universal Declaration of Human Rights (Universal Declaration of Human Rights 1948) as a starting principle: "all human beings are born free and equal in dignity and rights." In a similar vein, the International Covenant on Economic, Social and Cultural Rights (1966, Covenant) states in its preamble: "recognition of the inherent dignity and of equal and inalienable rights of all members of the human family is the foundation of freedom, justice, and peace in the world." Moreover, the Covenant goes on to claim that rights "derive from the inherent dignity of the human person." Dignity is the origin of rights and the basis for expressing equality. The African Charter on Human and Peoples' Rights (1981), on the other hand, refers to African peoples as "still struggling for their dignity and genuine independence," highlighting the difficulty associated with the notion of dignity: the tension between its "inherentness" and its need to be actualized. By looking back at colonialism, the African Charter establishes how colonialism had a detrimental effect on rights in Africa that seeded the ground for the contemporary human rights crisis, whereas this shared history has the potential to bring African countries together in a common human rights agenda (Lakatos 2020, 226–227).[1]

In western philosophy, Immanuel Kant first linked dignity to the notion of rights when he said that human beings "are under obligation to acknowledge, in a practical way, the dignity of humanity in every other man" (Gewirth 1998, 161). Kant's view can be contrasted to Joel Feinberg's, who argued that "the activity of claiming, finally, as much as any other thing ... gives a sense to the notion of personal dignity" (Feinberg 1970, 257). Therefore, whereas Kant places a burden on society to recognize the dignity of others, Feinberg places the emphasis on the individual's own sense of dignity. For Feinberg, dignity acquires meaning through the individual's act of claiming rights. On the other hand, the political theorist Jack Donnelly, who is a strong proponent of individual rights, argues that "any plausible account of human dignity must include membership in a society; people must be parts of social groups if they are to live lives worthy of human beings" (Donnelly 1989, 20).[2] Donnelly's definition of dignity is tied up with the notion of worthiness. "Human rights," he says, "are 'needed' not for life but for a life of dignity" (20). This "life of dignity," furthermore, is a "life worthy of a human being, a life which cannot be enjoyed without [human] rights" (20). Implied in Donnelly's discussion is the idea of actualization, of potentiality. Dignity must be realized through action. So, to quote him again: "human rights are a social practice that aims to realize a particular vision of human dignity and potential by institutionalizing certain rights" (20). If human rights address not "the way people are" but "how people might live," and if achieving a dignified life is the goal, then we can assume that dignity needs to be actualized (20). This point is emphasized because it demonstrates how important it is to incorporate dignity into the discussion of the processes by which human rights are actualized. The concept of dignity may be elusive because equality is never assumed. Indeed, in anticolonial literature from Africa, dignity is frequently identified as the mark of colonial power's arrogance. It becomes apparent in the way the official presence of empire carries itself and asserts its superiority. Thus, the District Commissioner in Chinua Achebe's *Things Fall Apart* expresses the opinion that his long years of service in Africa taught him not to "attend to such undignified details as cutting down a dead man from a tree. Such attention would give the natives a poor opinion of him" (1996, 147). In *A Grain of Wheat*, Ngũgĩ Wa Thiong'o describes Mr. Thompson's sense that the superiority of western culture rests on three principles, those "of Reason, of Order, and of Measure" (Ngũgĩ wa Thiong'o 1986, 53). All three, and especially "Measure," help present the colonial official in a dignified way to the Africans. In both these examples, the dignity of colonial officials is tied to their authority; they must appear dignified to claim authority. A satiric treatment of the same theme appears in Mongo Beti's *Mission terminée* (1957) where the educated African Jean-Marie feels that to maintain his authority as a symbol of Frenchness amidst the uneducated villagers of Kala, he must exert the effort to be a dignified drunk. The dignity of these three fictional characters (the District Commissioner, Thompson, and Jean-Marie) is at the expense of the dignity of the Africans who are seen as less dignified by comparison. This use of dignity to signify inequality is built into the etymology of the word because a secondary meaning of dignity is the concept of differential social ranks. A dignitary, after all, is a person of rank. Alan Gewirth calls such concepts of dignity "empirical" and argues that they are always comparative (1998, 162).

For Gewirth, the "empirical" concept of dignity refers to something we can observe about the person who has it. Gewirth explains: "In this sense, dignity is a characteristic that is often also signified by its corresponding adjective, 'dignified'; it is variously a kind of gravity or decorum or composure of self-respect" (162). This "empirical" idea is comparative, Gewirth argues, because the composure of an individual who acts with dignity is implicitly compared with its opposite, just as in the examples cited above. Therefore, when one speaks of dignity in this "empirical" way, one is acknowledging that dignity is a capacity "not always had by all human beings, let alone equally" (Gewirth, 162). Gewirth goes on to argue that Feinberg's way of linking dignity to the making of rights claims reveals that his notion of dignity is an empirical and unequal notion. You realize your dignity, or give it meaning, by making rights claims.

Gewirth opposes the "empirical" concept of dignity to the concept of "inherent" dignity by noting that the "empirical" concept defines human dignity as "consequent upon the having of rights" and, therefore, "not the ground for rights"; whereas dignity as "inherent" means that "'dignity' signifies a kind of intrinsic worth that belongs equally to all human beings as such, constituted by certain intrinsically valuable aspects of being human" (162). This is the concept that Gewirth identifies in the UDHR and the Covenants. Gewirth's distinction is useful because dignity is often deployed in both senses at once without awareness of how differently equality is treated by each concept. In this respect, the language of the African Charter is particularly interesting because, by talking about an ongoing struggle against colonialism and its legacy, it foregrounds the struggle to achieve dignity rather than declaring the dignity of African people as inherent and secure in principle. In the view of the writers of this charter, dignity is tied to the potentiality of a political struggle and the ongoing effort to realize equality from the experience of inequality. The African Charter dignifies such struggle, and hence highlights the agency of African people.

However, Gewirth also points out that the universal claim of inherent dignity is so broad that it is hard to justify and becomes almost meaningless. He identifies "a conflict between the high value accorded to inherent dignity and the egalitarian universality of its scope as indiscriminately characteristic of all humans amid their drastically diverse and unequal value" (163). Are Hitler and Stalin equally as dignified as Gandhi and Mother Teresa, he asks? (162). Gewirth concludes that the only meaningful way that a universal claim to inherent human dignity can be made (and he wants to make it) is to consider what he calls a person's "agency needs" (165). Falling back on what he learned through the "empirical" concept of dignity, Gewirth asks what "treating someone with dignity" means, and concludes that it means "to accord her certain kinds of consideration; to treat her as an end, not only as a means or object to be exploited; to treat her with respect for her basic needs, and for herself as worthy of having these needs fulfilled" (165). Gewirth, therefore, formulates an idea of inherent dignity that incorporates agency, and the trajectory of coming to fulfillment of one's dignity, in a social relation.

In "A Personal View of the Survival of the Unfittest," Head uses the word "unfittest" as a response to the multiple exclusions she experienced as a South African "colored" and a single mother refugee in Botswana. Her position on dignity closely parallels Gewirth's, as it depends on an idea of self-realization. In a reference to Darwin and the racist thinking that social Darwinism has spawned, Head asserts that the unfittest do survive (1995, 125). The question is: what do they become? In the language of South Africa's Truth and Reconciliation Commission (TRC), they are cast as victims in need of the restoration of their dignity. As Desmond Tutu explains, the TRC's goal of reconciliation addressed the need to "rehabilitate the human and civil dignity of victims," and it sought to do so by "allow[ing] those who came to testify to tell their own stories" (1999, 26). Returning to the issue of testimony, dignity, defined differently by Head than by the TRC, is the concept that frames her resistant subject position. It is this contrast that is striking: Head's idea that dignity is tied to self-realization, and the

TRC's notion (developed specifically to facilitate the post-apartheid transition) that it has the power to restore the dignity that has been stolen by the illegitimate regime of apartheid. Several decades of important history separate Head's essay from the Commission's work. Yet, they each reflect distinct orientations towards the historical agency of Africans that are relevant to the continuing efforts to historicize the transition after apartheid. With an eye on how historical agency is conceived, I turn first to the uses of the word dignity in a range of South African literary texts by Peter Abrahams, Alex La Guma, Nadine Gordimer, J. M. Coetzee, and, of course, Head.

Dignity and resistance to apartheid

In her essay, Head links the idea of the "unfittest" to a concept of dignity that she explains in the following terms:

> Though my whole life and thoughts are bent towards my country, Africa, I live a precarious existence, never knowing from one day to the next whether I shall be forced into an unwelcome and painful exile, never knowing whom it is I offend, who it is who demands absolute loyalty from me; to all, I can give nothing; to all, especially politicians and those still fighting for liberation, I ask an excuse for taking, prematurely, in advance of the chaos, dislocation and confusion around me, the privilege of a steady, normal unfoldment of my own individuality. I ask it. I have taken an advance on what I have not earned in any battlefield–human dignity (1995, 125).

Identifying her country as Africa (and not South Africa, her country of origin, or Botswana, her country of residence), Head marks her dispossession from the nation state and her embrace of a Pan-Africanist identity. Yet, as she notes, this identity is also rife with difficulty, as her belonging there is also threatened in large part because Africa in this sense is an idea rather than a reality, and it is an idea that has its strongest proponents in a kind of political activism that she was familiar with in South Africa: the Pan-Africanist Congress (Eilersen 1995, 47–48). Hence Head is claiming one kind of belonging and disclaiming another in this passage: she sees herself as African but not as political. Her life in rural Botswana, a far cry from the urban existence she lived in South Africa, would be an attempt to know Africa in this traditional sense. Dignity comes up in this passage as part of Head's rejection of politics and the embrace of everyday, ordinary life. Dignity is not something Head wants to wait for as a reward for a just fight; nor does she believe she needs to earn it. She claims it "in advance" of the fight (1995, 125).

Her definition of dignity in terms of self-realization, the "normal unfoldment of my own individuality," resembles the western philosophical concept. Gewirth, in *Self-Fulfillment*, argues that dignity is measured by the degree to which one has ownership of one's own goals and aspirations, and the extent to which one is able to realize these. For Gewirth, the violation of dignity is the violation of the individual's ability to express and pursue their self-fulfillment (1998, 169). Head introduces a further complication to this idea by problematizing the relationship between the individual and a political group struggling for a collective dignity. Political struggle, in the narrow sense of active membership in a political movement, compromises the individual's ability to attain self-fulfillment, according to Head (1995, 125). And, although dignity is realized in a process of self-realization over time, Head insists that this realization begins with an individual claim "ahead of the struggle" (125). She explicitly rejects the notion that dignity can be bestowed on the individual as a result of collective, political struggle. In this respect, Head's position differs from that of many anti-apartheid authors who argued that political struggle must come first.

Head's idea of dignity, therefore, complicates the relation between the individual and the community. Fiercely individualistic, she proclaims, "[t]o all, I can give nothing" (1995, 125). She asserts that she belongs first to herself, and this self-belonging underpins her dignity. The "normal un-foldment of [her] own individuality" takes place in resistance to the pressure to give up this individuality to a group or cause (125). At the same time, Head thought hard about how communal ties are forged, and she longed for community. As Rob Nixon has noted, Head set out to "improvise a sense of community and ancestry," creating a partly historical, partly invented Botswana as her home (Nixon 1995, 154). But the community she has in mind, unlike a political organization, does not subsume the individual; in-stead it allows the individual "unfoldment of self" in a lived network of relations (Nixon, 154).

Dignity is a word that recurs often in Head's autobiographical writings. In a piece published in the posthumous volume *A Woman Alone*, Head reports a conversation she had with a fellow artist who lived through the Nazi in-vasion of Poland before he settled in a small Welsh village. He had told her that he was driven by the need to find "a new name for human dignity," and hence his retreat to village life (quoted in Head 1990, 62). Speaking of her own writings about Serowe, the Botswana village where she lived, and comparing her experience in a village to that of her friend, Head writes: "I found a similar peace in Botswana village life and also drew large and dis-proportionate portraits of ordinary people. I meant that the immense suf-fering black people experience in South Africa had created in me a reverence for ordinary people" (1990, 62–63). The village evokes consolation in retreat to a life of the ordinary. The "new name" for human dignity pertains not so much to a different meaning for the word, but to new subjects: "ordinary people" exemplify the "new name for human dignity" (62). By referring to "ordinary" people, Head means black people as opposed to white people, rural as opposed to urban, illiterate as opposed to educated. The ordinary are the "unfittest." The democratizing impulse behind her use of dignity is evident here; it is the dignity of the "unfittest" that Head wants to proclaim (62).

Although disproportion and dignity do not seem compatible (dignity always seems to imply some kind of measure), Head's "disproportionate portraits of ordinary people" provide a kind of spotlight, a way to render visible and audible that which goes unnoticed (1990, 62). In *Serowe: Village of the Rain Wind*, which is replete with testimonies of villagers, the text functions as a stage for her subjects, an enlarged scope that helps disseminate a dignifying picture of village life. Head highlights ordinary life by paying attention to the kind of work villagers perform (Head, 1981, 42). The detailed accounts of how to make traditional clothes, tan skins, make pottery, build mud walls, and craft traditional stools all dignify ordinary life (Coundouriotis 2011, 38). Like her Polish friend who sought to heal from the trauma of Nazi aggression by retreating to a village, Head sought refuge in writing that connected her to the village community and a life of dignity denied her in South Africa. (Admittedly, the village refuge is more often true to the Serowe of her writing than to the Serowe of her experience where she was the target of overt discrimination as a single mother and colored South African.) Head's appreciation of the ordinary anticipates Njabulo Ndebele's seminal essay, "Rediscovery of the Ordinary," with its opposition of the ordinary to the overtly political. Ndebele, writing to reset the aesthetic agenda for South Africans after apartheid, contrasts the literature of the ordinary—depicting suffering through the roundly developed interiority of characters, to the literature of spectacle—which, he says, is a literature of political protest that "establishes a vast sense of presence without offering intimate knowledge; it confirms without necessarily offering a challenge" (Ndebele 2002, 137). Ndebele argues in favor of the moral complexity and humanistic depth of a literature of the ordinary, which he says "should be of political interest because they [ordinary people] constitute the very content of the struggle" (140). Head's "disproportionate portraits" reflect a similar engagement with "ordinary" suffering.

Head's preoccupation with human dignity in her autobiographical writings begins not from a sense of belonging, but from its opposite, her profound sense of homelessness. Anchoring a belonging to Africa is part of a lifelong literary and historical project for Head, a way in which to realize the "unfoldment of [her] own individuality" in defiance of the homelessness that politics have created for her. Other South African authors also resort to history to provide a basis for dignity in culture. However, Head's position is different in its emphasis on the individual, even though she also shows us that to speak of inherent dignity without an awareness of how dignity is accorded in relation is naive. Stripped of affiliations, as Head was, the individual is vulnerable, deprived of dignity in her very lack of affiliations. Dignity is a relation of self to others and is realized through affiliation.

Head's understanding of dignity brings into crisis the notion that dignity can be thought of apart, as an independent concept. Even when Head claims her dignity "in advance of the chaos," she acknowledges that she must "ask it" and thus address her community. The rhetorical construction of her statement implies the problem of recognition. Without the recognition of others (a crucial component of the African idea of dignity—Ubuntu—that I discuss below), dignity remains unrealized. The other examples from South African literature that I turn to (*Mine Boy, In the Fog of the Seasons' End, July's People, Disgrace*) debate more explicitly the boundaries between the group and the individual. Head removed herself from political exigency with her exile but remained a stateless person for most of the rest of her life. What of those in the midst of political struggle? How are dignity, agency, and self-worth related?

The extent to which Africans are depicted either as individuals or as representatives of their culture further complicates the way dignity figures into anti-apartheid literature. In a situation where racism and its explicit denigration of Africans undergirds the political structure, asserting the dignity of one's culture, whether through cultural or political nationalism, becomes urgent. Thus, much South African literature explores how cultural dignity and a sense of self-worth are interconnected. Peter Abrahams makes this point well in *Mine Boy*, a novel that examines how one becomes political and ties this process to self-understanding.

Mine Boy examines resistance to white rule in the context of the idea of universal humanity. When Paddy and his girlfriend Di (both white, both communists) discuss Zuma's potential for political radicalization, they argue about the extent to which he is a man, and by that they mean the extent to which he has self-consciousness (Abrahams 1989, 57).[3] Although the terms are jarring, this is not overtly about the exclusion of the African subject from humanity. Paddy and Di express their communist ideology, which associates self-consciousness with class-consciousness. Zuma, who has just arrived from the North to work in the mines in Johannesburg, makes the paradigmatic journey of South African fiction: from the rural to the urban, from ethnic identity to national identity, from accommodation to radicalization. Although Zuma seems to exemplify this narrative convention, the discussion about dignity in the novel raises questions about the validity of these binaries, which code the urban as more advanced. The binaries provide a yardstick by which to measure worth or, in Di's words, whether Zuma is a man, but dignity as a theme in the novel complicates this order of things.

Paddy, in defense of Zuma, points out that Zuma "has dignity and pride" before self-consciousness (Abrahams 1989, 68). Di replies sharply: "So has an animal ... You've got this all wrong. The man in your Zuma has not come out yet, so he looks beautiful and strong and perfect and has dignity, so you say that is your future native. That is not true" (68). Paddy succeeds in radicalizing Zuma by making him see that demands for justice are imperative to his dignity. When Paddy achieves this, it almost seems as if Di had been right—that Zuma was not yet fully human before his political radicalization and that he needed tutelage.[4] Yet, there is an alternative interpretation here that becomes evident if we decide that Paddy and Di mean two different things by dignity. When Paddy says that Zuma has dignity, he is replying to Di's charge that Zuma is too passive, that he does not assert himself. According to Di, Zuma does not ask for equality with whites. So, in this context, Paddy's reply that Zuma has "dignity and pride" is a way of saying that he indeed makes a claim. His dignity rests in the claim to his location as an African irrespective of any comparison to white culture. Eliza (the educated African woman to whom Zuma is attracted), on the other hand, shakes up Zuma by telling him that she "wan[ts] the things of the white people." She also knows history and explains that the Zulu fought heroically against the whites but were defeated (85–86). Before Zuma learns these things, he does not think comparatively. Zuma can be radicalized, however, because he is self-aware of his dignity, and when he learns from Eliza that his people lost in a war of self-defense, it is a blow. Di's emphasis on dignity as a kind of comportment or presentation betrays her correlation of dignity with authenticating the "native" (her word). Instead, Abrahams is at pains here to show that although Zuma may seem an authentic type to a European, his dignity is a matter of his humanity, not his exoticism.

Alex La Guma's *In the Fog of the Seasons' End* treats the problem of dignity in a similar circumstance where political passivity is opposed to radical action. Early in the novel, before we know Beukes's name or even the extent of his involvement in the struggle, Beukes tells a black nanny whom he has met by chance in a park: "I am not saying a person can change it tomorrow or next day. But even if you don't get what you want today, soon, it's a matter of pride, dignity!" (La Guma 1992, 11). The nanny, who is resigned to her lot, remains unconvinced of the need to break with the system because she likes her employers and does not mind her job. Beukes is telling her that dignity comes from a sense of self, which then determines one's relation to others. It is not guaranteed or protected by others we depend on, as the nanny thinks. Instead, the individual's own action affirms their dignity. For La Guma, as for Head and Abrahams, dignity depends on the individual's self-conscious agency. In a novel that graphically illustrates the torture of a freedom fighter, this affirmation of one's struggle for dignity is very important. It shows that although you can be violated and indeed killed, dignity is the meaning of resistance.

At the core of La Guma's novel is the problem of the absence of testimony. Elias is killed where only his killers are, out of view and in a separate realm from everyday life. Beukes, who survives to carry on the struggle, is not a witness to Elias's death and can only guess what has happened to his comrade. Coetzee remarked that Elias's "suffering and death" are a pivotal moment in South African literature. They "form a high point in La Guma's writing ... whose achievement is to demystify the torture chamber, inner sanctum of the terroristic state" (Coetzee 1992, 358). The narrator's account of the torture is premised on the fictionality of the text: a fictive narrative point of view closely follows Elias's experience. This narration does not meet the criteria of testimony; it also does not aim to be evidence or to authenticate facts. It seeks instead to dignify, to show how Elias's resistant stance dignifies his suffering. By resisting the interrogation and refusing to talk, he maintains his dignity throughout his torture. The survivor of this trauma (Elias's comrade, Beukes) seeks the realization of the equality he and Elias struggled for, which will also be dignity restored.

In *Long Walk to Freedom*, Nelson Mandela (giving his own testimony of his experiences) reflects on his time at Robben Island:

> Prison and the authorities conspire to rob each man of his dignity. In and of itself, that assured that I would survive, for any man or institution that tries to rob me of my dignity will lose because I will not part with it at any price or under any pressure. I never seriously considered the possibility that I would not emerge from prison one day (Mandela 1995, 391).

Mandela is asserting the power of his claim to dignity and casting himself as a survivor because he did not surrender his dignity. Mandela's position suggests that the claim to one's own dignity is more powerful than any restorative or rehabilitative effort. Moreover, it is important to note that both La Guma and Mandela do not ignore the relational component of dignity. Mandela's language (they want to "rob me") characterizes the assault as one based on an erroneous understanding of the relation of self to other: dignity is not alienable from a self that consciously holds on to it. This is not the same as "inherent" dignity, however, because it requires the self-awareness of the subject and an active purpose to claim one's dignity.

Like La Guma, Nadine Gordimer treats the figure of the servant but sets up a very different fictional circumstance, which also contrasts with Mandela's discussion of dignity. Whereas the apartheid that pits black and white inexorably against each other is the background of *July's People*, the characters she portrays try (and fail) to live in a sense of mutual recognition of human worth (1987, 57). Gordimer, like J. M. Coetzee in his post-apartheid novel *Disgrace*, is skeptical about the use of dignity as a political concept, seeing it as a mask for white, liberal moral superiority (1999, 57). At first, dignity seems a relative concept in Gordimer's work; this is most clearly demonstrated in an awareness of how English, as a language, encodes a relationship of moral difference in the conventional uses of the word dignity.

July's People, a novel about a fictional black revolution in South Africa, circumvents the testimonial mode on several fronts: it is set in some unspecified time in the future, it takes place in a rural backwater away from the revolution itself, there are no survivors because there is no closure, and there is no retrospective account of the revolution (Gordimer 1987, 38). Retrospection, which is actually a significant part of the novel, addresses only the life before the revolution, and not as testimony, but as revisionist history. The novel focuses largely on the dynamic between Maureen Smales and her servant, July, who has given the whole Smales family refuge in his rural home. Gordimer has characterized Maureen's situation as an "interregnum," citing Antonio Gramsci's use of the term in the *Prison Notebooks*. The novel's epigraph is: "The old is dying and the new cannot be born; in this interregnum there arises a great diversity of morbid symptoms." Through an intense engagement with her present moment—her totally transformed circumstances and her uncertain future—Maureen sheds layers of her past identity, but falls short of emerging into something new. The novel's ending has been deemed ambiguous by many critics because it is unclear whether Maureen regresses by reaching out to some familiar comforts or embraces a radically different future (Smith 1990, 143). I will not address this here. What is of interest is the central role that dignity plays in Maureen's revised understanding of her relationship with July. Not only does she attain a new sense of July's identity but she radically deconstructs her own. Maureen credits him with his own point of view and humanity only after she realizes that July does not depend on her for his dignity.

Thinking back on her life in the city, Maureen took pride in her treatment of July, for giving him liberties (social liberties primarily) that expressed her concern for him and her understanding of his humanity. In her new circumstances with herself and her family dependent on July, she no longer sees him as a servant. Yet, July confronts her with what she perceives as a puzzling insistence that he is her "boy:" "'I am the boy for your house, isn't it?'—he made a show of claiming a due" (Gordimer 1987, 71). To this Maureen replies defensively:

> What's the good of going on about that? It's six hundred kilometers over there … If I offended you, if I hurt your dignity, if what I thought was my friendliness, the feeling I had for you—if that hurt your feelings …. I know I don't know, I didn't know, and I should have known. (71–72)

At this point Maureen also doubts whether July's English is good enough for him to understand her meaning, especially the word dignity, although she is certain that he knows the concept: "If she had never before used the word 'dignity' to him it was not because she didn't think he understood the concept, didn't have any—it was only the term itself that might be beyond his grasp of the language" (Gordimer 1987, 72). Gordimer's point about dignity is couched in the problem of language: the unevenness of their relationship is mapped onto English, a language which July can only speak from the point of view of a black servant. However, the layers of misunderstanding between Maureen and July deepen here not because of July's imperfect English, but because of a difference of understanding of what is contested in this exchange. Maureen introduces the idea of dignity in response to July's jarring use of the word "boy," which she finds undignified. But July's claim that he is Maureen's "boy" is a claim on her trust: in the past she trusted him with the keys, but now she has objected to his taking the car keys. July is asking about trust; Maureen avoids answering him. The honest answer would have been that his request has aroused her suspicion, and in these new circumstances she doesn't know whether to trust him. Instead she brings up dignity, which (although she would not acknowledge this) raises the issue of his obligation to her for her dignified treatment of him, and extends the master/servant relation into the new setting as opposed to surpassing it as Maureen claims. Dignity, and the high moral tone in which it is talked about, are a mask for Maureen's avoidance of confronting her mistrust of July.

To her credit Maureen makes a self-realization along these lines when she figures out that the dignified way in which she used to treat July was in itself humiliating because it underscored his servant's dependence on her: "How was she to have known, until she came here, that the special consideration she had shown for his dignity as a man, while he was by definition a servant, would become his humiliation itself" (Gordimer 1987, 98). Maureen achieves a fuller realization that she cannot dignify July when, towards the end of the novel, they have another confrontation over trust (the Smales's gun has been stolen) and July in frustration starts shouting at her in his own language:

> Suddenly he began to talk in his own language, his face flickering powerfully. The heavy cadences surrounded her; the earth was fading and a thin, far radiance from the moon was faintly pinkening parachute-silk hazes stretched over the sky. She understood although she knew no word. Understood everything: what he had had to be, how she had covered up to herself for him, in order for him to be her idea of him. But for himself—to be intelligent, honest, dignified for her was nothing; his measure as a man was taken elsewhere and by others. (152)

Language here is crucially important, as English has been an impediment to equality; not because of July's limited mastery of the language, but because it is the language and instrument of the oppressor in which July cannot speak from the position of an equal. Gordimer goes out of her way to show that Maureen here does not understand July's exact words but she understands his meaning. Presumably the same would hold in the reverse situation; even if July does not understand some English vocabulary, he understands the meaning and, hence, when Maureen withheld language from him, she treated him unequally. Maureen's key realization here is that July's "measure as a man was taken elsewhere and by others," and, in other words, it was not up to her to make him a man, or dignify him (Gordimer 1987, 152). This realization powerfully suggests July's separate belonging; his identity has been centered elsewhere, rather than in the marginal and dependent condition of servitude. One can extrapolate from this exchange an explanation of race relations in

South Africa more generally. Gordimer makes an argument for cultural integrity and independence and, more importantly, for a South Africa that fosters ties among cultural groups that depend on mutual recognition of the autonomy of the other. For Gordimer, equality is key to a definition of dignity. Equality, whose ultimate political expression is democracy, is a guarantor of the dignity of individuals and the opportunity that Gewirth talks about in terms of self-realization. Without equality, dignity in the liberal, humanistic sense is a mask for a lie of mistrust.

Post-apartheid literature

Whereas Head, Abrahams, and La Guma seem more eager to uphold a notion of dignity, Gordimer questions the moral high ground that the concept carries with it and draws attention to the politicized uses of dignity. Gordimer thus anticipates a critique of the TRC's self-privileging position that it can restore dignity. What is learned from all four novels is that from the perspective of the anti-apartheid struggle, dignity has the most currency when proclaimed by the self and for the self. *Disgrace*, published during the TRC's tenure, goes a step further and depicts a character (Lucy Lurie) who disclaims dignity because she rejects her white privilege (Coetzee 1999, 57).

Coetzee, like Gordimer, links dignity to equality and wonders whether English does not perpetuate the inequality that makes it impossible to achieve dignified social exchanges. Thinking about how Petrus could tell his story effectively in English, David Lurie wonders:

> More and more he is convinced that English is an unfit medium for the truth of South Africa. Stretches of English code whole sentences long have thickened, lost their articulations, their articulateness, their articulatedness. Like a dinosaur expiring and settling in the mud, the language has stiffened. Pressed into the mould of English, Petrus's story would come out arthritic, bygone. (1999, 117)

Coetzee's imagery of age and decay portrays the English language not only as obsolete but as untruthful and hence a kind of obstacle. It is a hindrance to Petrus when he interacts with whites, but it is not relevant the rest of the time. Inevitably the dinosaur imagery reflects back on Lurie himself. It is his obsolescence, or that of his truth, that he recognizes here. English is tied to a political order that has been reversed in Lurie's eyes: blacks are more powerful than whites. Lurie reveals that he understands democracy as a loss of his white privilege. For Petrus, English falsifies his identity. In English, he is forced to express himself in a servile manner unfitting of his real circumstances, where he is relatively more powerful than Lurie, and more so than Lurie's daughter, Lucy. Consequently, part of the problem in the relationship among Lurie, Lucy, and Petrus is not only the absence of an adequate language but the longstanding and continuing habit of using a language that belongs to an obsolete order and that constantly distorts and confuses the present.

If language reflects inaccurately how power is distributed between Lurie and Petrus, one is led to wonder whether it does not also distort conversations between Lurie and his daughter. Their conversations are full of misunderstandings. Both struggle to find common ground in the meaning of actions and the language that describes them. One key point of conflict is naming Lucy's violation a rape. At first, she refuses to use the word and eventually relinquishes in an admission that she hopes will move her father to understand her notion of what rape implies. The disagreement between father and daughter here pertains to the degree that the actions of the violators are seen as personal or historical. Lucy asks, "'It was done with such personal hatred ... Why did they hate me so?'" and Lurie replies, "'It was history speaking through them ... A history of wrong. Think of it that way, if it helps. It may have seemed personal, but it wasn't. It came down from the ancestors'" (Coetzee 1999, 156). From this exchange, it might seem as if Lucy is holding the attackers accountable as criminals in an individual act of malice, while her father sees it as a hate crime against whites and thus more generally as a political action.

The meaning of these categories is confused fairly quickly when it becomes apparent to the reader that Lucy is thinking personally, but not individualistically. In fact, the category of gender is paramount to her. She thinks she is a victim of a hate crime against women. After her attack, her difficulty is not so much how to live as a white, but how to live as a woman alone. Of course, race is always relevant, but, for Lucy, gender is an added complication. Her father's language codes the attack as a race attack and he is entirely obtuse to the discourse of gender. The racial attack is an attack against his and his daughter's humanity. Lucy explains how she interpreted the men's hatred when she says "I think they are rapists first and foremost. Stealing things is just incidental. A side-line. I think they do rape ... Maybe, for men, hating the woman makes sex more exciting" (1999, 158).

This challenge provokes Lurie to think about the implications of rape in terms of his own experiences as a man, his "subjection" or "subjugation" of women, to use Lucy's words, and he realizes that he can understand the motivation of the rapists as men subjecting women: "he does understand; he can, if he concentrates, if he loses himself, be there, be the men, inhabit them, fill them with the ghost of himself. The question is, does he have it in him to be the woman?" (159–160). In answering his own question, Lurie rebels by rejecting the idea of subjection. Moreover, he dismisses gender as a significant category in favor of an abstraction of humanity that should be inclusive but that his daughter does not claim for herself. The difference in the father's and daughter's position is clearer if we paraphrase the narrator. When Lucy contemplates joining Petrus's household after the attack, she asks herself if she has it in her to be an African woman. By marrying Petrus, she accepts the African woman's subjection as her lot. As father and daughter debate their position on subjection, dignity emerges as a key idea. However, the question of why African women should have to accept their subjection to patriarchy is elided in the process.

Lurie wants to reject the inequality—the difference between the powerful and weak, the aggressor and victim—designated by man and woman. Moreover, to articulate his objection to this inequality, he resorts to history and the language of honor and shame and, by the end of the novel, to the language of dignity. Thus, in the contestations of meaning and language in history, dignity has a key role to play. Lurie's reply to Lucy sums this up: "You are on the brink of a dangerous error. You wish to humble yourself before history. But the road you are following is the wrong one. It will strip you of your honour; you will not be able to live with yourself" (Coetzee 1999, 160). Lurie, who saw the rape as historical and hence political in nature, wants his daughter to resist history and politics as too restrictive of individual identity. She does not have to sacrifice herself as an individual to these historical forces. Indeed, he sees such a sacrifice as a waste. Lurie believes in an individual who should, in the best of humanist tradition, transcend history. The individual's dignity should not be contingent upon historical right or wrong. For Lurie, human dignity is something that must be kept away from the contaminations of history and politics. Lucy, as a materialist, sees herself in the stream of history and is radical enough in her thinking to challenge the notion that dignity is a universal principle. Indeed, for Lucy, dignity has been historically a function of privilege and, hence, something she is willing to give up along with her privilege. Coetzee's triumph in the novel is that he turns Lucy's position into a powerful challenge of her father's privilege, a privilege marked primarily by his ability to use the aesthetic as a surrogate realm of experience from the historical.

In her idea of contrition, Lucy is willing to debase herself in order to right the wrongs of her white ancestry. After her rape and the assault of her father, she imagines accepting Petrus's offer of marriage and his protection. Petrus will then be obligated to take responsibility for the child that will be born of the rape (a child whose father is African). Lucy tells her father: "Perhaps that is what I must learn to accept. To start at ground level. With nothing. Not with nothing but. With nothing. No cards, no weapons, no property, no rights, no dignity" (205). Is the ground level that Lucy alludes to equality or something below? Is this really a productive beginning or does it reinstate a different kind of inequality, Lucy's dependence on Petrus? In what seems to be a violation of Lucy's individual identity, the feminist lesbian must enter into a polygamous marriage with an African man to ensure her personal safety on her property. Coetzee goes against the grain of liberal thinking in order to reveal the extent to which dignity functions in liberal discourses as a marker of privilege doing more to protect those who already have privilege than to ameliorate the conditions of those who do not.

But there are some added difficulties here besides the frustration that Coetzee seems to be expressing with white guilt. Is Lucy in a position to give up her dignity voluntarily or has she already been robbed of it? Is she giving up a claim here, or resigning herself to the logic of her changed circumstances? What has happened to her agency? Or, to put it differently, is her surrender of agency also an expression of agency? Although the willingness to assume the posture of subjection is presented by Coetzee as a more powerful instance of social repentance than that provided by the TRC's willingness to forgive perpetrators, Lucy's choices are ultimately only partially satisfactory because they function more as a foil to Lurie's own circumstances than as a separate set of issues. Coetzee wants the reader to compare Lucy's shame to her father's public humiliation. Lurie's sexual transgression, his nonconsensual sex with his student Melanie, is an act in which he was the aggressor. He admits he should be punished but stubbornly refuses to be shamed for it. Even as a perpetrator, he claims his dignity whereas Lucy disclaims hers.

Coetzee suggests that simply to assume dignity is not feasible because social relations are never equal. Hence, claims to all those things that Lucy lists (cards, weapons, property, rights, dignity) are markers of differential and unequal relations: one has rights or dignity only in relation to others who have no or fewer rights, more or less dignity. This is a deeply pessimistic estimation of rights that comes, for Coetzee, out of a profound disillusionment with the TRC, which he criticizes in the scenes portraying Lurie's hearings at the university. Coetzee's target here is the type of truth that the hearings try to elicit from Lurie. Whereas Coetzee intends a satiric parallel to the TRC, his concern is not with the apartheid past, but with the new mores that the TRC sets in motion. Lurie admits his sexual relations with the student, but that is not sufficient. He is asked to express contrition for his actions, something he refuses to do. Attacking the religious overtones of the TRC's doctrine of repentance and forgiveness, Coetzee has Lurie claim that "Before that secular tribunal I pleaded guilty, a secular plea. That plea should suffice" (1999, 205). But his plea is not sufficient because he is not facing a court of law (despite his insistence to the contrary). Lurie forgets that he has been told from the start that "[o]ur rules of procedure are not those of a law court" (48). The commission of inquiry wants to go beyond crime and punishment: "The criterion is not whether you are sincere. That is a matter, as I say, for your own conscience. The criterion is whether you are prepared to acknowledge your fault in a public manner and take steps to remedy it" (58). Coetzee is asking a question about truth here because the whole sequence of the narrative between these two statements revolves around Lurie's effort to find an appropriate language to recast the same events and culpability so it is acceptable to those in authority (48, 58). Neither his straightforward admission of guilt nor his "confession" are viewed as sincere enough (not "from his heart"), even though no controversy ever arises over the facts of the case (54). When the panelists contradict themselves and disclaim the importance of his sincerity, emphasizing instead his willingness to do public penance, the cause of truth has been sacrificed entirely.

One way to read this scene is to assume that Coetzee criticizes the TRC for not defining itself as a court of law. Coetzee depicts not a victim's testimony but a perpetrator's admission of guilt, in a scene where the commission's demands for contrition cloak the truth and consequently undermine the authority of the tribunal. The irony is that the perpetrator turns into a victim of a paralegal authority of questionable legitimacy. Lurie's stubborn insistence, despite evidence to the contrary that the commission is a court of law, plays up all the ways that the commission fails to adequately value facts. But Lurie's faith in the law is not necessarily principled as much as convenient. He expects the law to rescue him from unnecessary embarrassment, or indignity. "Why this thirst for abasement?" he asks of the commission (56). Provided he admits his guilt, the law would seek only a limited examination of his actions, preserving his privacy. The question then becomes whether it is Lurie's expectation that the law will preserve his privilege as well.

A glance back at Coetzee's *Waiting for the Barbarians*, is instructive. In this earlier novel, where Coetzee mounted his most damning attack on the apartheid state, the magistrate, like Lurie, kept hoping for the materialization of a court of law to try him. But the magistrate's idea that there was a legitimate legal authority in the empire is a mirage, an illusion which has anchored his complicity with empire. Is Lurie an echo of the magistrate here? Does his shrill insistence on the law reveal his complicity in the masculinist order of things? And what does this imply for his reaction to his daughter's victimization and her refusal both of the legal order and of dignity? In *Waiting for the Barbarians*, Coetzee also cautions against those in power who claim to recognize the "tone of truth" (1980, 5). The sadistic Colonel Joll arrogantly claims that he knows when his torture victims are telling him the truth because he recognizes the "tone of truth." Similarly, the commission of inquiry that tries Lurie presumes to be able to recognize the truth it is looking for—the truth of sincerity—through its interpretation of Lurie's tone. Truth seems elusive: Lurie wants to hide and the tribunal is too prescriptive. To use the TRC's language, there seems to be no "personal or narrative truth" in *Disgrace* (Coetzee 1980, 5).

Ubuntu and truth and reconciliation

But what is "narrative" truth? In her memoir of the South African Truth and Reconciliation Commission, Antjie Krog insists that she is looking for truth in story. She characterizes her own work as a reporter in the following way:

> I'm not reporting or keeping minutes. I'm telling. If I have to say every time that so-and-so said this, and then at another time so-and-so said that, it gets boring. I cut and paste the upper layer, in order to get the second layer told, which is actually the story I want to tell. (Krog 1999, 225)

When challenged that she is not being truthful, she replies:

> I am busy with the truth ... my truth. Of course, it's quilted together
> from hundreds of stories that we've experienced or heard about in the
> past two years. Seen from my perspective, shaped by my state of mind at
> the time and now also by the audience I'm telling the story to. In every
> story, there is hearsay, there is grouping together of things that didn't
> necessarily happen together, there are assumptions, there are exaggera-
> tions to bring home the enormities of situations, there is downplaying to
> confirm innocence. And all of this together makes up the whole
> country's truth. So also the lies. And the stories that date from earlier
> times. (225)

Krog structures much of her memoir as a dialogue between herself and
various interlocutors, putting many of her own statements in quotation
marks. The effect is that Krog's claim to truth is always qualified by the
acknowledgment of her authorship of the text. Like the TRC itself, she
synthesizes a multiplicity of points of view and circumstances into a narrative that represents her insight.[5] Yet, despite these qualifications, Krog
makes a strong claim to a larger truth when, just like a realist novelist, she
stands behind the totality of the varied and contradictory strands of story.
"All of this together," she says, "makes up the whole country's truth" (225).
For Krog, narrative can get at truth because it is complex enough to at least
intimate the multiplicity of points of view that make up a national history.
Krog is faulted for not reporting directly the testimony of witnesses; her
interlocutors privilege the witnesses' words over hers. Yet Krog, like the
TRC in its final report, wants to see the synthesis and seeks a truth that puts
the pieces together. What Krog calls "my truth" comes closer to the "whole
country's truth" than the fragments of testimony.

The Commission in its final report distinguished among four types of
truth, classifying "narrative truth" as one of the four types (Truth and
Reconciliation Commission of South Africa Report 1999, 112). By narrative
truth, also called "personal truth," the commission meant something different from Krog. It sought to recognize the importance of individual testimonies and the authenticity of each even within a larger context that might
undermine the claim to truth of any one individual story (112).
Furthermore, the Commission linked narrative truth and the act of testimony to the "healing" process of reconciliation. The act of telling one's
story in the public forum of the Commission enabled a collective recognition
of individual suffering while revealing the complexity of truth. The
Commission's language partly echoes Krog in its emphasis on a multilayered
truth, but also diverges from Krog in its privileging of individual testimony:

> By telling their stories, both victims and perpetrators gave meaning to
> the multilayered experiences of the South African story. These personal

truths were communicated to the broader public by the media ... The Act explicitly recognized the healing potential of telling stories. The stories told to the Commission were not presented as arguments or claims in a court of law. Rather, they provided unique insights into the pain of South Africa's past, often touching the hearts of all that heard them (Truth and Reconciliation Commission of South Africa Report 1999, 112).

Individual stories invoke pathos, which, in turn, create a new collective consciousness. The Commission in the same part of its text also highlighted the importance of African oral tradition, the cultural centrality of story-telling, to support its robust claim for the transformative effect of testimony. Testimony partakes of a larger project of collective memory, an essentially historical task.[6]

These two examples, a reporter's memoir and a truth commission's final report, provide somewhat divergent notions of narrative truth. Moreover, Krog asserts that historical truth can only be found in narrative whereas the Commission posits narrative truth as just one type of truth, the others being "factual or forensic truth," "social truth," and "healing and restorative truth" (Truth and Reconciliation Commission of South Africa Report 1999, 114). Can these other truths, however, exist beyond narrative, or explanatory structures? Philosophers, legal scholars, as well as historians will probably debate for years the validity of these distinctions and their political implications. It seems fairly clear that the claim that healing truth restores dignity implies a narrative: the story of healing, which according to Desmond Tutu, restores the victim's dignity. The act of giving testimony, therefore, is said to have a healing effect apart from the testimony's value to the larger narrative truth that is sought by the TRC. In fact, the Commission's report brings up dignity not in reference to narrative truth but to healing and restorative truth, which addresses not only the task of taking stock of the past but what the Commission saw as its work for the future. Restoration was to be achieved through "acknowledgment," which is "an affirmation that a person's pain is real and worthy of attention. [Acknowledgment] is thus central to the restoration of the dignity of the victims" (114). Truth as acknowledgment, or recognition, throws the emphasis back on the Commission as an agent and, indeed, as a storyteller.

The claim that the TRC would restore victims' dignity needs to be examined from the perspective of how testimony was actually handled by the Commission. Richard A. Wilson's (2001) ethnographic study of the TRC reveals several sobering facts about the actual uses of testimony. From a distance, one has the impression that all the proceedings of the commission were public, court-like occasions where victims had their day to tell their stories. However, as Wilson points out, after the initial phase of the Commission, the Human Rights Violations Committee collected testimony through a questionnaire administered in a private interview, which then enabled the Committee to enter information into a data base for a statistical tracking of violations.[7] Narrative and, more importantly, the centrality of the teller (a subject telling his own story) in the proceedings were sidelined. Furthermore, Wilson suggests that testifying became a confusing experience which was less than satisfying and hence could not live up to the high goal of restoring dignity (48).

Even when victims testified in a public hearing in front of a sympathetic committee, there were troubling aspects to the proceedings. As Wilson observes, the victims' testimonies emphasized their individual experience whereas Tutu and the Commission sought to "collectivize" the experience of suffering and subsume it into a "new national identity" that reflected reconciliation:

> Tutu was constructing a new national identity, that of a "national victim," a new South African self which included the dimensions of suffering and oppression. Thus individual suffering, which ultimately is unique, was brought into a public space where it could be collectivized and shared by all, and merged into a larger narrative of national redemption (Wilson 2001, 111).

The person testifying handed over his/her story to be appropriated and subsumed into this larger enterprise. The dignity restored, therefore, exacted the victim's consent to the new national identity; it could not be gained without this implied consent (Wilson 2001, 56–57). By contrast, Krog's synthesis, pegged to her metanarrative self-reflexivity, never pretends to speak for others even as it offers a possible articulation of a whole country's truth.

In her research on forgiveness, Martha Minow (1998) suggests that the problem lies in the handling of testimony rather than the goal of forgiveness. She uses language similar to Tutu's, placing a burden on truth commissions to actualize the dignity of victims. But her discussion of dignity is focused on forgiveness, not on "tell[ing] their stories in their own words" (Tutu 1999, 26). She understands forgiveness as an action carried out by the victims that has the potential to restore dignity by giving them agency. "Through forgiveness," she says, "victims can reassert their own power and reestablish their own dignity while also teaching wrongdoers the effects of their harmful action" (Minow 1998, 15). Victims are thus given an opportunity to determine closure and reclaim a power to act that redresses their loss of such power in their victimization. Furthermore, the victims are given a choice as to how to respond: they don't have to forgive (1998, 136).

Like Tutu, Minow speaks of a process of actualizing dignity. But while victims' agency is clear when they grant forgiveness, it is not so clear when it comes to describing the relation between testimony and dignity. In Tutu's formulation, the commission "rehabilitates" the dignity of the victims by giving them the opportunity to testify. Minow avoids the word dignity in her discussion of testimony (1998, 61–79). When she speaks more broadly of victims' responses (accepting the opportunity to testify could be one of various responses), then she, like Tutu, talks of dignity as something to be actualized for the survivors rather than something they actualize for themselves: "restoring dignity to victims after atrocity should at minimum involve respecting their own responses" (135). The listener accords dignity to the victim as they testify, therefore. The act of testifying is not dignifying in itself and leaves victims exposed and vulnerable. Retaining some control over the meaning of one's testimony seems crucial (Wilson 2001, 111–114).

The TRC's emphasis on restoration has been characterized as fiction; the Commission was in some sense the creator of a narrative truth. Thus, Daniel Herwitz speaks of reconciliation as an "ahistorical fiction," or "a way of picturing a deep unity that was not there" (Herwitz 2003, 42). Moreover, Herwitz and Wilson both critique Tutu's promotion of Ubuntu as an invented tradition that underpins the new nationalism. Its utility for the TRC was that it is antithetical to retributive justice (Wilson 2001, 10). Yet, to dismiss Ubuntu as an invention seems wrong. Ubuntu emphasizes a communal ethic very similar to dignity realized in relation. In the post-apartheid years, South African writers have leaned on Ubuntu frequently to criticize the wrong turns the country has taken, hence appealing to the concept's decolonial connotations. Zakes Mda, for example, credits his understanding of Ubuntu for giving him insight into his Afrikaaner characters in *The Madonna of Excelsior* (2004). To treat the history of the Immorality Act in a post-apartheid novel, he needed to "find humanity in those [he] found politically or morally reprehensible" (2008, 43). In an autobiographical reflection he notes how growing up under apartheid attitudes towards Ubuntu varied:

"You are not a person," was an accusation often heard directed at the inconsiderate, mean-spirited, and stingy. Responsible parents instilled the values of *ubuntu* in their children, but many of us discarded them with anger when we were faced with a world that had no place for compassion or generosity, or when we got "civilized" and adopted the Western value of individualism. Alternatively, we practiced selective *ubuntu*, making into persons only those we liked and confining the rest into the realms of nonpersonhood. (Mda 2008, 43)

By historicizing the term and discussing it as a lived concept, Mda wards off the kind of critique that surrounded the term because of its instrumentalization by the TRC, allowing it to be retrieved with fresh meaning.

Writing in protest, as many South Africans did at considerable personal risk during the apartheid years, was a proclamation of dignity and equality, which was not meant as restorative but as affirmative. The strongest, most affirmative instances of a claim to dignity come from novels of resistance. Moreover, the white critiques of liberal thought, on the other hand, point to how an insistence on dignity by whites, however universal the terms, underwrites their privilege. The kind of "subjection" that Coetzee imagines is, by contrast to the TRC's work, a more painful and consequential acknowledgment of an ethical call to retreat. But Coetzee does not become prescriptive. Retreat is also problematic. "Subjection," as Lucy explains it, is a self-negation of dignity. It stands in direct contrast to Bessie Head's position, as both a woman and a victim of apartheid, that dignity must be expressed as an ownership of self, a kind of self-belonging that is asserted in spite of oppressive conditions. Subjection, moreover, holds everyone hostage to the past. Apartheid's legacy looms large in Coetzee's novel, and its only antidote seems to be the traditional African family, which feels like a throwback unless we are meant to read it as an allegory of the new nation. The most troubling question posed by the novel is ultimately about the identity of Lucy's and David's violators. They remain mute and dehumanized, ciphers of evil that lack an adequate historical explanation. At the time of the TRC, the new in South Africa—which promised to dismantle the Manichean oppositions of apartheid—remained elusive. The critique of dignity shows the need for a new language of history in South Africa.

Notes

1 As Makau Mutua notes, historians should look for the "impetus of a universal conception of human rights" among those who struggled against "European tyranny and imperialism" rather than carrying on with the detrimental, Eurocentric "savages-victims-perpetrators" metaphor for human rights "which rejects the cross-contamination of cultures" and hence a multicultural approach (Mutua 2001, 205).

2 In regards to African conceptions of dignity and rights, Donnelly along with Rhoda Howard-Hassmann are frequently discussed together as two North American political theorists who believe that African rights are conceptions of dignity, not rights. This position problematically dismisses African ideas as possible foundational concepts of human rights (Lakatos, 2020, 219–220).

3 Throughout my discussion, I am regularizing the spelling of Zuma, which appears as "Xuma" in the novel except for when other characters address him as "Zuma" (68).

4 Ernst Bloch's (1986) defense of human dignity from a Marxist perspective resonates here. Bloch links dignity to the French Revolution, providing a supporting context for Abrahams's analysis of dignity and revolutionary consciousness.

5 Mark Sanders reads Krog alongside the TRC report and argues that the self-reflexivity of her account and its incorporation of numerous conversations "mimes" how the procedures of the commission, through questions and answers, arrived at its synthesis of the truth (Sanders 2007, 149).

6 See Teresa Godwin Phelps, *Shattered Voices: Language, Violence, and the Work of Truth Commissions* for a more detailed discussion of the role of stories as both instruments of justice and what she calls "carnival," the release of a "riot of emotion" through a public ritual that reorders the "chaos" into a national story (Godwin Phelps 2004, 113, 67–69).

7 According to Wilson, starting in August 1996, the Human Rights Violations Committee "adopted a mass survey style of format which completely abandoned

the original opening narrative section. The form could be completed in 30–45 minutes, and even by deponents themselves. Complexity was lost." Wilson quotes his interview with Themba Kubheka, the "chief data processor in the Johannesberg office," where Kubheka explains that "When we started it was narrative. We let people tell their story. By the end of 1997, it was a short questionnaire to direct the interview instead of letting people talk about themselves .... The questionnaire distorted the whole story altogether ... it destroyed the meaning" (Wilson 2001, 44–45).

Works Cited

Abrahams, Peter. *Mine Boy.* London, UK: Heinemann, 1989.

Achebe, Chinua. *Things Fall Apart.* Portsmouth, NH: Heinemann Educational, 1996.

"African Charter on Human and Peoples' Rights." Adopted 27 June 1981, OAU Doc. CAB/LEG/67/3 rev. 5, 21 I.L.M. 58 (1982), entered into force 21 October 1986. https://treaties.un.org/Pages/showDetails.aspx?objid=08000002800cb09f.

Beti, Mongo. 1983. *Mission terminée.* Paris: Éditions Buchet/Chastel, 1957.

Bloch, Ernst. *Natural Law and Human Dignity.* Translated by Dennis J. Schmidt. Cambridge, MA: MIT Press, 1986.

Coetzee, J. M. *Waiting for the Barbarians.* New York: Penguin, 1980.

Coetzee, J. M. *Doubling the Point: Essays and Interviews.* Edited by David Attwell. Cambridge, MA: Harvard University Press, 1992.

Coetzee, J. M. *Disgrace.* New York: Penguin, 1999.

Coundouriotis, Eleni. "An 'Internationalism of the Planted Earth:' Ronald Blythe's and Bessie Head's Ideas of the Village." *Comparative Literature Studies* 48, no. 1 (January 2011): 20–43. doi: 10.1353/cls.2011.0009.

Donnelly, Jack. *Universal Human Rights in Theory and Practice.* Ithaca, NY: Cornell University Press, 1989, www.jstor.org/stable/10.7591/j.ctt1xx5q2.

Eilersen, Gillian Stead. *Bessie Head: Thunder Behind her Ears.* Portsmouth, NH: Heinemann, 1995.

Feinberg, Joel. "The Nature and Value of Rights." *Journal of Value Inquiry* 4 (December 1970): 243–257. doi: 10.1007/BF00137935.

Gewirth, Alan. *Self-Fulfillment.* Princeton: Princeton University Press, 1998.

Godwin Phelps, Teresa. *Shattered Voices: Language, Violence, and the Work of Truth Commissions.* Philadelphia: University of Pennsylvania Press, 2004, www.jstor. org/stable/j.ctt3fh8vr.

Gordimer, Nadine. *July's People.* New York: Penguin, 1987.

Head, Bessie. *Serowe, Village of the Rain Wind.* London, UK: Heinemann, 1981.

Head, Bessie. *A Woman Alone: Biographical Writings.* Edited by Craig MacKenzie. Portsmouth, NH: Heinemann Educational, 1990.

Head, Bessie. *The Cardinals: With Meditations and Stories.* Portsmouth, NH: Heinemann, 1995.

Herwitz, Daniel. *Race and Reconciliation.* Minneapolis: University of Minnesota Press, 2003.

"International Covenant on Economic, Social and Cultural Rights," adopted 19 Dec. 1966, G.A. Res. 2200 (XXI), U.N. GAOR, 21st Sess., Supp. No. 16, preamble, U.N. Doc. A/6316 (1966), 993 U.N.T.S. 3 (entered into force 3 Jan. 1976). https://treaties. un.org/Pages/ViewDetails.aspx?src=IND&mtdsg_no=IV-3&chapter=4&clang=_en.

Krog, Antjie. *Country of My Skull: Guilt, Sorrow, and the Limits of Forgiveness in the New South Africa.* New York: Three Rivers Press, 1999.

La Guma, Alex. *In the Fog of the Seasons' End.* Oxford, UK: Heinemann, 1992.

Lakatos, István. "Implementing Universal Human Rights Standards in and by Sub-Saharan African States in the Shade of Local Traditions." *Human Rights Quarterly* 42, no. 1 (2020): 217–253. doi: doi:10.1353/hrq.2020.0007.

Mandela, Nelson. *Long Walk to Freedom.* Boston: Little, Brown and Company, 1995.

Mda, Zakes. 2008. *"Justify the Enemy: Becoming Human in South Africa."* Boston Review. (1 May 2008): 42–44.

Mda, Zakes. *The Madonna of Excelsior.* New York: Farrar, Straus and Giroux, 2004.

Minow, Martha. *Between Vengeance and Forgiveness: Facing History after Genocide and Mass Violence.* Boston: Beacon Press, 1998.

Mutua, Makau. "Savages, Victims, and Saviors: The Metaphor of Human Rights." *Harvard International Law Journal* 42 (2001): 201–245.

Ndebele, Njabulo. "Rediscovery of the Ordinary." In *Readings in African Popular Fiction,* edited by Stephanie Newell, 134–140. Bloomington: Indiana University Press, 2002.

Ngũgĩ wa Thiong'o. *A Grain of Wheat.* Revised Edition. Portsmouth, NH: Heinemann, 1986.

Nixon, Rob. "Refugees and Homecomings: Bessie Head and the End of Exile." In *Late Imperial Culture,* edited by Román de la Campa, E. Ann Kaplan, and Michael Sprinker, 149–165. London, UK:Verso, 1995.

Sanders, Mark. *Ambiguities of Witnessing: Law and Literature in the Time of a Truth Commission.* Stanford: Stanford University Press, 2007.

Smith, Rowland. "Masters and Servants: Nadine Gordimer's *July's People* and the Themes of her Fiction." In *Critical Essays on Nadine Gordimer,* edited by Rowland Smith, 140–152. Boston: G. K. Hall and Co, 1990.

Truth and Reconciliation Commission of South Africa Report. Vol. 1. Cape Town: Truth and Reconliation Commission, 1999.

Tutu, Desmond Mpilo. *No Future without Forgiveness.* New York: Doubleday, 1999.

"Universal Declaration of Human Rights," adopted 10 Dec. 1948, G.A. Res. 217A (III), U.N. GAOR, 3d Sess. (Resolutions, pt. 1), at 71, U.N. Doc. A/810 (1948), reprinted in 43 Am. J. Int'l L. 127 (Supp. 1949). https://www.un.org/en/universal-declaration-human-rights/.

Wilson, Richard A. *The Politics of Truth and Reconciliation in South Africa: Legitimizing the Post-Apartheid State.* Cambridge Studies in Law and Society. Cambridge, UK: Cambridge University Press, 2001. doi: 10.1017/CBO9780511522291.

2 Congo cases

The stories of human rights history

That human rights history constitutes an identifiable genre becomes apparent when we consider the growing body of work that either tries to tell the history of the human rights movement or examines particular historical events through a human rights lens.[1] The human rights lens frames the historiographical project as an exposition of crimes against humanity.[2] Human rights history uses the frame of crimes against humanity to analyze contemporary history where it might be instrumental in making the case for legal prosecution or, alternatively, to revisit events from the deeper past and renarrativize them through its criteria.[3] The two centers of gravity (histories of the human rights movement and histories of crimes against humanity) reveal divergent ideas of what human rights history is, but they also work in synergy to highlight an emphasis on narrative, which characterizes both. My focus is on the latter type of human rights history (histories of crimes against humanity), with texts about the Congo as my particular example. I contend that human rights history is shaped by a story of reading in which the author takes evidence previously ignored or misconstrued but pertaining to well-known events and uses the evidence to renarrativize the events, providing a new story with a human rights–inflected moral center. This process of identifying crimes against humanity by narrating a discovery made through reading ultimately serves the larger enterprise of legitimating the history of the human rights movement by arguing for its capacity to create a broad constituency of people who can see past wrongs in a new light and who are empowered by this recognition to participate in the effort to prevent the repetition of such wrongs.

Stories of reading, instances in which the author refers to his or her own act of reading, illuminate the ways in which reading is a form of experience. Jonathan Culler defines "stories of reading" as our coming to awareness of an agency that lies in the text itself. We experience reading as if the text has the power to act on us, to transform us, yet

> it proves no easier to say what is in the reader's or a reader's experience than what is in the text: "experience" is divided and deferred—already behind us as something to be recovered, yet still before us as something

to be produced. The result is not a new foundation but stories of reading, and these stories reinstate the text as an agent with definite qualities or properties, since this yields more precise and dramatic narratives as well as creating a possibility of learning that lets one celebrate great works (1982, 82).

The boundaries between text and reader are blurred, since it is only in reading that both come to life; and, as reading is an experience over time, it can never be fixed. Instead, the story of reading is incorporated in the form of the text. The human rights history refers to reading, asking us to imagine someone else's reading while we ourselves are reading. In this imaginative act, we see ("constitute" is Culler's word) the text as an agent acting upon the reader. Thus, our access to the text's agency is highly mediated. Furthermore, it is this kind of layering that takes up much of the energy of human rights history and where its potential to bring the reader to awareness (its "possibility of learning") lies.

Culler's terminology gives us a fresh approach with which to examine the instrumental uses of narrative in human rights discourse. In our stories of reading, we constitute the text as an agent that has wrought change upon us and given us experience. Moreover, Culler deliberately calls this a "reinstatement" of agency, hinting at the infinitely renewable passage to new stories of reading at each occasion of reading. Stories of reading have an empowering effect, giving the reader of human rights history a sense of expansiveness, which comes from the recognition these texts ask us to give. This recognition is often duplicated by the actors in these histories who themselves undergo a recognition/conversion experience for us to see. In texts of human rights history, therefore, we might find accounts of the authors' stories of reading, moments when they recognize something new in a familiar narrative that enables them to recast the entire narrative in a different light. In addition, we might also find the representation of the moral awakening of the key actors. The recognition by the author of what he or she already knew is a key narrativizing moment for human rights, one that seeks to cast atrocity as a truth denied and now urgently foregrounded in order to create a delayed but forceful response.

Furthermore, human rights history as a genre distinguishes itself from the human rights report. Unlike the report, it does not claim to be the first to expose abuses. Instead it revisits an already known history and tells it differently.[4] As "history," such texts have the advantage of more extended hindsight than a human rights report, but this is not the only difference. A human rights report, like human rights history, seeks to shift our sense of scale; something unimportant becomes important. The report does this so as to create an awareness of emergency. By making us conscious that we have misread the past, human rights history provides instead the satisfaction of having set things right, affirming our participation in this change by our act of reading and situating the experience of reading as an end in itself.

As I have noted, the impact of reading is foregrounded by the story of reading dramatized within the text of human rights history. The author must tell us of his own reading experience, making form into content, as Hayden White explains:

> I move from the consideration of history as an object, a content, the form of which is to be perceived by the historian and converted into narrative, to that in which the form provided, the narrative actually produced, becomes a content, an object of reflection on the basis of which a truth about history-in-general can be asserted on rational grounds. And this raises the problem of the possible content of that truth and the form its affirmation must take (1973, 93).

White famously reverses our assumptions of how historical narrative is constituted. We do not glide from reality to narrative but travel through story first. He urges us to see narrative as the form of history, its content, thus enabling us to reflect on the truth of "history-in-general" as a subsequent step. As Edward W. Said put it, "Facts do not at all speak for themselves, but require a socially acceptable narrative to absorb, sustain, and circulate them" (1994, 254). Such framing and narrativizing of events is constantly being renewed. The emplotting function of the historian negotiates forms of stories as instruments which mediate the process of arriving at historical understanding. White insists that "every historical narrative has as its latent or manifest purpose the desire to moralize the events of which it treats" (1987, 14). Human rights history as a genre is able to revise and retell familiar stories because its main motivation lies in the remoralizing, emplotting function rather than the exposition of new facts. To turn to Said once again, "where are facts if not embedded in history, and then reconstituted and recovered by human agents stirred by some perceived or desired or hoped-for historical narrative whose future aim is to restore justice to the dispossessed?" (1994, 267).

This sketch of human rights history as a genre is, of course, provisional, and what follows here is an analysis of three texts, of which only the first, Adam Hochschild's *King Leopold's Ghost* (1999), is paradigmatic. The other two, Bryan Mealer's *All Things Must Fight to Live: Stories of War and Deliverance in Congo* (2008) and Georges Nzongola-Ntalaja's *The Congo from Leopold to Kabila: A People's History* (2002), both come up short of the narrow focus on crimes against humanity. But they do show us a lot about how stories of reading condition the form of human rights history. All three texts are part of a cluster of books about the Congo that began appearing in the mid- to late 1990s and reflect a resurgent interest in the history of Central Africa after the 1994 Rwanda genocide and its deeply destabilizing consequences for the entire region. My three examples attempt to recast the Congo's history by resisting the persistent construction of the Congo as the "heart of darkness," with Hochschild and Mealer making explicit references to Joseph Conrad's novel. For Nzongola-Ntalaja, the Congo as "heart of darkness" is one of the underpinnings of imperial history in the nineteenth and twentieth centuries that must be cast aside by shifting the focus to the Congolese people as historical agents.[5] Hochschild interprets the "heart of darkness" theme as the story of the moral conversion of the witness. Mealer, who unlike the other two is a journalist rather than a historian, demonstrates his awareness of the narrative conventions of writing about the Congo by imitating several of them (including the adaptation of *Heart of Darkness* into a story of war in the film *Apocalypse Now*), confirming the centrality of renarrativizing to human rights discourse.

In my examination of these texts, I delineate three types of emplotment for human rights that are not intended as an exhaustive typology but rather as a preliminary mapping. Each of the three types of plot presents a different construction of the heroic. The first type is the moral crusade which is temporarily thwarted but holds strong promise of fulfillment in the future; the second is the witness of a lone journalist or rapporteur who tells of a seemingly unending and unassimilable series of horrors but positions himself as a redeemer witness struggling to create a vision of hope; and the third is the collective story of a democratization movement which constructs a heroic people whose efforts also fall short but must be sustained.

All three types of emplotment put emphasis on what the story moves toward, on the kind of closure it proposes, despite the setbacks that are part of the historical account of events. In human rights history, there is an a priori investment in the progressive narrative of human rights as a movement. The closure of the narrated events often takes the form of a setback that is perceived as having contributed to previous misreadings of these events but is now pegged against the larger progressive narrative. The key questions, therefore, become: how big is the setback of the moral crusade in relation to the pace of human rights progress? How permanent is the sense of failure in the rapporteur's despairing witness? How long do the people have to wait for democracy? Moreover, emplotment is also implicated in the imagination of place. This is perhaps most glaring in the case of the rapporteur who enters the Congo as an outsider with a distinct sense of arriving at a topos called the "heart of darkness" and then leaves it behind to give witness to an audience that perceives itself as distant and different. By contrast to the rapporteur, Hochschild emphasizes his research in European archives, and Nzongola-Ntalaja is a Congolese activist and historian. Insofar as all three texts respond to the "heart of darkness" motif, they must confront the disjuncture it creates between two places that posit distinct and irreconcilable narrative possibilities. Conrad's novel dramatizes the idea that a lie fractures the historical, retrospective narrative of the civilizing mission. His protagonist, Marlow, tells one story to his listeners on the Nellie and another to Kurtz's Intended. The narrator in turn frames this lie, the double story, making it seem permanent, a static feature of the reality itself. Exposing the lie is the narrator's motivation for telling Marlow's story, but by repeating and failing to explain it, the story launches the lie anew. Human rights history thus can be said to be haunted by a permanent doubling: the version appropriate back home and the version discovered in the field, or the library. Negotiating this doubling, returning to the blind spot of the lie and exposing it, is a productive gesture that seems infinitely renewable. In what follows, I examine in turn the three texts of Hochschild, Mealer, and Nzongola-Ntalaja and posit my own stories of reading in an attempt to elucidate how the genre of human rights history works.

The moral crusade: revelation and concealment

In her review of *King Leopold's Ghost*, Michiko Kakutani summarizes Adam Hochschild's contribution to the literature on late nineteenth-century Congo with the succinct "Kurtz wasn't fiction," thus highlighting Hochschild's defense of Conrad's historical evidence (1998). The irony of a historian defending the evidence deployed by a novelist should not be lost on us, yet this reversal of authority is less surprising than it seems, as the borders between narrative history and the historical novel have always been porous. A modernist text that foregrounds ambiguities of meaning and troubles our sense of the real, *Heart of Darkness*, however, has been read not for its historical reference but for its groundbreaking style, achieving its cultural influence as a tale of interiority for which the novel's setting serves as metaphor.[6] On the basis of such a reading, Chinua Achebe rejected the novel as racist, arguing that it treated the African experience as background, its people as a prop (2006, 339). The return to the real signaled by Hochschild's reading of the novel has had a wide influence and has created a shift in pedagogy, changing how the novel is read in the college classroom.[7] This turn to the historical probably does little to satisfy Achebe's objections, however, as it still fails to show Africans as historical actors, even as it puts the spotlight on the evil deeds of imperialism and its discourse.

In *King Leopold's Ghost*, Hochschild's story of reading goes as follows. He recounts how he first read about the death of millions in a text in which Mark Twain was cited as a participant in the movement to eradicate slave labor in the Belgian Congo. In a direct address to his reader, Hochschild admits his embarrassment at his ignorance of Congo's history despite the widely published nature of these facts and his own firsthand knowledge of the Congo. He had visited Congo in 1961 to interview a CIA agent about the role of the United States in Patrice Lumumba's assassination (Hochschild 1999, 3). In this story of reading, Hochschild minimizes the value of his travel experience and privileges his role as a researcher of the archive instead. Furthermore, by casting doubt on one's ability to know the Congo by going there, he makes an ironic reference to the inscrutability of the "heart of darkness" as an actual place. His deepening understanding of the Congo's history gelled when he realized that he already knew the Congo's history from Conrad's novel (3). Thus, his recognition took the form of a reinterpretation of the novel, which he had read before as Freudian allegory, hence "fiction," and now suddenly recognized as history (3). The Congo as "heart of darkness" is placed urgently in front of us as that which we have forgotten. Although it acquires a past, it has a static quality, reappearing in a similar guise, one in whose darkness we now recognize our complicity.

But even the recognition of our complicity that Hochschild foists on us is not new, since Kurtz as a character confronted us with it and we (like Hochschild) have encountered him before, although we have repeatedly mystified him with other meanings. The already-told is available for reanimation in a new narrative because it is haunted by the uncanny specter of complicity, which draws us back to it. Hochschild warns us that we are living the consequences of the "great forgetting" of Congo's colonial history (292). His text, however, exhibits a paradox typical of human rights histories. Although he can point to a number of other prior texts that contain the facts of his narrative, he claims to be telling the story against the pressures of forgetting. The bibliography of scholarly works from which Hochschild draws legitimates his effort, while at the same time he presents this body of work as constituting a forgotten history. *King Leopold's Ghost* is a synthesis, but more importantly a retelling, a reinflection of previously told stories.[8] It is situated in a chain of stories that take on a pattern of revelation and concealment, the identification of which becomes Hochschild's task.

Hochschild's account pits ambitious imperialists, Leopold and the explorer Henry Morton Stanley, against the crusaders of conscience, most prominent among them Edmund Morel and Roger Casement, to tell the story of what he calls the "first great international human rights movement of the twentieth century" (1999, 2) His narrative is composed of finely crafted portraits of individual actors that assess their moral caliber, ambition, and capacity for leadership. Stanley is first sketched sympathetically, made unfamiliar to the reader by reference to his real name (John Rowlands), Welsh origins as an abandoned "bastard" child, and his ability to rise beyond his limited means. Stanley's capacity to reinvent himself, however, leads Hochschild to defamiliarize him once again. He deconstructs the heroic explorer by confronting us with the instrumental role Stanley played in helping Leopold establish his exploitative and violent hold over the Congo. Hochschild repeatedly contrasts Stanley's tolerance for violently subjugating Africans to the awakened conscience of the witnesses to this abuse, the moral crusaders of what eventually became the Congo Reform Movement.

Stanley and Leopold both are affected by the failure of the ethos of domesticity and sentimentality. Hochschild identifies Charles Dickens's influence in Stanley's early sentimental narratives of himself, which capture the sense of shame he was fleeing (24). Leopold is portrayed as seeking refuge from an unhappy marriage in his imperialist ambitions. Unlike his cousin Victoria, who symbolized domestic sentimental values, Leopold's royal household was emotionally dysfunctional. By characterizing Stanley and Leopold in terms of the failure of the domestic and the sentimental,

Hochschild displays his own awareness of how genre becomes content. The moral crusade, like the imperial adventure, provides a contrast to the domestic, but it takes its protagonists reluctantly away from the hearth. It is a sacrifice of the ordinary life in order to safeguard its values for others. Edmund Morel, an ordinary man with "an ailing mother and a wife and growing family to support," radically redirects the trajectory of his own life when confronted by evil. He comes to exercise a high degree of moral influence, bringing to light the exceptional nature of the "ordinary" (1).

In what amounts to yet another story of reading, Hochschild discovers the phrase "crimes against humanity" in the writings of George Washington Williams (112). An African American who was at various points a soldier, a minister, a lawyer, and, most importantly for Hochschild, a "pioneer among American historians in the use of nontraditional sources," Williams was one of the first to raise the alarm about Leopold in an Open Letter addressed to the monarch and published in 1890 (Hochschild 1999, 104). Having gone up the Congo River and discovered that the colony described by Stanley as exemplary was far from that, Williams outlined an indictment of Leopold's policies. To demonstrate how thorough Williams was, Hochschild gives a detailed synopsis of the pamphlet, reproducing its salient points as a list that takes up two pages of his own text. The list brings to light what was once known and then concealed, so that Morel a few years later had to rediscover the same facts (109–111). Williams used the phrase "crimes against humanity" (the phrase that "seems plucked from the Nuremberg trials") in a letter to the U.S. Secretary of State (112). Hochschild turns to Williams not to discover the facts about the abuses but to link the type of reporting that Williams was doing to the moral lens of "crimes against humanity." Because of Williams's standing as the first to decry Leopold's abuses, his use of the phrase puts the entire campaign against Leopold under the umbrella of this term. It is Hochschild's recognition of this convergence that makes his text paradigmatic of the discourse of human rights history.

When Hochschild talks about Williams's outrage at the abuses he witnessed, he does not hesitate to assert that "Williams's concern was human rights" (109). The term does not seem anachronistic to him, and by applying the label "human rights" he is interpreting Williams's actions. Hochschild's interpretation is what the reader wants from his text. Reading *King Leopold's Ghost* provokes a powerful identification with those who protested the horrors, and only secondarily and as repetition does it teach us that such horrors occurred. It tells us the story of a moral crusade, the Congo Reform Movement, and is itself a moral crusade for a particular type of historical practice that seeks to apply a human rights lens to the past's "crimes against humanity."

The paradigmatic heroes of Hochschild's human rights history—Edmund Morel, Roger Casement, and Jules Marchal—are portrayed as readers. The book begins with Hochschild's account of how Morel intuited that atrocities were occurring by wondering about the evidence that was in plain sight on the docks of Antwerp, but which no one else seemed to be probing. If ships were bringing valuable cargo from the Congo and only taking back "officers, firearms and ammunition" to Africa, then, Morel concluded, no trade was taking place (2). Deeper into Hochschild's text, we learn that Morel came to scrutinize the activity on the docks after examining the accounts. By carefully reading the numbers, he concluded that the figures he compiled for his employer, the Liverpool firm Elder Dempster, and the figures published by the État Indépendant du Congo were discrepant (179). To understand what the difference in figures was telling him, Morel scrutinized the activity on the docks, which he now saw as evidence of slave labor in plain sight. The shipments of ammunition from Antwerp back to the Congo could only mean that extreme coercion was taking place. Morel linked two places, two geographies, and different moral orders by reading the books. Without his ability to make a narrative out of double-entry accounting, the visual evidence would not have been intelligible.

The value of the Congo Reform Movement, Hochschild concludes, was to "put a remarkable amount of information on the historical record" and to create a "tradition," or as he explains, "a way of seeing the world, a human capacity for outrage at pain inflicted on another human being" (304–305). We as readers of Hochschild now locate ourselves in that "tradition," and we are beneficiaries of the historical record, which is there to be mined over and over. Both of these objectives (creating a historical record and a "way of seeing the world") propose a long-term effort in which a dynamic of revelation and concealment plays itself out. Hochschild's history can be read as a chronological account of one witness after another coming forth with his revelatory story of reading, only to have it be forgotten or somehow hidden from view until it is rediscovered by a later figure to become his story of reading and revelation.

Hochschild's narrative of Casement's contribution to this chain of stories follows the pattern of revelation and concealment. But Casement was primarily the reader of his own text, at once revealing and concealing what he discovered in his negotiation of different genres of writing. Casement transformed the language of his diary, in which "his horror pulses through the cryptic pages," into the "formal and sober" language of his report, inventing in the process, according to Hochschild, the style of the human rights report of the future (202–203). The historian after Casement, who can read both the diary and the report, is privy to another revelation: how Casement shaped the rhetoric of his testimony. Casement's place in this chain of stories is also important because of his encounter with Conrad in the Congo. Hochschild suggests that Casement's stories "see[m] to have darkened Conrad's vision of colonialism in Africa" (197). In a letter that is often quoted, Conrad said of Casement: "He could tell you things! Things I have tried to forget, things I never did know" (Hochschild 1999, 197). The contradictory impulses of revelation and concealment are apparent in Conrad's statement, as is their willfulness. Those things "I never did know" could be either things he literally never knew about or the things he did not want to know about. The phrase does not resolve this ambiguity for the reader; it does not tell us whether the speaker embraces his new knowledge. For Conrad, the ambivalence marks Europe's pervasive complicity in the violence of imperialism in Africa. As Hochschild reminds us, "Conrad said it best, 'All Europe contributed to the making of Kurtz'" (283). But it is telling that Hochschild associates the Conradian sensibility of at once noting and denying moral unease not with modernist aesthetics but with Conrad's experiential difficulty processing what he saw and heard in the Congo. By contrast to Conrad, Hochschild navigates the same territory with moral assurance. Differences between the two texts are hard to ignore. The awakening experienced by the witnesses to atrocity is rendered by Hochschild as a form of heroism, whereas Conrad exhibits less confidence in the meaning of Marlow's experience. His frame narrative with two endings is a conceit which repeats the pattern of revelation and concealment: the frame reveals the lie, but the lie still succeeds in hiding its substance, since the revelation amounts to the fact that a lie was told without providing an explanation of Kurtz's experience.

Hochschild further illustrates the pattern of revelation and concealment with the example of the Commission of Inquiry Report from 1905, a report produced for Leopold to dispel Morel's and Casement's accusations, but which instead strongly corroborated them. Although "couched in bland and bureaucratic language," the report's evidence was explicit and, even more importantly, was drawn from interviews with Congolese (1999, 251). The archive with the Congolese's testimony was inaccessible to scholars until the 1980s. The African witnesses are not quoted directly in the report, which summarized the findings, transmitting them in "generalities" (255). So whereas the pressure exerted by the Congo Reform Movement prompted the production of the report and the creation of an archive that would not otherwise have been available, the exclusion of the Congolese's direct witnessing in the report silenced their voices, which remained hidden away in the archive awaiting rediscovery.

The Belgian diplomat and historian Jules Marchal did the most significant archival work underpinning Hochschild's history. The beginning of his story follows a familiar pattern. Posted at the Belgian embassy for Ghana, Liberia, and Sierra Leone in the 1970s, Marchal saw a reference in a Liberian newspaper to the millions of Congolese dead at the beginning of the century (Hochschild 1999, 297). At first, as a Belgian official, he sought to deny this statistic as defamatory, but as he looked more closely into the evidence, he became aware that the official record instead had been distorted. Thus, Marchal's commitment to this project begins as a story of reading that led him to work on recovering and recreating the record of the atrocities. Because Marchal's archival work uncovered interviews with Congolese, he helped bring into play in this chain of stories their voices. His reading of the Liberian paper showed once again how the truth was in plain sight in one domain, circulating as an uncontested fact in an African newspaper, while hidden in another, cast out of view in the European archive. Marchal had to wait eight years to gain access to the records collected for the Commission of Inquiry Report.

Belgium's identity as a historical victim of the Germans placed the country's history beyond scrutiny and facilitated the forgetting of the truth about its imperial rule (Hochschild 1999, 296). By contrast, the Congolese remember the turn of the century as "the overwhelming," a powerfully allusive term that intimates a different kind of erasure (300). The moral crusades of Morel and Casement and, later, Marchal also aimed at an overwhelming of sorts but fell short of creating a lasting urgency about the issue. Hochschild, moreover, links an African forgetting to the lack of recognition of the Congo Reform Movement. The poverty of the African collective memory of the atrocities is a consequence of the more culpable forgetting by the European and American publics of the Congo Reform Movement and what it revealed about Belgian rule. Hochschild's narration of Marchal's efforts to restitute the historical record turns Marchal into the crusader for the African memory of the period. Marchal's significance in the chain of stories also lies beyond *King Leopold's Ghost*. Hochschild was instrumental in the publication of an abridged translation of another of Marchal's works related to the history of atrocity in the Congo, *Lord Leverhulme's Ghosts*, which examines the period from 1910 to 1945 and the extraction of palm oil. The analogous titles of Hochschild's and Marchal's (translated) work link the two texts, reversing our sense of their order of publication, since we now identify *Lord Leverhulme's Ghosts* as coming after Hochschild.[9] Once again the dynamic of revelation and concealment is foregrounded. *Lord Leverhulme's Ghosts* comes to light as a result of Hochschild's reading. The text is an exposé of another player in Congo's colonial history, Leverhulme, who is both new (we had forgotten about him) and familiar, in the mold of Leopold. The chain of stories moves backward, retrieving texts from the past, before it moves forward to expose the new. By making Marchal's text available in English and in a form more closely analogous to his own text, Hochschild extends the tradition, strengthening his own claim to it by becoming a link in the chain.

The redeemer witness

The redeemer witness seeks to salvage the progress narrative, to find evidence of change for the positive. He searches for evidence that will cast aside the topos of the "heart of darkness" and its association with crimes against humanity. The act of witnessing, an "I must see for myself" imperative, is the action. Thus, the redeemer witness does not seek to transform, or intervene, but to see and report. Journalists who report on human rights abuses want to "say something that was true" (Dawes 2007, 166). However, truth alone does not redeem, especially when the "truth" confirms Congo's regression since independence, an impression which accompanies the image of Congo as static and unchanging. Bryan Mealer plays with this stereo-typing language, characterizing Kinshasa as a city that "seemed to have frozen in time and crumbled with the thaw" (2008, 53). Stasis produces regression, whereas we learn from one of Mealer's translators on the boat trip up the Congo River that "the most important thing is forward progress" (199). The literal and metaphorical here travel together, and Mealer's quest becomes focused on finding signs of progress in the form of "recovery" from the war (150).

All Things Must Fight to Live stitches together a single narrative out of multiple trips to the Congo which Mealer took from 2003 to 2007, inter-rupted by text in italics that describes his personal life in the United States in the interludes between trips to the Congo. The personal narrative progresses from romance to marriage to home ownership in spite of the danger of their derailment due to Mealer's long absences and stress as a war reporter. Furthermore, the Congo experience is integrated into this narrative of the self through a fiction of containment. Containment of the war stories, the dark material of Mealer's experience in Congo, is presented explicitly as the book's last gesture:

So I gathered [the stories] up for one last hurrah, and led them down the path to the dark place at the end. And there on the trail sat the box I'd opened so long ago. I folded each story into the collective memory and placed them down inside, then closed the lid. And without looking behind me, I walked off into the trees (2008, 296).

The "dark place at the end" is one more repetition of the "heart of darkness" motif. Stories of this place, although already published during his years as a war journalist, should stay in a "box," under a "lid," at the "dark place in the end" lest they contaminate his determination to be hopeful, as Mealer walks "into the trees," now away from the "dark place." Mealer turns the forest into a metaphor for the personal journey, transformed by its distance from the dark stories sealed in the box and left behind, mimicking the archive.

Conrad's novel enables the coherence of Mealer's personal narrative by serving as a place marker for the unassimilable, represented by Kurtz. Mealer can allude to the "heart of darkness," just as he can allude to Leopold's horrors through Hochschild and to the challenges of the Congo River environment through Stanley. The past revelations of others license his act of concealment, distancing him from his role as war journalist. Mealer faults himself and journalists in general for being unable to make the war in the DRC relevant to the West during this period (2008, 94). His own presence, his "bootprints" on Congolese soil, have sunk "below the ca-mouflage," the meaning of their traces left for someone else to uncover (xiv).

Mealer's war reporting (the first three chapters of the book, which I will contrast with the last two) exhibits the classic problems of ethnographic authority, revealing a text that lies about its own assurance in producing an "objective" account of a static other. His way of narrating events often obscures the influence of his own role in creating the conditions for his witness. The best intentions to be truthful are put at risk by the imperative to follow a script, which despite its rhetoric of overcoming is determined by the opposition that divides the places of anomy and civilization. These very categories (anomy, civilization, war front, home front) are the lens through which the redeemer witness sees, trapping him in their polarities.

Reporting on the war, Mealer systematically borrows from his sources and recasts the narrative from an unattributed point of view as this is what happened, especially when it addresses acts of extreme violence. Thus the book's opening recounts the events of the Drodro massacre on 3 April 2003, from an omniscient perspective.[10] The gruesome details of the Lema warriors' atrocities are presented from an omniscient point of view, although the reader learns subsequently that the incident occurred before Mealer's first visit to the region, and hence we can assume that he acquired the details from others. Mealer describes acts of cannibalism: "Down the road, survivors kept still in their hiding spots while several warriors opened the chest of a dead man, cut out his heart, and ate, blood streaming down their wrists" (2008, 2). We also learn that "others saw ... a lone warrior crouched in the road, feasting on the open organs of a man he'd just killed" (33). Exhibiting yet another kind of doubleness typical of human rights history, Mealer's text feels like a composite, part reporting and part memoir. In a memoirist aside, therefore, he reports that his translator, Johnny, confessed to having witnessed this second incident: "I saw them do it" and "I never believed it was true, but ..." (38–39).[11] Johnny's point of view is the closest surrogate for Mealer himself. The Western discourse about Africa is marked by such disclaimers, in which Western observers disclaim their proximity to violence while soliciting an alternative type of participation through the act of narration, inviting the reader's consumption of the story as "a surrogate for the performance of violence" and a confirmation of mastery (Coundouriotis 1999, 54). The pleasure in such fascination is one manifestation of the mastery over the other enacted through reading. The narrative relies on Johnny not so much as a Congolese subject but as an intermediary who can verify the most atrocious acts without Mealer being sullied.

Events are difficult to assimilate into story, especially in accounts of war in which the norms of behavior are violated. As White points out, "narrative becomes a problem only when we wish to give to real events the form of story. It is because real events do not offer themselves as stories that their narrativization is so difficult" (1987, 4). However, despite the impression of immediacy created, Mealer in his war reporting is recounting events that are often transpiring at an elusive distance, especially when the action is in the forest. He turns the resistant real into story by aligning his narrative with what's been said before. Retrieving the terrifying rebel commander "Cobra" from the forest, therefore, echoes the narrative of getting Kurtz out of the forest. Each repetition, however, is anticlimactic. After much tension and fear, "Cobra" emerges, alive and ready to negotiate.

After several years of reporting on the war, Mealer "decided [he] never wanted to see it again, not there anyway, and if [he] continued to pursue this death and decay, then death and decay would forever be [his] memory of Congo" (2008, 150). To change his memory of Congo becomes his goal. In the last two chapters, therefore, he abandons his war reporting in order "to see those places that weren't bleeding or blown to hell ... to meet people whose lives were moving a little ways forward" (150). He undertakes two journeys to the interior, one by boat and one by rail (Chapters 4 and 5), self-consciously following in the footsteps of Stanley and Leopold, and continuing to make references to Hochschild's history as well as Stanley's travel accounts and Conrad's novel.

The boat journey up the Congo River to Kinsangani enables Mealer to experience Congo at eye level instead of from above, which was how he had experienced it being flown in and out of war zones, escaping back into the helicopter whenever he reached his limit. Ironically, he goes on the river "to finally plant [his] feet on the ground," seeking an intimate eye-level view (2008, 159). This terrain has returned to the status of the primeval, the unexplored; it is "now uncharted territory" (153). It conceals the past, and revisiting it is akin to exploring its history: "A journey upriver was like breaching the very vine-choked memory of the land" (152). The tension between the "vine-choked memory of the land" and "uncharted territory" points to the landscape's ability to conceal. Mealer sets himself up to enter the landscape as if he were the first because, by regressing, the terrain has become similar to what it was when Stanley encountered it. The Congo seems to erase its own history. The eye-level view is frustratingly opaque, uncharted and unyielding. In this circumstance, Mealer relies on his experience as a reader to guide him. To show us how this works, he describes his translator, Séverin, an electrical engineer by training, reading Hochschild and copiously taking notes during the boat journey, eager to learn the history of the interior and understand the unfamiliar surroundings.

Upon his arrival at Kisangani (the real setting of *Heart of Darkness*'s "Inner Station"), Mealer confirms that it "was hardly fiction," echoing Hochschild's gesture of relying on Conrad for a measure of the historical Congo (2008, 204). Failing to find the progress he is looking for at the end of the boat journey, he rejects the validity of his quest: "I realized I'd risked life and limb looking for something that didn't exist, some modern notion of progress that didn't even apply. Like Buisine had said, there was nothing even before the war. And there was certainly little now" (218). The disappointment and anticlimax, characteristic of the narrative as a whole, are a lapse to the old views about the Congo, the ones that Mealer presumably is trying to disprove. They become an occasion for his renewed effort.

When he undertakes the rail journey, Mealer gives himself a second chance to find the positive, even though it will assume a different guise than progress.

The railroad captures most dramatically the imperial, colonial, and post-colonial histories of the Congo. Its construction was a high act of empire that enabled the more efficient exploitation of the Congo, as well as the implementation of colonial rule and discipline. As Mealer experiences it in 2007, the railroad has deteriorated considerably, and, barely functioning, it is dangerous and unpredictable. Yet he can still describe the train's forward momentum as reenergizing, inspiring a deep desire for arrival: "And just as this was about to happen, as the twitch of despair crawled up my arm, the Rénové [the name of the train] blasted her whistle down the tracks, so brash and strong it lifted the top of my skull and brought me back around" (2008, 280). The train, which is carrying refugees returning home from the war, shifts the witness's eye to focus on the emotional reunion of one family. Having done something for "his conscience" by showing a different side of the Congolese, "who only seemed to suffer and bleed in the news," Mealer decides he can now leave (150). Once again the literal and the metaphorical travel together in Mealer's text. The homecoming of one father is symbolic of a restoration that proves the people's endurance. The return home is also the arrival at the destination. In this war-torn country, being able to get back to where you were and pick up the pieces of your life is a kind of success, a bucking of the backward slide.

Despite constantly reminding us of his literary sources, Mealer insists that he tried to write around Conrad's novel. In an interview, he has described his dilemma thus:

> I try to make it a point with Congo to try to move past the *Heart of Darkness* references. It's so easy, you know, an instant association. And while I think I had an easier time going up the road [around Livingstone Falls] than Conrad did—I didn't see the bodies chained to poles, or the skeletons on the road—it's a really hard trip. It's really hard, man. I guess it's as hard as you want to make it (Bures 2008).

He admits, furthermore, that he had trouble understanding what he had accomplished in his many trips to the Congo: "When I got out of there, I felt that I'd really accomplished something, though at the same time, I wasn't really sure what I'd accomplished" (Bures 2008). Mealer's next project, the best-selling *The Boy Who Harnessed the Wind* (co-authored with William Kamkwamba, 2009), fulfills his objective to provide an uplifting story about Africa. *The Boy Who Harnessed the Wind* reinvents the figure of the male African child lodged in the imagination of the American reading public—through books such as Ishmael Beah's *A Long Way Gone* (2008)—as the violent child soldier, recasting him as an ingenious inventor and successful entrepreneur, an American-style hero.[12] As the Nigerian novelist Chris Abani notes, "William will challenge everything you have thought about Africa, about young people, and about the power of one person to transform a community. This beautifully written book will open your heart and mind."[13]

In this book, Mealer is able to place his redeemer witness not only in relation to Africa but to global warming, and hence present Kamkwamba in the context of an emerging planetarity. Furthermore, on his YouTube posting, Kamkwamba proclaims that the book is a message to Americans telling them they can achieve whatever they set their mind to. An American cliché gives Kamkwamba's story its shape, or "figuration."

In the stories of Congo, by contrast, tragedy was everywhere. Mealer tells of one exception, the successful escape of Séverin, who goes to Belgium to study. There, Mealer tells us, Séverin is "seeing the true world" (2008, 294). The "true," Mealer claims, rather than real world, thus indicating the metropole's moral superiority despite the contradiction that the "true" also reveals the exploitation that this world rests on. Séverin immerses himself in the life of young people in Europe, "where all they seemed concerned about is maximum pleasure," and where they remain willfully ignorant of what is happening in Congo (294). He does not feel compelled to tell them. Mealer's complicity with Marlow's lie becomes suddenly transparent, and it is Séverin, as portrayed by Mealer, who takes on Marlow's role as carrier of the lie.

The democratizing movement

Mealer also reported on the historic elections of 2006, the country's first in 40 years. Resident mostly in Kinshasa during the period running up to the election, Mealer hesitates to be hopeful and prompts his reader to expect political chaos and more violence. After the elections, as I showed above, he searches for the elusive "recovery" by traveling once more to the interior and, failing to find it, plants further doubts in the reader's mind about the success of the elections. Given the complicated logistics of carrying out a fair democratic election in the DRC, Mealer's distanced, impressionistic view provides too few specifics from which to understand the political dynamics of the democratizing process. Published in 2002, Georges Nzongola-Ntalaja's history does not take into account the events central to Mealer's narrative, but it gives us rich background to help us appreciate more fully their significance.

Nzongola-Ntalaja's importance is not his function as a native informer but rather his deployment of a different historical sensibility. He aims to make perceptible what Ariella Azoulay calls a "potential history" that "restore[s] within the order of things the polyphony of civil relations and forms of being-together that existed at any moment in history without being solely, let alone exhausted by, the national division" (2013, 565). Azoulay appeals to us to imagine a historical practice that opens our view of the past to the potential held by a heterogeneous group of stakeholders, as opposed to a practice that constructs the past retrospectively, either as the story of the winners or the victims. "Potential history" maps the road not taken but still detectable in retrospect and hence potentially available to be taken anew. Nzongola-Ntalaja appropriates the convention of people's history to write the story of the Congo as a struggle for democracy whose potential lies at least partly in the continuity of an ongoing effort. His story of reading is a story of reading anticolonial theory, more specifically the work of Amilcar Cabral, and of jettisoning the "heart of darkness" paradigm in order to foreground the historical agency of the Congolese people. Imperialism, Cabral argues, "is the negation of the historical process of the dominated people" (1973, 14). National liberation is not "simple decolonization" but a restoration of the people to their historical role (Nzongola-Ntalaja 1984, 48). As a people's history, Nzongola-Ntalaja's text is not simply writing back to empire. Instead, it envisions a Congolese national narrative addressed to the Congolese as a nation entangled in the global history of empire and its consequences. Congolese citizens are portrayed as rights claimants, struggling for self- determination.

As Nzongola-Ntalaja explains it, the narrative of Congo is one in which the two phases of the struggle against imperialism outlined by Cabral (a struggle against foreign domination followed by one against class domination) are intertwined and continue to run concurrently after independence (1984, 47). A people's history restores our understanding of the people as historical agents. This reclamation of agency also enables a critical examination of past events by attributing at least some responsibility for these events to the people. Thus, Nzongola-Ntalaja seeks to explain "the failure of the Congolese democracy movement, particularly the culture and class interests of those who have assumed its leadership and the constraints of the international environment," in hopes of setting forth a better process (2002, 253).

A Congolese political activist and academic historian, Nzongola-Ntalaja develops his view of the people's struggle in a sustained narrative from "Leopold to Kabila." Cabral, as Nzongola-Ntalaja explains, argues that "for a dominated people, genuine liberation implies the fact of regaining not only one's historical personality as a free people but also one's own initiative as a maker of history" (Nzongola-Ntalaja 1984, 44). "Maker of history" in this context gains a double meaning, referring both to the agency of the people in actual historical circumstance (Cabral's primary meaning) and to the work of the historian, the making of the historical narrative. Conveying how this secondary meaning of "maker of history" is actualized constitutes Nzongola-Ntalaja's story of reading. His work intervenes in the imperialist historiography of the Congo, appropriating a human rights discourse in order to convey his point of view as a Congolese political activist.

Human rights are no longer seen through the lens of crimes against humanity but as part of the struggle for "freedom from foreign control and expanded democratic and economic rights" (Nzongola-Ntalaja 2002, 121). Resisting the "crimes against humanity" frame is a significant gesture by the postcolonial historian, which we can appreciate by considering the contrast between the narrative frame of war and that of crimes against humanity. As Kenneth W. Harrow points out, "war implicates all its combatants into a generalized hell," whereas "genocide and crimes against humanity pit evil forces against its victims," drawing us ("humanity") to the side of victims, which can only account inadequately for the complex historical agency of all involved and their entanglement with one other (2013, 7). The "generalized hell" of war (portrayed by Mealer, in fact) is not useful to Nzongola-Ntalaja either, and he chooses a third path, the struggle for civil, political, and economic rights carried by a democracy movement.

The historian's authority is dependent on his effectiveness as storyteller, or moralizer; yet, as Said has pointed out, this narrative authority also depends on a power dynamic reflected in a disparate "permission to narrate" among different constituencies. Exposing facts about atrocities does not suffice to constitute a national narrative if the Congolese do not figure as subjects and as historians. As we noted, facts do not speak for themselves but need to be embedded in appropriate vehicles for their dissemination, such as socially acceptable stories that enable their readers' recognition. Although Nzongola-Ntalaja's political project of achieving democracy is incomplete, his historiographical project against colonial inscription is realized to the degree that he can successfully seize the "permission to narrate," which he does by hanging his narrative on human rights discourse. Nzongola-Ntalaja makes gains in rendering to the people their "historical personality" by showing how the long history of Congolese resistance translates into a human rights struggle.

Compared to Hochschild's or Mealer's, Nzongola-Ntalaja's text has a less pronounced metanarrative quality. Yet, its framing as a people's history gestures toward its appropriation of certain recognizable narrative conventions. Writing from a sense of acute crisis during a civil war in the late 1990s, Nzongola-Ntalaja tries to buck the pressure of thinking in apocalyptic terms of the end of the nation and instead brings the story of Congo in line with the larger postcolonial narrative of the African continent, which shows in broad strokes how national independence is followed by neocolonial rule and authoritarian regimes, renewing the struggle for social justice and self-determination. Nzongola-Ntalaja hopes to rescue the Congo's narrative from incoherence by highlighting a repetitive pattern of events, which helps demonstrate the continuity of the ongoing struggle. Furthermore, repetition falls into the configuration of revelation and concealment. Analysis of one period of history leads to the revelation of its similarity to a previous period, uncovering a whole sequence of concealments that suppressed the Congolese national narrative. Thus the period of 1963–1968, which marked the "first major resistance against the postcolonial state," is understood as a "revival of the mass democratic movement of 1956–1960" (2002, 121). Nzongola- Ntalaja calls 1963–1968 the "second independence movement," this time a struggle against the neocolonial state (2002, 121). By 1999, when "external forces were financing their war effort in the DRC with revenues from the Congo's own resources," we have repetition once more; "the Congo was witnessing history repeat itself. The struggle for democracy had once again become synonymous with the struggle for national liberation" (Nzongola-Ntalaja 2002, 141). The incomplete project of national liberation is sustained through the "afterlives" of its failed efforts, "an imagined but as yet unrealized future" (Wenzel 2009, 7). Repetition also marks the succession of oppressors. Mobutu is the successor to Leopold, "a new king for the Congo, and the true successor of King Leopold as the owner of the country and its resources" (Nzongola-Ntalaja 2002, 141). Because Mobutu owed his longevity in power to external sponsorship, the struggle for democratization was a struggle for independence from neocolonialism, despite Mobutu's nationalization of most sectors of the economy. Nationalization did not put these resources at the disposal of the people but turned them into Mobutu's private wealth. His regime is presented by Nzongola-Ntalaja as mimicry, a resurrection of Leopold as an African. Nzongola-Ntalaja covers in detail the ways in which Mobutu's regime failed and intensified the "extractive and repressive functions" that linked the former colony to the metropole. The postcolonial state, moreover, "proved inferior to the colonial state [which followed Leopold's death in 1908] in terms of meeting the needs of the population" (2002, 151). By 1993, the starting point of the current crisis, the economy was destroyed (151). In outlining the factors that held Mobutu in power (the security forces, wealth, outside support), Nzongola-Ntalaja also stresses that "no rule is sustainable in the long run without popular legitimacy and support" (165). He explains the narrative of the declining popular support for Mobutu's regime, which culminates in the emergence of the democratic movement in the mid-1990s (165). By emphasizing the upsurge from below, Nzongola-Ntalaja gives the lie to the portrayal of the Congolese people monolithically as victims of colonial and neocolonial rule or the barely human inhabitants of an anomic, regressive, violent "heart of darkness." There is no triumphant ending, however, as Kabila, too, takes his place in a series of patriarchal oppressors.

Additionally, Nzongola-Ntalaja resists the narrative which turns Patrice Lumumba into a martyr and seeks to make sense of history outside the frame of the "myth of an indefatigable fighter for national liberation and unity," a myth which is counterproductive because it aids the perpetuation of political rule as personality cult (2002, 247). When discussing the early 1990s, "with so many public services broken down, and so much time spent on finding food or making ends meet," Nzongola-Ntalaja points out that strikes may not have had the same effect as before but "traditional solidarity mechanisms continue to help people survive" (2002, 257). His attention to these "traditional solidarity mechanisms" that have evolved since Leopold's rule enables him to stress continuity once more and delineate a narrative thread that foregrounds the people's historical agency.

White argues that the "true" needs narrative to become "real": "the very distinction between real and imaginary events that is basic to modern discussions of both history and fiction presupposes a notion of reality in which 'the true' is identified with 'the real' only insofar as it can be shown to possess the character of narrativity" (1987, 6). Nzongola-Ntalaja must make the people "real" through narrative in order to establish their "truth" as a nation. The people are made into a character of the historical narrative (like *le peuple* in histories of the French Revolution, for example). They are conceived through the theoretical frame of Cabral, which enables Nzongola-Ntalaja to break down the exceptionalism of the Congo as "heart of darkness" and place the country in the larger context of human history.

Conclusion

The three types of stories that I have sketched here provisionally as examples of a distinct genre that I am calling human rights history (the moral crusade, the redeemer witness, and the people's history) share in common a strong sense that, as stories, they must enact their moral point of view. They are written not in a distanced, objective manner but from a situated and committed perspective, which urges us to reconsider that which is presumably already known. These types of texts thus share an awareness of responding to an existing literature which they invite their reader to reinterpret along the lines of their argument. To make their point, the authors tell their readers their own stories of reading and testify to the transformative experience of reading, inviting their readers in turn to experience their texts in a similar way.

These histories also grapple with uncertain outcomes. For Hochschild, the Congo Reform Movement did not have a large enough impact to stem abuses in the Belgian Congo. Mealer's memoir fails as a transformative narrative of the Congo and concocts a lie of arrival out of a very poignant but singular scene of family reunion. The repeatedly deferred fulfillment of the people's struggle threatens the momentum of Nzongola-Ntalaja's narrative. Keeping the people's agency in view not only for himself but for those outside Congo, who are ever ready to succumb to the conventional representations of it, continues to be a significant challenge much after the publication of his history.

Each of these texts also aims to be uplifting, to provide some kind of positive satisfaction for the reader. This effect is not facile but rather a function of our stories of reading human rights history. If stories of reading aim at "creating a possibility of learning," then reading in itself should result in a new awareness, which could be characterized as an experience of reconciliation, a balancing of accounts in which different versions of history are compared and realigned, redressing disparities in emphasis. The stories of reading in Hochschild's text, for example, demonstrate that we already knew about the extent of the atrocities in the Congo even though we had overlooked how we had come to this knowledge. We had put it aside in the archive without making further use of it. Hochschild reconciles the imbalance between the magnitude of the atrocities committed and the faltering campaign to eradicate this evil, a campaign which turns out to have been transformative of the way in which we imagine a more just future and act to realize it. By lending itself so easily to repetition, the "heart of darkness" narrative, Mealer shows, is not immutable; it can be updated, its lie reformulated. Nzongola-Ntalaja reconciles the imbalance between the rhetoric of liberation theorists such as Cabral and the bleak post-independence reality of the Congo by downplaying the importance of Lumumba as shaper of Congolese history and foregrounding the heroic resilience of the people. These kinds of textual reconciliations bring into alignment our old reading and our new and go some way toward positing the genre of human rights history as form.

Notes

1 In the prologue to his own such history, Samuel Moyn gives an overview of this body of work and concludes that it is "recasting world history as raw material for the progressive ascent of international human rights." (2010, 5). Afshari (2007) has critiqued the biases of this literature, showing that the compulsive telling and retelling of the field's origins constitute a fairly obvious enterprise of legitimation that also reflects considerable anxiety.

2 Crimes against humanity originate in the laws of war and concerns over violations of the laws of humanity. They were first construed "as violations of customary international law," and the phrase was used, for example, by Great Britain, France, and Russia in 1915 to condemn the Turks in the massacre of Armenians. Their present legal form has been systematically documented after World War II to describe crimes against civilians in war (Paust 2009).

3 An example of the first type is Gilligan (2010). The longer retrospective (and more encompassing geography) is deployed by Kiernan (2007). Kiernan applies genocide to ancient as well as twentieth-century history. The conventional project of world history (an examination of civilization) is reconceived as a study of mass violence. A third type may also be discerned in texts which take a form somewhere between biography and narrative history, such as Metaxas (2007); or Balakian (1998), in which "uncovering" involves a "story of reading," a trope which is the focus of my analysis below.

4 Gilligan (2010) provides a fine example. Divided into two parts, "The Crimes" and "The Response," her book takes on a form which reflects not only what happened but what could/should happen in the framework of international human rights law. Gilligan explicitly indicates that she is writing in a particular key ("tragedy") and draws our attention to her focus on atrocities against civilians and how these constitute war crimes. Using international legal criteria as her lens, she reinflects the narrative of the second Chechen war (1999–2005) as a story of crimes against humanity.

5 Nzongola-Ntalaja is not alone in this effort. See Chinua Achebe, "An Image of Africa" (2006), whose angry response to Conrad's novel is standard college reading. See also V. Y. Mudimbe, *The Invention of Africa: Gnosis, Philosophy and the Order of Knowledge* (1988), which is a key text in the theoretical and cultural deconstruction of the "heart of darkness" motif. Mudimbe's work as a Congolese novelist further addresses this dynamic.

6 See, for example, the influential reading in Leavis (1954, 196–197), as well as Watt (2006) and Brooks (2006).

7 The greatly expanded "Backgrounds and Contexts" section of the Norton Critical Edition of the novel, fourth edition (edited by Paul B. Armstrong) demonstrates this shift.

8 The secondhand nature of Hochschild's narrative, both a function of his insistence on using Conrad's text as a frame and his use of mostly already published accounts and known archival material, has been noted widely by his reviewers; yet it does not detract from the high regard accorded to his work, especially for its narrative style. Kakutani (1998), for example, praises Hochschild for his use of known sources, which he "has stitched together into a vivid, novelistic narrative that makes the reader acutely aware of the magnitude of the horror perpetrated by King Leopold and his minions." She notes his "tightly controlled anger" and the power it gives the narrative and repeats, as her closing remarks, that Hochschild, "like other historians before him," wants to ensure that Leopold's crimes are not forgotten. See also Clay (1999), who notes that Hochschild "transforms" history into a "page turner." Another reviewer also feels compelled to stress the narrative superiority of the text as a means of defending it against charges of unoriginality. Thus he says, "Hochschild's reliance on an exhaustive array of previous works on this subject does not make his book any less a 'must read'" (Hymans 1999). Silverman (2000) describes Hochschild as the "strong moral center in his work," privileging his voice over the material itself. With Hochschild's example, the work of human rights history seems to lie in the reinflection of known narratives. For a dissenting review, see Mitchell (1999). Mitchell raises problems with Hochschild's use of his sources.

9 The book was first published as Jules Marchal, *Travail forcé pour l'huile de palme de Lord Leverhulme, vol. 3, L'histoire du Congo: 1910–1945* (Borgloon: Bellings, 2001).

10 These events are recounted in Gerard Prunier's authoritative history of central Africa since the Rwanda genocide (2009, 291–92).

11 Human Rights Watch reported acts of cannibalism in Ituri in 2003 (Van Woudenberg 2003). Mealer (2008) acknowledges the author of this report, Anneke Van Woudenberg, but does not mention the report itself. It is interesting to note how differently HRW handles the reporting of cannibalism. First, they caution that the press tends to sensationalize these acts whereas it underreports the horrific and massive killings happening on a much larger scale. Moreover, HRW tries to frame its report by explaining how such acts become possible in a time of war. These acts were "part of a larger political and ritual context" historically not unique to Congo, and they are evidence of the toll that years of "constant threat" take on human beings who seek whatever means to survive they can (213).

12 Beah's memoir was promoted by Starbucks and sold in its cafés.

13 See Abani's blurb, found "Inside the Book" at http://www.amazon.com/Boy-Who-Harnessed-Wind-Electricity/dp/productdescription/0061730335.

Works cited

Achebe, Chinua. "An Image of Africa." In Joseph Conrad, *Heart of Darkness: A Norton Critical Edition*, edited by Paul B. Armstrong, 4th ed., 336–349. New York: Norton, 2006.

Afshari, Reza. "On Historiography of Human Rights: Reflections on Paul Gordon Lauren's. *The Evolution of International Human Rights.*" *Human Rights Quarterly* 29, no. 1 (February 2007): 1–67. www.jstor.org/stable/20072787.

Azoulay, Ariella. "Potential History: Thinking through Violence." *Critical Inquiry* 39, no. 3 (Spring 2013): 548–574. doi: 10.1086/670045.

Balakian, Peter. *Black Dog of Fate: An American Son Uncovers His Armenian Past.* New York: Broadway, 1998.

Beah, Ishmael. *A Long Way Gone.* New York: Farrar, Straus and Giroux, 2008.

Brooks, Peter. "An Unreadable Report: Conrad's Heart of Darkness." In Joseph Conrad, *Heart of Darkness: A Norton Critical Edition*, edited by Paul B. Armstrong, 4th ed., 376–386. New York: Norton, 2006.

Bures, Frank. 2008. "Bryan Mealer: War and Deliverance in Congo." *World Hum* 10 June 2008. http://www.worldhum.com/features/travel-interviews/bryan_mealer_war_and_deliverance_in_congo_20080610.

Cabral, Amilcar. *Return to the Source: Selected Speeches*, edited by Africa Information Service. New York: Monthly Review Press, 1973.

Clay, Rebecca. "Review of *King Leopold's Ghost: A Story of Greed, Terror, and Heroism in Colonial Africa*." by Adam Hochschild. *Wilson Quarterly* 23, no. 1 (Winter 1999): 103–104.

Conrad, Joseph. *Heart of Darkness: Authoritative Text, Backgrounds and Contexts, Criticism*. Edited by Paul B Armstrong, 4th ed., A Norton Critical Edition. New York: W.W. Norton, 2006.

Coundouriotis, Eleni. *Claiming History: Colonialism, Ethnography, and the Novel.* New York: Columbia University Press, 1999.

Culler, Jonathan. *On Deconstruction: Theory and Criticism after Structuralism.* Ithaca, NY: Cornell University Press, 1982.

Dawes, James. *That the World May Know: Bearing Witness to Atrocity.* Cambridge, MA: Harvard University Press, 2007.

Gilligan, Emma. *Terror in Chechnya: Russia and the Tragedy of Civilians in War.* Princeton: Princeton University Press, 2010.

Harrow, Kenneth W. "The Amalek Factor: Child Soldiers and the Impossibility of Representation." *Postcolonial Text* 8, no. 2 (2013): 1–20. Web. https://www.postcolonial.org/index.php/pct/article/view/1737.

Hochschild, Adam. *King Leopold's Ghost: A Story of Greed, Terror, and Heroism in Colonial Africa.* Boston: Mariner Books, 1999.

Hymans, Jacques Louis. "Review of *King Leopold's Ghost: A Story of Greed, Terror, and Heroism in Colonial Africa*." by Adam Hochschild. *History* 27, no. 2 (1999): 82. doi.org/10.1080/03612759.1999.10528338.

Kakutani, Michiko. 1998. *"Genocide with Spin Control: Kurtz Wasn't Fiction."* New York Times, 1 September 1998. https://www.nytimes.com/1998/09/01/books/books-of-the-times-genocide-with-spin-control-kurtz-wasn-t-fiction.html.

Kiernan, Ben. *Blood and Soil: A World History of Genocide and Extermination from Sparta to Darfur.* New Haven: Yale University Press, 2007.

Leavis, F. R. *The Great Tradition.* New York: Doubleday, 1954.

Marchal, Jules. *Travail forcé pour l'huile de palme de Lord Leverhulme*, vol. 3, *L'histoire du Congo: 1910–1945*. Borgloon: Bellings, 2001.

Mealer, Bryan. *All Things Must Fight to Live: Stories of War and Deliverance in Congo.* New York: Bloomsbury, 2008.

Mealer, Bryan, and William Kamkwamba. *The Boy Who Harnessed the Wind: Creating Currents of Electricity and Hope.* New York: Morrow, 2009.

Metaxas, Eric. *Amazing Grace: William Wilberforce and the Heroic Campaign to End Slavery.* New York: Harper, 2007.

Mitchell, Angus. "Review of *King Leopold's Ghost: A Story of Greed, Terror, and Heroism in Colonial Africa*." by Adam Hochschild. *History Today* 49, no. 8 (August 1999): 52.

Moyn, Samuel. *The Last Utopia: Human Rights in History*. Cambridge, MA: Harvard University Press, 2010.

Mudimbe, V. Y. *The Invention of Africa: Gnosis, Philosophy and the Order of Knowledge*. Bloomington: Indiana University Press, 1988.

Nzongola-Ntalaja, Georges. "Amilcar Cabral and the Theory of the National Liberation Struggle." *Latin American Perspectives* 11, no. 2 (Spring 1984): 43–54. www.jstor.org/stable/2633520.

Nzongola-Ntalaja, Georges. *The Congo from Leopold to Kabila: A People's History*. London: Zed, 2002.

Paust, Jordan J. "Crimes against Humanity." In *Encyclopedia of Human Rights*, edited by David P. Forsythe, 421–428. Oxford: Oxford University Press, 2009. doi: 10.1093/acref/9780195334029.001.0001.

Prunier, Gerard. *Africa's World War: Congo, the Rwandan Genocide, and the Making of a Continental Catastrophe*. Oxford: Oxford University Press, 2009.

Said, Edward W. "Permission to Narrate." In *The Politics of Dispossession: The Struggle for Palestinian Self-Determination, 1969–1994*, 247–268. New York: Pantheon, 1994.

Silverman, Sue William. 2000. "Interview with Adam Hochschild." *Fourth Genre: Explorations in Nonfiction* 2, no. 2 (2000): 203–218. doi:10.1353/fge.2013.0114.

Van Woudenberg, Anneke. "Covered in Blood': Ethnically Targeted Violence in Northeastern DR Congo." *Human Rights Watch* 15, no. 11 (2003): 1–57. www.hrw.org.

Watt, Ian. "Impressionism and Symbolism in Heart of Darkness." In Joseph Conrad, *Heart of Darkness: A Norton Critical Edition*, edited by Paul B. Armstrong, 4th ed., 349–365. New York: Norton, 2006.

Wenzel, Jennifer. *Bulletproof: Afterlives of Anticolonial Prophecy in South Africa and Beyond*. Chicago: University of Chicago Press, 2009.

White, Hayden. *The Content of the Form: Narrative Discourse and Historical Representation*. Baltimore: Johns Hopkins University Press, 1987.

White, Hayden. *Metahistory: The Historical Imagination in Nineteenth-Century Europe*. Baltimore: Johns Hopkins University Press, 1973.

3 The child soldier narrative and the problem of arrested historicization

An argument revisited

In *The Wretched of the Earth*, Frantz Fanon describes the incomplete process of cultural and political decolonization that characterized the immediate independence period as yielding a nationalism that is "only an empty shell, a crude and fragile tragedy of what it might have been" (1968, 148). Africanist postcolonial theory renames Fanon's assessment of the failures of decolonization, "arrested decolonization." Simon Gikandi uses the phrase, for example, in reference to Kenya and applies it to the stalemate caused by the trauma of the Emergency, whose scale of violence "called into question the nationalist romance of restoration" of the Gikuyu people even as independence was becoming reality, leaving Kenyans, therefore, unable to capitalize on the historical momentum of the liberation struggle (2000, 72). Furthermore, "arrested decolonization" is reflected in the displacement of the production and study of African literatures outside of Africa (Jeyifo 1990, 33, 40). This trend has accelerated with the demise of African publishing houses, one element in the complicated phenomenon that Charles Larson (2001) has called the "ordeal of the African writer."

The recent proliferation of African child soldier narratives largely reflects the new shape of African literature, written and marketed outside Africa. Arrested *historicization* offers a way to understand the narrowing down of historical scope compared to earlier African war novels. Child soldier narratives are symptomatic of an arrested historicization in part because they become trapped in a rhetorical effort to restore the childhood innocence of their narrator. As a result, they generalize a condition of African childhood characterized by victimization, voicelessness, and lack of agency that obfuscates and makes it harder to access the historicity of armed conflicts.

The new child soldier narratives since 2000 borrow from the self-help model of the recovery narrative, deploying the language of addiction and thus privileging a view of the individual that is significantly abstracted from culture and society. Whereas psychoanalysis has played a key role in the understanding of the postcolonial condition, nowhere more prominently than in the work of Fanon himself, the recovery paradigm focuses less on analysis and more on the production of a self. Key to the process of recovery is the subject's "appropriation" of story elements from existing narratives.

Olivier Taieb et al. posit that such appropriation from the existing literature on addiction is "necessary to enable the subject to organize his or her life, to give it intelligibility, and to attempt to become 'coauthor as to its meaning' " (2008, 994). Taieb et al. (2008) draw from Paul Ricoeur's theory of narrative identity, connecting it to a goal of the addiction literature: "constructing a non-addict identity" through the production of an autobiographical narrative. Furthermore, McIntosh and McKeganey summarize a number of earlier clinicians who argue that, for recovery, the "capacity of the individual to maintain a narrative of his or her biography is an important component of that process." Taieb et al. point to Alcoholic Anonymous (AA) where a "newcomer has to reconstitute his identity through the AA story model" (2008, 1503). This process mimics the Ricoeurian refiguration of reality by encouraging the identification and appropriation of a socially acceptable narrative for the self (995). Although Taieb et al. use Ricoeur to point out the risks involved in the process and show that the task of appropriation does not always go smoothly, for child soldiers this is a generative route (995). Traumatized by chaotic and extreme violence, child soldier survivors have little recourse to complex historical and political explanations of what got them where they are. Many, if not most, are also addicted to drugs, which makes the recovery narrative all the more appealing (Singer 2006, 111).

What we find frequently in these narratives is child soldiers presented as victims. The responsibility for committing atrocities is largely disclaimed as abuse the child has suffered or the result of drug addiction from which the child must be rehabilitated. The problem of responsibility in the war shifts to the task of recovery. The discussion of responsibility, moreover, then shrinks in scope, focusing on isolated individuals and their trauma. In his widely read memoir, former Sierra Leonian child soldier Ishmael Beah (2007) explains how he came to write his book only after he was helped to understand through therapy (for drug addiction) that the acts he committed were not his fault. Beah claims that at first he was very resistant to the idea that he was not at fault; "I hated the 'It is not your fault' line," he tells us, but eventually he came to accept it (2007, 160). In interviews, Beah explains how, when they first enter therapy, the children would often attack the caretakers (stabbing them, etc.), resisting their rehabilitation. When the same caregivers returned repeatedly after such attacks and said "It's ok, it's not your fault," then the child soldiers saw the consistency in the caregivers' behavior and learned to trust. These difficulties made huge demands on the therapists and only extremely self-sacrificing and committed caregivers in rehabilitation centers could give child soldiers back their ability to trust other human beings (The Hour 2007; CBS News 2007). The effort involved also transforms the child soldier's self-perception from that of combatant to victim. The mechanism necessary to accomplish this shift entails some willful overlooking of the child soldier's violence, albeit now exhibiting itself in a controlled circumstance (the stabbing of the caregiver becomes the issue, for example, rather than the killings and maiming of the war itself).

Beah's memoir has come under significant scrutiny for its veracity (Sherman 2008), but it is important and influential as it offers a clear arc of the child soldier story. For example, to justify his participation in the war, Beah emphasized his physical suffering during the period between the destruction of his village and the time he joined an armed unit. This interlude when the child is adrift appears in most narratives. Beah explains how he had little choice but to join, stressing necessity rather than outright coercion, and putting his narrative in line with the findings of researchers who understand that children "volunteer" when they find they have no other option for survival (Singer 2006, 62). The distinction between volunteering and forceful recruitment often used to gauge responsibility is a misguided criterion for understanding the complexity of the passage into war. Ugandan former child soldier China Keitetsi, for example, describes her victimization in these terms: "My childhood is long forgotten. Sometimes I feel as if I am 6 years old and sometimes as though I am 100 years old because of all I have seen" (2002, 7). Her identity is both arrested at six years old when her abuse began and also burdened with too much experience, making her feel much older than her years. By her own admission, Keitetsi tries to recover her own sense of innocence and, by means of her narrative, to "single out the abused from the abuser" (2002, 7).

The theme of a lost childhood serves to mainstream these narratives as it is also a prevalent theme in most stories of children in war. In her bestselling war memoir, *The House at Sugar Beach: In Search of a Lost African Childhood* (2008), *New York Times* journalist Helene Cooper is nostalgic and unapologetic about her childhood as an upper-class Liberian. She presents her story as a victim's narrative, drawing the reader's sympathy. Moreover, Cooper charges Samuel Doe's forces, her mother's rapists, with having "successfully hijacked [her] childhood" (2008, 340). Traumatized children of war, rich and poor alike, share the experience of a lost childhood and yearn for its restoration despite the passage of time. Memoir offers an avenue for reconstructing the childhood and also making a defiant gesture against the violence of war. Cooper, moreover, is both victim and savior, returning to Liberia as a US-based journalist to reclaim her family's "house" of memories. She recreates in writing a past, functional Liberian society whose memory can promote the country's recovery from war. Whereas Cooper turns from victim into benefactor (or from agentless child to accomplished and agentic adult) through her writing, the child soldier changes a combatant's identity into a victim.

Although in the eyes of their communities child soldiers are often not seen as victims, they are frequently cast in human rights discourse as the victim-perpetrators par excellence. This human rights framing, as noted, offers a refiguration of their real experience. What we read in child soldier narratives, where telling one's story is presented as part of the therapy, does not correspond to the experience of the vast majority of child soldiers. In real life, instead of storytelling, the communities insist on rituals of purification. As one subject explains: "If a person goes to fight a war, he becomes another person, because he learns how to kill other people, even his own mother and father ... During that time he only thinks of killing... When he returns he has to be treated to become his own self again" (Honwana 2006, 105, ellipses in the original). Such rituals of purification "do not involve verbal exteriorization of the traumatic experience of war" because "people would rather not talk about the past" (Honwana 2006, 108, 121). Restoration to a previous self, however, is also the goal here since the stated aim is for the child "to become his own self again." The reluctance to talk about the war experiences highlights the main contrast: that narratives such as Beah's, which are marketed as authentic, are mediated through the process of therapy provided by international organizations, and thus they incorporate a certain kind of talk as an extension of their portrait of the child soldier.

Whereas seeing yourself as a victim restores a degree of innocence that enables the reclamation of childhood, victimhood also becomes the condition of possibility for talking about violent acts. Thus Honwana explains:

> The recovery narrative sets the stage for a reversal of the child's soldier's trajectory: [H]aving started out as victims, many of [the child soldiers] were converted into perpetrators of the most violent and atrocious deeds. Yet such a linear progress does not fully represent the complex, intertwined and mutually reinforcing acts of violence of which they were both victims and perpetrators. Some boy soldiers were most victimized in the very act of murdering others; the more closely connected they were with their victims, the more intense and complete was their own victimization. But their identification with those whom they mercilessly killed was not redemptive; rather, it wed them more irrevocably to the identity of soldier." (2006, 73)

Plotted as recovery, the child soldier narrative suggests there is a path out of that identity, contradicting the trajectory of the historical experience. The first person narrative attempts a new self-fashioning through a number of already available narrative conventions that can be grafted onto the combatant's story, one of which is the recovery narrative. Such narratives encode explanations of the past, which are obscured, however, by the focus on the therapeutic effectiveness of storytelling and the demand for closure. In foregrounding history, I do not look for verisimilitude or reportage, but for the historical imagination implicit in these narratives and their metaphors. What assumptions do they make about individual agency? Are there political claims in their representational strategies of historical subjects? With the two memoirs by Beah and Keitetsi in mind, I read child soldier narratives in the context of a more encompassing genre, the African war novel. At the end, I turn to two film treatments of the child soldier figure to extend the reading and show how the big screen strikingly distills these narrative elements.

The child soldier and the war novel

A cluster of works (two novels and two films) by artists with ties to Nigeria fall within the child soldier victim paradigm. In Uzodinma Iweala's *Beasts of No Nation* (2005), the child soldier is victimized not only by being recruited to fight but by being forced into sex with his commander. Adapted into film by Cary Joji Fukunaga (2015) for Netflix, Iweala's novel disseminated the African child soldier story to a wide North American audience. Chris Abani's *Song for Night* (2007) offers a child soldier narrator who speaks after he has died and become a victim of the war. Abani's empathetic treatment is most impactful in its refusal of realist time and place. Newton Aduaka's film *Ezra* (2007) offers an additional perspective by substituting the rehabilitation motif (particularly prominent in the film adaptation of Iweala's novel) with a portrayal of a truth commission aimed at healing and closure.

Whereas fictional texts such as Iweala's and Abani's have been swept up into the genre of human rights fiction,[1] there are other child soldier novels that refuse this framing and, thus, resist the appropriation of African war narratives by human rights discourse. Two texts in particular stand out for explicitly rejecting the pedagogic and didactic agenda of human rights: Emmanuel Dongala's *Johnny Chien Méchant* (2002) and Ahmadou Kourouma's *Allah n'est pas obligé* (2000). Although they experiment with temporality, Iweala and Abani essentially follow the convention of the child soldier narrative which is told retrospectively by a "former" (for Abani, deceased) child soldier. Dongala instead creates two narrators who speak in the present during the war and Kourouma creates a circular narrative that begins and ends with the same words, proposing an endless loop. The retrospection of his child soldier narrator, who speaks very self-consciously as an expert witness explaining the general condition of child soldiers as well as his own story, is thus destabilized: it is a voice that comes from experience but cannot distance itself from that experience as it seems trapped within it. Moreover, both Dongala's and Kourouma's novels are cynical about humanitarianism. They explicitly foreground the agency of the child, which manifests itself in ownership of his brutal actions and the refusal of help or rescue. This independence also manifests itself in particularly vulgar and profane language, recalling earlier uses of irreverent, violent, and scatological language in African novels. In the work of Sony Labou Tansi, for example, profane language was a subversive tool against the oppression of the authoritarian state, targeting its claim to make the world (Thomas 2002, 60).[2] This type of irreverent child soldier narrative fits within the earlier convention of resistance literature that its language evokes. Through challenging, irreverent language, the authors attempt to convey the agency of child soldiers who are otherwise described as subjects who have been acted upon: kidnapped, drugged, and made to do things. The focus on language also raises one of the vexed questions of interpretation of the African novel more broadly: how allegorical are these child soldier novels?[3]

Dongala pits good against evil by deploying two competing first-person narrators, a sixteen-year-old innocent girl and a vicious sixteen-year-old boy soldier. This strategy clearly invites allegorical interpretation, yet critics' insistence on the novel's realism forecloses the allegorical approach. If we see Dongala as intent on questions such as "How can these children ever have a normal life? How can they become responsible adults, loving parents?" (Cazenave 2005, 62), then we expect the novel to be sociological and psychological. However, questions about history and agency do not have to preclude an allegorical presentation of war. Nor does the novel's engagement with history have to assume realism and verisimilitude. The exaggerated polarities of Dongala's fictional world are in themselves a commentary on the world he depicts rather than a literal transcription of its realities. These two models for framing the war novel, human rights and postcolonial resistance, cover some of the same historical ground, but are emplotted differently. Thus, Dongala and Kourouma's texts critique the child soldier identity as constructed by the international discourse of human rights.

A wider frame brings into view some important continuities with earlier war novels. Ken Saro-Wiwa's *Sozaboy: A Novel in Rotten English* (first published in 1985) is the most widely recognized precursor to the contemporary child soldier narrative. The novel's pidgin and its urgent testimonial style are openly imitated by Iweala in *Beasts of No Nation*. Another less recognized influence is Wole Soyinka's *Season of Anomy* (1974), which bears directly on both Iweala and Abani's novels. Soyinka uses the phrase "beasts of no nation" to condemn the condition of a war-ravaged population and to show how, without the nation-state and a sense of belonging, man loses his humanity. In Abani's *Song for Night*, the mute peasant figure from Soyinka's novel returns as My Luck, a child soldier narrator who speaks as a ghost haunting the nation from the dead. He tells us that in life he was mute, his tongue severed when he was twelve so that he would not scream if injured scouting for land-mines. In the novel's opening lines, he announces curiously: "What you hear is not my voice. I have not spoken in three years." This device of presumed voicelessness allows Abani to explore the mind of a silenced subject. My Luck's narration is full of anachronisms and inconsistencies, elements that destabilize the novel's historical reference similarly to the invented nations of Soyinka's novel. The indeterminacy of time and place in *Song for Night* (these are Ibo characters, but there are references to Lexus cars, so it cannot be Biafra in 1967, for example) suggests the kind of flattening out of time that occurs in memory where the past is part of the present consciousness. Thus, Abani seems less concerned with recreating the specifics of a particular conflict or historical period and more with the ways in which the memory of the Nigerian Civil War grafts onto his awareness of West Africa's civil wars of the 1990s where child soldiers become a more prominent issue.

Iweala's borrowing from Soyinka, on the other hand, highlights the difference in their treatment of war. In Soyinka's novel, the phrase "beasts of no nation" is in quotation marks, the accusing words of one character, witnessed and assented to by another (1974, 296). By protesting the conditions of war, the leper and Ofeyi are safeguarded from becoming "beasts of no nation," and a consciousness of their humanity is preserved. In Iweala's novel, the nation has disappeared as a meaningful term. Not only has the government collapsed in the unnamed country where the novel takes place, but the reason for the fighting has no explanation beyond what is necessary for basic survival in the reining anomy. Unnamed, as opposed to fictitious, countries in fiction are a way to generalize, to speak in broad and unspecific terms, and hence the context here serves to justify the extremes of the child soldier stereotype (Shringarpure 2016, 309). You fight to live; war is a total condition, a way of life, not a cause in the name of something. Agu's testimonial narrative in *Beasts of No Nation* acknowledges the new person that the child soldier has become in war; a transformation presented as a devastation of his personhood.

Secure in their sense of self, Soyinka's characters turn outwards, resisting and accusing others of being "beasts of no nation." Iweala's protagonist precariously turns inward and collapses onto the self that, at some point after the war, he must begin to salvage in a rehabilitation camp. Agu confesses to his therapist that he fears his story will present him not as a human being at all, but as a beast (Iweala 2005, 142). He has internalized the judgment that men are beasts in war, whereas Soyinka's characters pass this judgment on others in a gesture that expresses their own resistance to war. The human rights frame defines the conditions that Agu must meet to be redeemed: he will be judged by the sincerity of his revelations, which is never in doubt. As an icon of suffering, the child soldier turns out to be similar to all children in the discourse of development. Laura Suski explains how "As the poorest of the poor, children function in the discourse of development as testaments to international suffering. As deviants from modern childhood, their fundamental narrative role is to plead for the restoration of their childhoods" (2008, 207). Evident here is once again how the child soldier aids generalized, unspecific characterization. Yet Agu's plea will not be fulfilled even if his narrative humanizes him; the promise to be restored to childhood can only be frustrated. Although the child soldier's rehabilitation might depend on restoring some measure of his identity, the narrative itself can only function as a Derridean supplement, or substitute, for that which cannot be reclaimed in actuality (Derrida 1974, 155). The insistence on retrieving childhood innocence also carries a political danger in that it infantilizes the former combatant, preventing him from reaching adulthood. It ignores a wider context where a struggle for political liberation or empowerment might be taking place and an active (adult) citizenship with rights might become possible.

Iweala adopts Soyinka's view that war is literally bestializing: human beings, according to Agu, turn into animals and even look like animals (2005, 93). Thus Agu describes being raped by analogy to the same sex intercourse of goats: "he was telling me to kneel and then he was entering inside of me the way the man goat is sometimes mistaking other man goat for woman goat and going inside of them. If you are watching it, then you are knowing it is not natural thing" (85). Agu, anxious that rape dangerously feminizes him in a terrain of hypermasculinity, fears what he sees as the unnaturalness of same sex intercourse, which he stresses as a way to talk about the violation. The language of bestiality enables the rape's telling. The descriptions of Agu's repeated rapes in the novel are extensive and the insistent rehearsal of Agu's powerlessness, his complete loss of control over his body, underscores his subordination. Later, when Agu kills, he is unambiguously already a victim in the reader's eyes and becomes a channel through which his commander's violence passes.[4] There are no victims' victims (a premise for rehabilitating the child soldier in *Ezra*, for example); the subjects killed by Agu are the victims of his commander.

In *Destination Biafra* (1983), Buchi Emecheta provides another precedent: how to narrate rape in war. Her feminism, however, shapes an empowered protagonist who contrasts sharply with the narrator personas of former child soldiers. Debbie is raped by Federalist soldiers on her way to Biafra. Because, as a member of the Nigerian elite, she is an unlikely victim in an unlikely place, her mother tells her to lie about the incident and deny it happened. The mother is convinced no one will believe her daughter anyway. But when Debbie realizes that she has a story to tell that no one will believe, she becomes particularly motivated to talk about her rape. She finds the opportunity when she reaches London and testifies at a public event meant to raise concern for Biafra's humanitarian crisis. The story no one will believe, like Agu's perverse victimization ("not a natural thing"), gains traction outside its national context. It is spoken about in the international setting of humanitarian and human rights campaigns. Yet, the story of rape does not suffice as an instrument of political change. In Emecheta's novel, Debbie's disappointing experience testifying about her rape convinces her to go back and reengage in the conflict. She does not abandon her goal to tell the story of the war, but changes genres, turning away from the personal story to a broader historical narrative of the suffering of the Biafran people. While Emecheta and Iweala share an awareness that stories of war gain traction because of their sensational content, Emecheta's turn to history is notably absent from Iweala's portrayal of Agu who, at the end of the novel, addresses his therapist instead. The tendency of child soldier narratives to individualize suffering is apt to obscure the political context (Shepler 2006), whereas Debbie's focus on the collective foregrounds the political.

Emecheta's themes reappear in Chimananda Ngozi Adichie's *Half of a Yellow Sun* (2006), which (unlike Iweala's and Abani's texts) is very explicit about its historical setting during the Nigerian Civil War. Adichie handles the child soldier narrative with ambivalence. Although she narrates the events of Ugwu's forced conscription and traumatic experience (including his participation in a gang rape in which the narrator is at pains to preserve the subjectivity of the victim), like Emecheta, Adichie foregrounds Ugwu's plans to write a history. This narrative is not a personal testimonial of his experience, but a collective narrative whose title is "The World Was Silent When We Died." The accusation inscribed in Ugwu's title calls out the international community for its passivity during Biafra's humanitarian crisis. For a twenty-first-century reader, however, Ugwu's title also resonates with the circumstances of the Rwanda genocide, an event from whose media iconography Adichie borrows liberally to depict the pogroms against Ibos in Northern Nigeria, which immediately preceded the war. To strengthen this analogy between Rwanda and Nigeria in 1966–1967, Adichie also alludes to earlier anti-Tutsi violence in Rwanda in 1959–1961 and draws a parallel between Tutsis fleeing Rwanda with "tiny parts of their mauled babies" as keepsakes and a similar incident experienced by one of her protagonists. When Olanna escapes back "home" to the East after witnessing the violence in the North, she finds herself sitting in a train next to a woman who was traveling with her daughter's head in a calabash (Adichie 2006, 82). The sight is deeply shocking and traumatizes Olanna, who is only able to tell what she saw to Ugwu, her servant. The occasion of Olanna's testimony to Ugwu is the moment when Ugwu discovers his attraction to history and his ability to draw out the witness of others.

Parallels between the Holocaust and the pogroms against the Ibo have been made before, and Adichie repeats such allusions here, but it is the discussions of genocide in Africa that frees her to talk about the Nigerian Civil War in a new way. Analogies between the earlier outbreaks of violence in Rwanda and the Nigerian Civil War are not common in the literature of the Nigerian Civil War. Furthermore, Adichie depicts the characters in the novel discussing the genocide of the Herero in German South West Africa in 1904 (2006, 50). This genocide was understudied until it was given prominence by Mahmood Mamdani in his history of the Rwanda genocide, where he discusses the massacre of the Herero as the first genocide of the twentieth century (2001, 12). Through her references to Rwanda, Adichie implicates herself in the emplotments of human rights fiction while keeping her distance from the child soldier narrative, wary of its politically disempowering implications. Ugwu will not write about his own experience as a child soldier. Instead he will collect the testimonies of others.[5]

Throughout her novel, Adichie is intent on undermining the fixity of terms such as victim and savior, asking her readers to see these as transient rather than identitarian. Makau Mutua's critique of the "savages, victims, and saviors" metaphor of human rights is ubiquitous in the postcolonial critique of human rights, and it is important that he speaks of metaphor, not identity. In a politically ambivalent gesture, Adichie renders the upper-class, educated professional woman into the traumatized, suffering victim, and the "savage" (Ugwu as child soldier) becomes the "savior," historian of the people. According to the metaphor (and Mutua's use of the plural), people are victims of savage states and hence must be saved by good states exhorting them, and even disciplining them, to adopt human rights norms. The target of the critique is the cultural arrogance that presumes the moral superiority of the West and an inclination to savagery of the rest of the globe (Mutua 2001, 202). Dismantling the ideology is key: "the savior is ultimately a set of culturally based norms and practices that inhere in liberal thought and philosophy" and work to extend the project of colonialism (204). It is not entirely clear that, writing about war, Adichie breaks clean from the metaphor of human rights. What she does effectively is dissociate it from its Western savior so as to create a more complex and historically anchored portrayal of civilians and combatants.

Writers take up the categories of savages, victims, saviors as interchangeable masks that require a certain degree of complicity by the reader to be legible. Thus, they have the potential to be inverted if contemplated through a changed moral lens. A much earlier work, Thomas Mofolo's Sesotho classic *Chaka* (1986, first published in 1925), attributes the production of the savage metaphor to missionary influence. Mofolo emphasizes Chaka's childhood acculturation to violence, making the novel an important precursor to the child soldier narrative. He also foreshadows the typical relationship between abusive commander and child soldier in Chaka's connection to his mentor, the witch doctor, Isanusi. Isanusi guides Chaka's war strategy but also gives him the drugs he needs to execute the war and transform into nothing less than war itself. The transformation of Chaka, his demonization, initiates an enduring motif in the literature, that of the "male warrior as war personified" (Coundouriotis 2014, 26). The violence is of genocidal proportions as Isanusi advises Chaka to "let your spear be your hoe," deploying an agricultural metaphor for mass killing that correlates with what Ben Kiernan identifies as genocidal ideology's "fetish for agriculture" (2007, 2).[6]

Mofolo's Isanusi is at the same time a spectral presence of the colonizer's violence. His origins and real name are obscure; he comes from afar and brings magic powers to Chaka.[7] Moreover, Isanusi insists on being given his due when Chaka succeeds, in effect robbing Chaka of the kingdom he created. One can decipher here a historical argument about the *mfecane*, the wars that profoundly disrupted Southern Africa in the early nineteenth century and for which Chaka is usually held responsible. The novel seems to attribute the instigation of the *mfecane* to the meddling of a foreign power that exploited Chaka's sense of injustice and desire for redress to provoke war and increase its outside influence.

In *Sozaboy*, Saro Wiwa recreates Isanusi's duplicity in the character Manmuswak, who is Mene's nurse and torturer at different points in the novel.

Both characters (Isanusi and Manmuswak) are also precursors of the Commandant in *Beasts of No Nation.* "Everybody is enemy in this our war," a character says in Saro-Wiwa's novel, indicating that the conflict ("our war") is not between sides but pits everyone against each other (Saro-Wiwa 1994, 137). Sozaboy's helplessness is most acute in his interactions with Manmuswak because he has trouble recognizing him as either savior or savage. This blurring shapes how such figures convey their status as surrogate fathers as well. In a sense, they produce this version of the child through their presence.

Moreover, the child soldier figure contributes fuel to Mutua's metaphor and the challenge is how to retrieve the narrative of the child soldier from the operations of the metaphor. According to Mutua, "the metaphor of the victim is the giant engine that drives the human rights movement. Without the victim there is no savage or savior, and the entire human rights enterprise collapses" (2001, 227). *Sozaboy* can be disentangled from the child soldier narrative if we see it as a misreading of its protagonist. The term "sozaboy" refers to Mene's low rank in the Biafran army, his political disempowerment, and his childlike status as an uneducated peasant. Although Mene is young and inexperienced, the text offers contradictory information about his age. Apprentice drivers (Mene's occupation at the beginning of the novel) could be middle aged in real life (Ojo-Ade 1999, 65).[8]

Depictions of child soldiers can be compared to other constructions of the child in African literature that represent village life nostalgically. In such texts, the child is a thin allegory of the emerging African nation in the years leading up to independence. Like Camara Laye in his fictional autobiography, the child is on his way to be educated and will subsequently become alienated from his traditional culture. The narrative of childhood, therefore, attempts to recuperate this loss of belonging after the full impact of a western education is felt. The child soldier narratives instead tell of an interrupted education, reflecting bitterly on the lost opportunity that holds them back. Thus, Saro-Wiwa's novel focuses on this disappointment and satirizes village life with its narrowness and lack of opportunity.

Ironic treatments of the child soldier

The interrupted education is *Sozaboy*'s strongest similarity to the genre. Since promises of modernization and development at independence flowed from assumptions about the superiority and presumed universality of western education, the postcolonial civil wars are the extreme consequence of their nonfulfillment. It is not surprising that for both Kourouma and Dongala the interrupted education is a rupture that the child soldier seeks to heal. Kourouma's Birahima in *Allah n'est pas obligé* grieves the disruption of his education and carries with him four dictionaries that he uses obsessively to check the meaning of words. Dongala's Johnny admits to being seduced into child-soldiering by the words of a "professor," an "intellectual." His own education, although cut short, is a bit more advanced than that of his peers, and he constantly reminds himself of his own superiority on these terms (Anyinefa 2006, 93). Like Birahima, Johnny also collects books. Saro-Wiwa, Kourouma, and Dongala all in some measure satirize the boys' exaggerated respect for the educational system inherited from the colonizer. The satire is directed at the presumed superiority of the West and modernity, which now hypocritically condemn postcolonial conflicts despite their complicity in the economic interests that fuel the violence. Kourouma takes the satire a step further when he has Birahima repeatedly eulogize fallen child soldiers and thus mock the child soldier narrative itself.

The child soldier narratives also present the interrupted or missed education as a significant marker of poverty. What ties Dongala's two sixteen-year-old antagonists (Johnny and the innocent Laokolé) to each other is their shared experience of poverty, not only in individual but also in national terms; they are children born into the precarious economy of an underdeveloped nation. Laokolé's interest in and talent for science, moreover, demonstrates that the education missed is not only the education in the colonizer's culture but in technical know-how as well. Johnny's most cherished possessions are surprisingly the books he collects as war booty; an eccentric choice in his circumstances, but one that hints at a possibility for his advancement, a possibility never actualized. While Johnny's brutality makes it very difficult to empathize with him, his characterization is not without humor. As Odile Cazenave argues, humor is a type of "echoing" that:

> exposes Johnny Chien Méchant's flaws, his weakness, his truancy, his false excuses, etc. In doing so, Dongala deconstructs the whole process of de-humanization of children turned adult soldiers: at heart, Johnny Chien Méchant is still a boy, a child, who does not want to confront certain realities, who wants to pretend he is a real chief, a real 'Chien Méchant,' when his first nickname is 'Gazon' (lawn) and the members of his gang are contesting his authority. (2005, 63)

Although the humor makes Johnny seem vulnerable (and perhaps child-like as Cazenave argues), this is only by comparison to the other child soldiers, whose perspective the narrative does not adopt and who would not spare Johnny if they had a chance. Furthermore, Dongala's double narrative repeats the same events from the viewpoints of Johnny and Laokolé, two voices and tonalities, and succeeds in creating two failed versions of nationalism: Johnny's tribalism and Laokolé's Western-influenced, modern idea of the nation-state. Both nationalisms are fictions that don't hold up. Johnny's tribalism is a facade; he adheres to it selectively at his convenience. And Laokolé's experience of civil war shows her that the nation has a weak hold on the state.

When Johnny and Laokolé finally meet in the novel's climactic confrontation, Johnny tries to deny to Laokolé that he is a killer by calling himself an intellectual and showing her his books. Laokolé flings a Bible at him and stuns him enough to gain the advantage in their fight and eventually kill him. The heavy-handed symbolism in this confrontation of good versus evil is perhaps less stable than it first appears. Whereas it seems as if Johnny gets punished by a higher power (the Bible), it is also possible to see the Bible, turned into a weapon of opportunity, as emptied of all its content and its moral and cultural authority debunked, as it too does violence in the war. By flinging a Bible, which is only a heavy object in this case, Laokolé is hence freed from the moralizing authority of the colonial culture's Christianity that would ask her to remain nonviolent or, worse, to turn the other cheek. Laokolé's fury instead is evident, complicating the view of her as innocent and certainly lifting her from typical victim status. She beats Johnny to death avenging his violence against women in particular: "I began stomping, crushing, kicking with all my might, aiming my blows at those genitals that had humiliated so many women. I thought of the twelve-year-old girl in the camp; I thought of my daughter [a child she adopts], whom he'd nearly flayed alive with lashes from his belt; and I rammed him ceaselessly between the legs. I trampled, pounded, pulverized his groin" (2006, 320). Further destabilizing established categories, Dongala depicts the humanitarians (the United Nations and nongovernmental organizations) in a particularly negative light. In the novel, they are identified primarily by barriers and walls that close off their compounds to the displaced. Their actions are arbitrary as they select who to save, abandoning the majority. Thus, collectively, humanitarians are incapable of fulfilling the promises they hold out to civilians and appear cruel (Dongala 2006, 67, 157–159). By freeing herself from the oppressor Johnny, Laokolé is also freed of her dependence on outside intervention.

Dongala avoids any suggestion of the recovery narrative. The ending of his novel conforms to another cliché, however. It invests hope in a child who symbolizes the good that might come out of the war despite its destructiveness. Thus, Laokolé is filled with aspiration for her "daughter," an orphan she meets by chance and protects from Johnny's beating immediately before her final confrontation with him. She adopts the girl and names her Kiessé, meaning Joy. There is a feeling that this new beginning is only possible because of the justice rendered in killing Johnny, but Dongala does not moralize here. He refers instead to the "Joy at being alive. Joy at having survived. Joy at continuing to live" (2006, 320). More importantly, as a mother, Laokolé is no longer a child, and there is no effort to recover her childhood. In the desire to move forward and the embrace of a new beginning, the impulse to historical retrospection is absent.

Johnny fetishizes books, and Kourouma's Birahima derives his satiric power from the use of his half-knowledge to highlight the absurdity of the language of war. His obsession with dictionary definitions of French slang exposes the link between language and violence. Moreover, being trapped in borrowed, ill-fitting terms, he forces a reinflection of language to articulate experience from his perspective. For Kourouma, as for Saro-

Wiwa before him, one of the lessons that needs to be taught is that language too can be a space of empowerment, but it must be owned by its user, transformed and tailored to its speaker's experience. Inserting oneself in the dominant language as Mene and Birahima do partially redresses the humiliation and disempowerment of their experience and lays a foundation for a sense of justice.

Kourouma's dictionaries also allude ironically to a convention of the autoethnographic novel in Africa, the glossary of African words. *Sozaboy*, which was initially self-published by Saro-Wiwa's own Saros International Publishers and only later picked up by Longman, has a glossary in the back such as we find in earlier African novels. For Saro-Wiwa, the purpose is presumably to explain pidgin to a non-West African audience, although ironically it is a dictionary that translates one form of English into another. Critics usually attribute the glossary to Saro-Wiwa's desire to reach an international audience (Ojo-Ade 1999, xv), but in the larger context of the African novel as a form, Saro-Wiwa is being self-reflexive and extending his satire to address the earlier autoethnographic genre.

As noted, Kourouma, gives his novel a circular structure. Birahima's narrative ends with an account of how he came to tell the story of his life. Thus, the last page of the novel launches the beginning of the novel, the text being identical. The reader is left with a sense that he or she hasn't gotten anywhere, having only arrived once again at the story's beginning so that it can repeat. The pessimism implicit in this circularity suggests that we have not found a way out of the problem of child soldiers. The realization that the story is worth rereading softens this sense of failure, however. Birahima is a particularly compelling narrator and his narrative has incorporated along the way the stories of many other child soldiers, such as those he eulogizes. Kourouma effects an artful broadening of the individual narrative that, along with the obsessive parsing of terms ("humanitarian peacekeeping," "ethics," "decency"), destabilizes the genre (2007, 126–127). The gesture at retrospection, which ends by compulsively restarting the retrospection, subverts the linear narrative of recovery that Honwana critiques in her ethnographic work. The recovery narrative is easily assimilable to the classic novel of education, a genre whose boundaries Kourouma is certainly testing. John Walsh describes Kourouma's novel as a "deformation of the African Bildungsroman in French," not only because of Birahima's interrupted education but also because of Kourouma's unaccommodating attitude toward assimilation, which is reflected in his irreverence towards the French language (Walsh 2008, 185). But if the Bildungsroman traditionally ends in compromise and the hero's acceptance of limits on his nonconformity, it also creates a momentum to move forward, albeit on a conventional path. The obsessive repetition of the story of childhood that Kourouma sets up inhibits such moving forward and exposes the arrested historicization of the child soldier narrative, drawing critical attention to it. Perhaps the messy contingencies of history seem more accessible in the ironized space of such novels that have multiple perspectives compared to the overly insistent sincerity of the child soldier narrative in the human rights literature.

The child soldier in film

Sincerity is the hallmark of the cinematic treatment of child soldiers as well. Aduaka's feature film *Ezra* and the film adaptation of Iweala's *Beasts of No Nation* amplify the pitfalls of this sincere mode of narration that has come to dominate and which is Kourouma's very particular target. Overall, *Ezra* is the better film as it has a keener historical awareness and succumbs much less to the tendencies of generalization and broad characterization of dysfunction in Africa. Its portrayal of a female child soldier who is on a par with the male protagonist also makes an important effort to complicate the narrative. The story begins in an all too familiar way as Ezra's village, presumably in Sierra Leone, is attacked by rebels while he is attending school. He ends up in the rebel army where he is trained, brutalized, and given drugs. The apogee of violence comes when Ezra participates in the destruction of his own village, killing his father. The viewer also gets an "insider's" view of the rebel camp and an exposé of the illegal diamond trade. However, these predictable elements are complicated by two narrative threads: the retrospective, which comes from Ezra's testimony to a truth commission, and the romance between himself and Mariam.

The film is not historically accurate in its depiction of the truth commission. In the Sierra Leonian truth and reconciliation process, children did not testify (Rosen 2012, 288). However, the truth commission frame serves an interesting function in the film: it makes explicit that the human rights intervention is not the same as the humanitarian one.[9] The senior commissioner keeps reminding Ezra that he does not need to defend himself because he is not in a court of law. All that is required of him is to speak the truth so that the events can be documented and closure achieved. Thus, human rights is about truth and reconciliation. Ezra is a very resistant witness, however. It does not help that the first question he is asked is his age, which effectively underscores his status as a child and thus as someone not responsible for his actions. Ezra refuses to answer and suggests that his sister knows his age. Hence, the film makes him look immature and petulant as if it is insistently calling him a child against Ezra's self-presentation as a grown-up. He asserts that he does not remember the attack on his village and insists that he was fighting a war for justice; the lack of education leads kids to war, moreover, he says. The commission's work seems to be to rediscover the child in Ezra. The pressure exerted on him causes Ezra to collapse and next we see him admitting to a therapist the things he did.

The humanitarian angle is different and a bit more subtle, although it also leads to a dead end. It connects to the romance plot of the film. Once Ezra and Mariam are pregnant, they decide to give up their weapons and rejoin the civilian world. Escaping is not easy and what the film does best of all is portray the precariousness of this return. Giving up their guns, Ezra and Mariam are in danger from the rebels for desertion. As regular civilians in a refugee flow, they are also extremely vulnerable. Thus, in an ironic twist, we see them fleeing from gunmen at a checkpoint and Mariam is killed. There will be no new child here, and Ezra and Mariam will not shift like Laokolé to being parents. Putting down their weapons and becoming civilians, the child soldiers almost inevitably became victims. However problematic the guns, they were able to survive as long as they held them. The loss is eloquent in the film and bitterly ironic. It also speaks to the near impossibility of an effective humanitarian mission to protect lives.

If the truth commission carries the recovery plot in *Ezra*, Fukunaga's film puts the emphasis directly on psychological rehabilitation. At the end of the film, Agu is in a rehabilitation center for child soldiers, an idyllic setting photographed in soft tones that envelop the children in safety. The center represents home, school, and family at once, although all is not peaceful. There are references to the difficulties the children are facing and Agu is sullen and resistant to therapy. Once he begins to talk, however, he is restored to childhood so that in the final scene of the film he joins the other children playing in the ocean. This comes after Agu had said towards the end of the war section of the film that he could never go back to doing "child things" after all he had seen. Thus, the impossible does happen and, given the film's bleakness, it feels like a miracle that Agu can be a child again.

Fukunaga's film aims to retain the humanity of the characters, especially with its references to family. It therefore departs from Iweala's text, which focuses relentlessly on the dehumanization of war. Whereas the film's excesses of violence refer back to the book and hover on the edge of being purely gratuitous in their iconography of savagery, the storyline and characterization hew a more sentimental line, stressing family, especially father-son bonds, and the child's abandonment. The opening sequence of the film (which is not part of the novel) depicts Agu's life before he became a combatant. What would be more typically the village setting from before the war is here a humanitarian buffer zone with a vibrant community of locals who have also put their resources into helping refugees. This is most definitely 'civilization:' we see family, church, and benevolent, productively engaged adults who are community building.[10] Agu's father, a former teacher, is in charge of taking care of the refugee camp. Humanitarianism sustains this bubble in the middle of a war. In Agu's voice-over narration, he explains there is no school because of the war, and so the children must figure out how to occupy themselves.

Agu leads his friends in a pretend game of "imagination tv" where he uses a hollowed out television set as a stage for his friends to perform. The opening scene of the film in fact is shot through that broken screen, a frame-within-a-frame hinting that the safety of the buffer zone is make-believe. Like the "imagination tv," this real does not hold. Once the buffer zone is abolished, the family is split: mother and baby sister go to the city as refugees; the men, including young Agu, stay behind until they are attacked, and Agu, the lone survivor, runs into the bush and eventually into the rebels. What follows (Agu's war experience, which is the longest sequence of the film) takes place in another type of bubble, or enclosed world, which also proves ephemeral although this is not apparent immediately. It swallows up Agu in a whirlpool descent into violence.

This long, brutal middle section of the film arguably becomes the story of Agu's commander, played by Idris Elba. Elba dominates the film with his powerful, psychologically nuanced performance. He is such a draw though that he takes our attention away from Agu, who at times is just one of the many child soldiers in the unit. Therefore, the film contains the child soldier story within a larger narrative that follows the conventions of war narration more broadly; child soldiers are one dysfunction of war among many. The Commandant is a disgruntled officer, cheated by the higher ups of his monetary reward and promotion. He proclaims his loyalty to his troops to whom he is father and they, all together, are family. Bonds become complex and include forced intimacy. The Commandant rapes Agu asking him to "do this for [him]," hence drawing him close like a special son. The traumatic effect of this assault is evident in the remarkably expressive performance by Abraham Attah. Agu's loyalty is not absolute and the final break with the Commandant comes after the unit goes rogue, following the Commandant's defection from the political leadership that wants to remove him. The troops abandon the Commandant, and although Agu vacillates—threatening the Commandant with his gun, then standing as he watches the other combatants march off—he too follows them out of the forest.

The dominance of the Commandant and the viewer's engagement with him (which becomes almost sympathetic) makes sense of Agu's near absolute subjugation to this man. Yet, we need to get beyond psychology and its sentimentalizing narrative structures. The Commandant is the author or creator of this world in the forest: he has fashioned its dress code, rituals, behaviors, doctrine. In that, he has a strong cinematic antecedent in Coppola's Kurtz from *Apocalypse Now*. This is most striking when Agu encounters the Commandant for the first time and the angles of the camera echo the cinematography of *Apocalypse Now*: the camera is situated low and pans up to capture the troops and the Commandant, who comes down to Agu and kneels to look him in the eye. Agu then joins them by climbing up to the camp, as the camera remains below the group. To the extent this becomes another heart of darkness narrative, it invokes the humanitarian response even as the depiction of humanitarianism in the film reveals its weakness. Personalizing all that is evil in one figure, drawn so as to repulse and attract, serves a familiar aesthetic project to shore up a civilizational mission. The film also calls for better fathers and, in other words, less corrupt political leadership.

There are several sightings of UN peacekeepers in the film, but the force remains peripheral until the retreating combatants run into the blue helmets and surrender. There was an earlier missed opportunity to interrupt and save Agu and the other children, however. Walking along a road fully armed, the combatants are passed by a UN convoy that includes a photographer who we see shoot photos of the child soldiers, evoking images that we remember from the reportage of the civil wars in West Africa. Moreover, there is a white woman in the van who holds the children in her sustained, pained gaze. Agu notices and looks back, following the convoy with his eyes as it moves past. This scene indicts humanitarianism's politics of looking. It misses what is in plain sight: children needing rescue. Perhaps Fukunaga intends to break into a different type of looking and narrative. Although purporting to go beyond the snapshot, the film does not avoid the pitfalls of arrested historicization. Compared to *Ezra*, which attempts to account for the protagonists' ten years as a child soldier, we have little sense of time in *Beasts of No Nation*.

In sum, framed as a human rights literature, the child soldier narrative is too often sentimentalized and co-opted by ideas of the self that accommodate a largely first world, distant reader. The complexity of the historical, political, cultural, as well as individual circumstances of child soldiers requires a less literal, more ironic, and even allegorical method of narrative representation. Recent works, including films, come up short when they focus too exclusively on a portrayal of individual suffering without proper contextualization. An abstracted figure of the child soldier cast against a background of the "dark continent" has been commodified as the new authenticity out of Africa. Indeed, the most successful narratives (those by Kourouma and Dongala, for example) are the ones that take this abstracted figure and parse it, examining it as an invented discourse about Africa.

Notes

1 James Dawes provides the best definition of this genre, which arises alongside a multifaceted "global human rights culture." This literature has formed "a self-contained set of texts sharing key formal properties, an emerging global subgenre that can help structure high-school and college teaching and research, and that can illuminate urgent questions about the relationships among representation, beauty, ethics, and politics" (2007, 190). In his work on US fiction, Dawes defines the "novel of human rights" further according to plot structure: such novels deploy a "justice plot" or an "escape plot" (2018, 22).

2 Looking ahead to the discussion below of Fukunaga's *Beasts of No Nation*, Agu's politeness is striking by comparison. He is obedient, respectful, and polite to a fault with his Commandant. His language is direct and simple, childlike in that sense, but never profane.

3 Jameson (1986) argued that all third-world novels are allegories of the nation. He was widely rebuked for his overgeneralization, which seemed to erase the value of the individual stories and the real in novels (Ahmad 2008). However, allegorical interpretation can help us tap into the historical imagination of these texts which

resist colonial discourses of the real. In the ongoing debates about third-world nationalism, Jameson's thesis continues to be relevant (Szeman 2006).

4 The film version changes the sequence so that Agu kills first and is raped later. This makes the rape (a single event, rather than recurring as in the novel) a touchtone of Agu's suffering as a child soldier, whereas his behavior as a killer is somewhat normalized by falling into the background.

5 For a fuller discussion of Ugwu as historian of the people and the implications for human rights see Coundouriotis 2014, 229–231.

6 Kiernan argues that, historically, land has been more than an economic motivation for genocidal violence. The idea of one group's racial superiority feeds directly into a sense of entitlement over land, to the extent that genocidal violence fetishizes land: "Genocidal conquerors legitimize their territorial expansion by racial superiority or glorious antiquity at the same time as they claim a unique capacity to put the conquered lands into productive agricultural use" (2007, 29).

7 Isanusi's appearance is often misread. His exotic dress and strange physical features place him in a long line of figures with strange appearance who are misperceived as somehow particularly African, whereas they bear all the signs of the globalized culture of capital. The Liberian war lords in their dresses and purses, the child soldiers with teddy bear back packs, etc., carry the accessories of a global market.

8 One question pertains to Mene's age. Although there is general agreement that Mene is young, it is unclear whether he is a child, which legally would mean under eighteen years old. Moreover, the International Criminal Court considers conscripting children under fifteen a war crime (Kamara 2019, 28). Another question is whether the identity of the child, such as we understand it, holds. Kourouma has argued that the child is a recent identity in Africa; he dates it to the 1990s with urbanization and the proliferation of street children who were vulnerable to conscription (Borgomano 2002, n.p.).

9 Olivier Barlet notes that the Inquiry Commission (as it is called in the film) is a gesture towards a popular genre: "the trial formula so common in American films." Aduaka, according to Barlet, does something similar with the film's romance yet at the same time, by mixing these elements with "disarticulated narrative" (the nonlinear flashbacks, Ezra's amnesia, etc.), he asks the audience to be more active in engaging with the complexity of the characters (2016, 83). Similarly, Kenneth W. Harrow reads *Ezra* as a part of a larger trend of mixing the high and the low in African cinema, pointing more specifically at the film's over the top violence (2013, 29).

10 The buffer zone is also a nation as the community makes a claim to the land they are on against the state's decision to abolish the buffer zone and move the war front. Earlier in the film, a similar assertion of ownership of the land is made in a dispute between Agu's family and a squatter on their land who objects to the land being given to the refugees, displacing her.

Works cited

Abani, Chris. *Song for Night*. New York: Akashic, 2007.

Adichie, Chimamanda Ngozi. *Half of a Yellow Sun*. New York: Knopf, 2006.

Ahmad, Aijaz. *In Theory: Classes, Nations, Literatures*. London: Verso, 2008.

Anyinefa, Koffi. "Les enfants de la guerre: adolescence et violence postcoloniale chez Badjoko, Dongala, Kourouma et Monénembo." *Présence Francophone* 66, (2006), 81–110.

Apocalypse Now. Directed by Francis Ford Coppola. Paramount Pictures, 1979.

Barlet, Olivier. *Contemporary African Cinema.* Translated by Melissa Thackway. East Lansing: Michigan State University Press, 2016.

Beah, Ishmael. *A Long Way Gone: Memoirs of a Boy Soldier.* New York: Farrar, Straus and Giroux, 2007.

Beasts of No Nation. Directed by Cary Joji Fukunaga. Netflix, 2015.

Borgomano, Madeleine. "Being a child in Africa." *Mots Pluriels* 22 (September 2002). Web. http://www.arts.uwa.edu.au/MotsPluriels/MP2202edito2.html.

Cazenave, Odile. "Writing the child, youth and violence into the Francophone novel from Sub-Saharan Africa: The impact of age and gender." *Research in African Literatures* 36, no. 2 (June 2005): 59–71. DOI: 10.1353/ral.2005.0109.

CBS News. *Eye to Eye: Ishmael Beah.* 2007, 4 June 2007. Web. Available: https://www.cbsnews.com/amp/video/eye-to-eye-ishmael-beah/.

Comaroff, John, and Jean Comaroff. *Of Revolution and Revelation,* Vol 1. Chicago: University of Chicago Press, 1991.

Cooper, Helene. *The House at Sugar Beach: In Search of a Lost African Childhood.* New York: Simon Schuster, 2008.

Coundouriotis, Eleni. *The People's Right to the Novel: War Fiction in the Postcolony.* New York: Fordham University Press, 2014.

Dawes, James. *That the World May Know: Bearing Witness to Atrocity.* Cambridge, MA: Harvard University Press, 2007, www.jstor.org/stable/j.ctt13x0m08.

Dawes, James. *The Novel of Human Rights.* Cambridge, MA: Harvard University Press, 2018.

Derrida, Jacques. *Of Grammatology.* Translated by Gayatri Chakravorty Spivak. Chicago: University of Chicago Press, 1974.

Dongala, Emmanuel. *Johnny, Chien Méchant.* Paris: Le Serpent à plumes, 2002.

Dongala, Emmanuel. *Johnny Mad Dog.* Translated by Maria Louise Ascher. New York: Picador, 2006.

Emecheta, Buchi. *Destination Biafra.* Glasgow: William Collins Sons, 1983.

Ezra. Directed by Newton I. Aduaka. California Newsreel, 2007.

Fanon, Frantz. *The Wretched of the Earth.* Translated by Constance Farrington. New York: Grove, 1968.

Gikandi, Simon. *Ngugi Wa Thiong'o.* Cambridge Studies in African and Caribbean Literature. Cambridge, UK: Cambridge University Press, 2000. doi: 10.1017/CBO9780511554117.

Harrow, Kenneth W. *Trash: African Cinema from Below.* Bloomington: Indiana University Press, 2013.

Honwana, Alcinda. *Child Soldiers in Africa.* Philadelphia: University of Pennsylvania Press, 2006.

Iweala, Uzodinma. *Beasts of No Nation.* New York: Harper Collins, 2005.

Jameson, Fredric. "Third-World Literature in the Era of Multinational Capitalism." *Social Text* 15, (1986), 65–88. DOI: 10.2307/466493.

Jeyifo, Biodun. "The Nature of Things: Arrested Decolonization and Critical Theory." *Research in African Literatures* 21, no. 1 (Spring 1990): 33–48. www.jstor.org/stable/3819299.

Kamara, Mohamed. "In Search of the Lost Kingdom of Childhood." In *Research Handbook on Child Soldiers,* edited by Mark A. Drumbl and Jastine C. Barrett, 28–51. Northhampton: Edward Elgar, 2019.

Keitetsi, China. *Child Soldier: Fighting for My Life.* Durban: Janana, 2002.

Kiernan, Ben. *Blood and Soil: A World History of Genocide and Extermination from Sparta to Darfur*. New Haven: Yale University Press, 2007.

Kourouma, Ahmadou. *Allah n'est pas obligé*. Paris: Seuil, 2000.

Kourouma, Ahmadou. *Allah Is Not Obliged*. Translated by Frank Wynne. New York: Anchor, 2007.

Kourouma, Ahmadou, and Madeleine Borgomano. "À L'écoute de Ahmadou Kourouma: On est toujours un enfant pour des personnes plus âgées que vous." *Mots Pluriels* 22 (Septembre 2002). Web. http://www.arts.uwa.edu.au/MotsPluriels/MP2202mb.html.

Larson, Charles R. *The Ordeal of the African Writer*. London, UK: Zed, 2001.

Mamdani, Mahmood. *When Victims Become Killers: Colonialism, Nativism, and the Genocide in Rwanda*. Princeton: Princeton University Press, 2001. www.jstor.org/stable/j.ctt6wq0vm.

McIntosh, James, and Neil McKeagney. "Addicts' Narratives of Recovery from Drug Use: Constructing a Non-Addict Identity." *Social Science and Medicine* 50, no. 10 (May 2000): 1501–1510. DOI: 10.1016/s0277-9536(99)00409-8.

Mofolo, Thomas. *Chaka*. Translated by Daniel P. Kunene. London, UK: Heinemann, 1986.

Mutua, Makau. "Savages, Victims, and Saviors: The Metaphor of Human Rights." *Harvard International Law Journal* 42, no. 1 (Winter 2001): 201–245.

Ojo-Ade, Femi. *Ken Saro-Wiwa: A Bio-Critical Study*. New York: Africana Legacy, 1999.

Rosen, David M. *Child Soldiers: A Reference Handbook*. Santa Barbara, CA: ABC-CLIO, 2012.

Saro-Wiwa, Ken. *Sozaboy: A Novel in Rotten English*. Essex: Longman, 1994.

Shepler, Susan. 2006. *"Can the Child Soldier Speak?"* Paper delivered at Humanitarian Responses to Inflicted Suffering, University of Connecticut, Human Rights Institute, October 13–16, 2006.

Sherman, Gabriel. "The Fog of Memoir: The Feud Over the Truthfulness of Ishmael Beah's *A Long Way Gone*."*Slate*, (2008). 6 March 2008. Web. http://www.slate.com/id/2185928/.

Shringarpure, Bhakti. Review of *Beasts of No Nation*, directed by Cary Joji Fukunaga." *African Studies Review* 59, no. 2 (September 2016): 307–310. Project MUSE. https://www.muse.jhu.edu/article/629903.

Singer, P. W. *Children at War*. Berkeley: University of California Press, 2006.

Soyinka, Wole. *Season of Anomy*. New York: Third Press, 1974.

Suski, Laura. "Children, Suffering, and the Humanitarian Appeal." In *Humanitarianism and Suffering: The Mobilization of Empathy*, edited by Richard Ashby Wilson and Richard D. Brown, 202–222. Cambridge, UK: Cambridge University Press, 2008.

Szeman, Imre. "Who's Afraid of National Allegory? Jameson, Literary Criticism, Globalization." In *On Jameson: From Postmodernism to Globalization*, edited by Caren Irr and Ian Buchanan, 189–211. Albany: State University of New York Press, 2006.

Taieb, Olivier, Anne Rehav-Levy, Marie Rose Moro, and Thierry Baubet. "Is Ricoeur's Notion of Narrative Identity Useful in Understanding Recovery in Drug Addicts?" *Qualitative Health Research* 18, no. 7 (July 2008): 990–1000. DOI: 10.1177/1049732308318041.

The Hour. *Ishmael Beah–Child Soldier.* 1 May 2007. Web. http://www.youtube.com/watch?v=5K4yhPSQEzo.

Thomas, Dominic. *Nation-Building, Propaganda, and Literature in Francophone Africa.* Bloomington: Indiana University Press, 2002.

Walsh, John. "Coming of Age with an AK-47: Ahmadou Kourouma's *Allah n'est pas obligé.*" *Research in African Literatures*, 39, no. 1 (March 2008): 185–197. DOI: 10.1353/ral.2008.0007.

4 Improbable figures
Realist fictions of insecurity

Novels that depict the effects of prolonged and extreme insecurity often include improbable figures, characters in which they invest a hope for the future in order to burst out of a seemingly predetermined plot of gloom and doom. Characters such as Toloki in Zakes Mda's *Ways of Dying* (1995), Ahl in Nuruddin Farah's *Crossbones* (2011), and Kotchikpa, the boy narrator in Uwem Akpan's "Fattening for Gabon" (2008) each navigate a terrain of insecurity to improbable ends. Unlike magic, which can make the real more poignant (Rushdie 2014), improbable figures are not fantastic but realistically drawn characters that surprise and, simply put, seem improbable although they inhabit a recognizable setting and claim to be real. The improbable is used to draw attention to aspects of the real that are overlooked, especially the uncertainties of historical contingency.

The improbable figure makes us question how historical contingency works by surprising us with the outcome of events and our response to them, bringing us back repeatedly to a fresh confrontation with the real. When things do not turn out the way we expect and characters who should have succumbed to, or been determined by, their insecurity turn out to be resilient, inventive improvisers of the new, we take a second look at those circumstances we thought we understood. This second, retrospective look is at the core of literary realism's historical and revisionist gesture. Thus, the improbable breaks new ground because it calls on us to recognize something presented as real even though unexpected. A new understanding is evoked by breaking a predictable chain of causality. The reader's satisfaction comes less from recognizing the familiar or from an amplification of a sense of the quotidian and more from an emphasis on the break with the expected. The real suddenly is foregrounded as the other side of catastrophe, where everything has changed. And, although the real is now located in the prolonged insecurity that follows catastrophe, the improbable therein makes palpable a new sense of potentiality for the future.

Improbable figures frequently, therefore, occupy the scenes of humanitarian disasters or emerge from the consequences of human rights abuse. Stories of survival against the odds in events of mass violence are frequently circulated as improbable but true. Reporting on the horrors perpetrated by ISIS, Tim Arango (2014), for example, presents the experience of an Iraqi soldier, Ali Hussein Khadim, as "his improbable story" of surviving a mass execution. In this case, the militants posted video of the atrocity and the improbable survivor was able to identify himself in the images as "No. 4 in this line" (Arango 2014). He was left for dead among the victims. Readers familiar with realist novels of war will not be entirely surprised by stories like Khadim's. Such novels repeatedly have rehearsed situations in which the living emerge out of a heap of corpses. Who can forget the protagonist of Honoré de Balzac's *Le Colonel Chabert* (1832)? Taken among the dead at the Battle of Eylau and buried, Chabert climbs out of the grave and attempts a return to society, although his efforts fail. Society is too invested in the more probable scenario of his death in battle to believe in the fact of his return. In Arango's journalistic reporting, Khadim is interviewed with his family after the atrocity, apparently restored to his previous life: "back now at his family home here in Southern Iraq ... while taking a break from harvesting dates in his uncle's orchard" (Arango 2014). Such ordinary life was almost foreclosed, yet, the reporting shows us, here is continuity, survival.

The arc of Arango's journalistic narration puts all the emphasis where Balzac did not: in restoration and a celebration of a return to the ordinary, punctuated by the comforting image of agricultural life. The difference that emerges in this diachronic and cross-media comparison alerts us to a key emplotting device of the fictional genres of the real, which resist gestures of restoration as closure and instead point either to its failure, as in Balzac, or to the possibility of breaking through to something new, an impulse evident in the contemporary fiction of insecurity. To maintain the appearance of restoration, Arango keeps at bay a widely discussed alternative that confronted former veterans like Khadim: many veterans were forced to reenlist and become subject once again to the precarity of conflict.[1] Arango's story instead focuses on the restoration of normal life. Contemporary African realists more frequently take a different tack. They depict an escape from death that extends the improbable into a future unimaginable before the crisis rather than a future that looks like the past. Although a departure from nineteenth-century strategies of emplotment that tended toward disillusion, the emphasis on a sustained trajectory of the improbable into the future is not out of line with realist fiction's commitment to history. The commitment to portray change and subjects who are agents in that change directs the novelist's effort at dismantling plots that conform to a predictable and hence ideologically driven pattern of crisis followed by restoration.[2]

Thus, the improbable is a narrative figure that tries to capture the space of the new within insecurity and to examine it as a chronotope neither of stagnation nor of increasing deterioration, but of history making, of social change. Chronotope designates the way time and space intersect in the imaginative engagement with the real, with M. M. Bakhtin's emphasis falling in particular on the thickness of time and how it informs any consideration of space (1981, 84–85). Furthermore, "it is precisely the chronotope that defines genre and generic distinctions" by signaling various kinds of emplotment (Bakhtin 1981, 85). An acute awareness of temporality permeates the chronotope of insecurity and the improbable figure that emerges therein. What Peter Hitchcock (2010) has called the "long space" of the transnational, postcolonial novel applies, especially in the example of Farah, whose *Crossbones* is the final novel of a trilogy.[3] Such works "invoke time as an aesthetic apparatus for the production of space" (Hitchcock 2010, 10). Situated facing forward and backward in time, "Janus-faced" in a moment of crisis, the long space" also marks the "irruption of local history into the truncated temporalities of globalization and transnationalism" (Hitchcock 2010, 10, 9). By drawing attention to that which surprises, the improbable provides an outside, imagined diachronically as potentiality, to the all-encompassing claustrophobia of the insecure, usually conveyed as a dys-functional topos. The imaginary traversed by the improbable figures of this new realism occupies parameters shaped by multiple discourses of the real, such as journalistic media and NGO practices of collecting and disseminating testimony.

The improbable intervenes to change the representational strategies of narrating atrocities, veering away from adherence to what one might call the hard-core real, true to life and explicit.[4] The improbable, moreover, locates the center at the margin, a gesture that is expected of postcolonial texts, and performs "globalectically" to world the novel in a way that reflects the kind of reciprocity that Ngũgĩ wa Thiong'o (2012) has argued is necessary for abolishing aesthetic and political hierarchies inhibiting the full impact of the literature. Globalectics is a visual metaphor for dialogue among literary voices and rests on a presumption of equality through which the world is seen anew: "Globalectics is derived from the shape of the globe. On its surface, there is no one center; any point is equally a center. As for the internal center of the globe, all points on the surface are equidistant to it—like the spokes of the bicycle wheel that meet at the hub" (Ngũgĩ 2012, 8). These novels that capture the imaginary of insecurity set in motion some-thing akin to what Ngũgĩ calls the "equality of potentiality of parts," sig-naling the way they can open into the future instead of closing off with narratives of catastrophe (2012, 8).

Improbable figures in fictions of insecurity are symbols of hope that also open up a space of critique and change our sense of the future. They stretch realism's historiographic scope by imagining more broadly what we mean by historical contingency. This dynamic is best understood by close reading of particular novels. But before turning to these, I want to es-tablish more firmly the narrative model of emergency to which these novels respond and the antecedents of the improbable in canonical theorists of realism such as Georg Lukács (1980), Fredric Jameson (2013), and Njabulo S. Ndebele (1994).

Insecurity and the temporality of emergency

The idea of emergency is a powerful regulatory force that amounts to a worldview, what Craig Calhoun calls the "emergency imaginary" (2004, 376). According to Calhoun, our understanding of the global order rests on the expectation that it is essentially regular and predictable, and thus we are sensitized to interruptions or unexpected events. Moreover, when such disruptions make us aware of a sudden surge in large-scale human suffering, we are compelled to intervene to set things back on course. As Calhoun explains: "'Emergency' is a way of grasping problematic events, a way of imagining them that emphasizes their apparent unpredictability, abnormality and brevity, and that carries the corollary that response—intervention—is necessary. The international emergency, it is implied, both can and should be managed" (2004, 375). The framing of events as emergencies becomes an essential feature of those events; emergencies only appear unpredictable. Or, put differently, operating from the premise that emergencies are sudden and unpredictable disasters produces phenomena called emergencies (Calhoun 2004, 377). Therefore, the "emergency imaginary" can mask the structural weaknesses that make societies prone to crisis by presenting a temporality of sudden interruption, or eruption, that veers strongly in response back to the preexisting order. Humanitarian organizations have the "social capacity to designate a situation as an emergency" and hence to shape our sense of reality (Barnett and Weiss 2008, 42).

Because it indicates an interruption of normal temporality, emergency forces us to reconsider our relationship to time. But it also implies a particular spatial organization. Calhoun has called the perspective of humanitarianism the "view from nowhere" because it is founded on the fiction of a distanced point of view that separates the global North from places of crisis, obfuscating the ways in which it is implicated in what happens in the global South (2004, 376). Such distancing makes it possible to construct the real as a conventional distanced view and works against the globalectic imagination, which presumes a radius with multiple spokes. Furthermore, Luc Boltanski's (1999) influential thinking on "distant suffering" shows how distance allows for a triangulation among three figures: the person suffering, the spectator to that suffering, and the observer of the dynamic between the two. This third figure is characterized as an "introspector" because he can enter the mind of the spectator and describe how the spectator processes the suffering he is viewing. As a result the "person who reports and the spectator are no longer one and the same" (Boltanski 1999, 43). In narrative theory, the problems Boltanski alludes to make up some of the tricky ground differentiating the concepts of focalization and free indirect discourse, both of which inform the practices of realism.[5]

Calhoun's "nowhere" and Luc Boltanski's "distance" point to the ways in which emergency produces space, dividing it between a safe proximity and dangerous realms further away. Yet, problems of temporality also trouble the imaginary of emergency. Demarcating the beginning and end of a disruptive event designated as a humanitarian emergency is difficult in practice. The "emergency imaginary" produces robust terms with which to declare the onset of a crisis, such as "abnormal" and "sudden" (Fearon 2008, 52). However, those saving lives on the ground have difficulty bringing such interventions to a close. The expectations for what a return to normal might be in such conditions are unclear as the intervention may only push back to a previous stage of an ongoing crisis, failing to alleviate suffering in a satisfactory way. As Calhoun notes: "Many 'emergencies' develop over long periods of time and are not merely predictable but are watched for weeks or months or years before they break into public consciousness" (2008, 83). Identifying a new crisis, distinguishing it as different from what has already been going on, further complicates the timeline of humanitarian intervention. Such problems of temporality are highly pertinent for theorizing the narratives of crisis and insecurity.

Whereas crisis has a less clear temporality than emergency and is more expansive, both terms "prioritize the present over the past and future" (Redfield 2013, 14). Foregrounding the "present" complicates the temporality of the "emergency imaginary" in more ways than simply making us aware of the tension between emergency response and development projects, the latter of which clearly aim to shape the future.[6] Intervention involves a prolonged stasis in an expanded "present" outside a normal temporality. Emergency might present a rapidly moving timeline of worsening conditions that must be halted through intervention. Once the intervention is underway, the danger of getting caught up in a downward spiral of destruction is more feared than stagnation. Along these lines, emergencies are often theorized as states of exception.[7]

The improbable figures that occupy the novel of insecurity surprise because they do not obey the rules of representation from such states of exception. They are not disturbing figures such as Primo Levi's "Muselmänner," deprived of their humanity to become "non-men" (Levi 1996, 90), but are consoling figures instead. The improbable dismantles the assumption of an inescapable stagnation in crisis and returns the communities in crisis to a temporality of individual lives. Improbable figures make a radical gesture of reclaiming the meaning of these lives for the individuals who live them, foregrounding those individuals as autonomous actors and releasing them into a more open future.

Novels of insecurity explore what it feels like to live in crisis conditions and allow the characters to discover and frame the terms of the crisis. Despite the extent to which humanitarian organizations aim to be surrogate witnesses for the populations they serve (Fassin and Rechtman 2009, 192–94), a perspective from below remains elusive in their accounts. The distance such humanitarianism maintains between a purported us and them frequently yields an "ironic spectator" who displaces the conventional idea of a humanitarian actor. The "ironic spectator" participates in an "elliptical form of communication that remains silent on the vulnerable other so as to gesture towards the knowingness of the West" (Chouliaraki 2013, 176). How to avoid this pitfall is a challenge. Erica Caple James's (2010) ethnographic work in Haiti fills an important gap in the literature on humanitarianism because it provides a nuanced perspective on how insecurity is framed by its victims, accomplishing this in part by suggesting a different approach to the temporality of insecurity.

James's emphasis is from the start on the new that emerges out of insecurity. Under the conditions of long-term insecurity, she reports, Haitians "formulated new political subjectivities as apparatuses of terror and compassion intervened in their lives" (2010, 1). In the years following the restoration of democracy on October 15, 1994, "Haiti continued to be plagued by political and criminal violence, called ensekirite (insecurity), in everyday discourse" (James 2004, 128). The climate was one of "pervasive fear and 'nervousness'" (a term James borrows from Michael Taussig) (128). In James's evocative terms, insecurity was both "acute" and "chronic" for the subjects in her study—those "viktim" who had suffered political violence during the coup years of 1991–94 and had to endure the insecurity that followed in an already traumatized condition (128). Ensekirite contrasts sharply with the notion of humanitarian emergency that deploys the purportedly apolitical "view from nowhere" about a distant place to create a sharply delineated moment of disruption. James further elongates the time frame by historicizing her study in the context of Haiti's experience of political instability since its independence in 1804. The implications of her ethnography carry forward as well, past the end of her study, as they persist in the aftermath of the earthquake of 12 January 2010.

James's emphasis on the compounding effect of long-term insecurity and fear is most useful for reading the novels of insecurity. More than a number of different emergencies following each other, the period examined as one extended sweep of time gains coherence as a different kind of history, one of compounding effects, resulting in profound changes that for some time remain unassimilable to our story telling. Unassimilable may not be James's term, but it corresponds with James's emphasis on trauma. If insecurity evokes a discomforting randomness that feeds the terror it produces, the telling of its history aims to demystify and explain. Such are the conventional tasks of realism in its classic, nineteenth-century form when it was closely associated with the genre of narrative history. Distance evokes objectivity and the expansiveness of the form sought, in Lukács's words, "to uncover and construct the concealed totality of life" (1971b, 60). A narrative of prolonged insecurity with compounding effects might find it difficult to attain such transparency, yet the improbable figure is situated where reaching for such transparency can be transformative. Moreover, to find the antecedent to the improbable we need to look at the discussion of typicality of realist texts and the horizon of expectations typicality creates regarding historical contingency.

Typicality and contingency

In his writings on realism and the historical novel, Lukács argues that the novel should "evoke the totality" of social relations (1983, 139). The particular must give an "immediate impression of an entire society in movement" (139). Readers of Lukács have usually stopped here, remembering that he calls for the novel to "give central place throughout to all that is typical in characters, circumstances, scenes, etc." (139). What tends to be overlooked is that Lukács qualifies typicality as something that sounds almost like its opposite. His discussion takes place in the context of a comparison of the novel to drama. Characters in drama "must be directly and immediately typical," or, in other words, they must be instantly recognizable by the audience as a type, and the action must "concentrate upon one central collision" (1983, 140). The novel, however, provides a different experience of the real. It unveils reality in increments as process, showing what Lukács calls "an entire society in movement." Thus, the "typical quality of a character in a novel is very often only a tendency which asserts itself gradually, which emerges to the surface only by degrees out of the whole" (140). In *Studies in European Realism* (1964), Lukács goes further and acknowledges that the crystallization of a typical figure represents an unusual congruence of qualities. Novelists after Balzac and Stendhal "confuse the typical with the average," whereas the masters of the form "regard as typical only figures of exceptional qualities, who mirror all the essential aspects of some definite stage of development" (1964, 71).

The typical in the aesthetic of realism, therefore, must not be confused with the stereotypical. The typical is not a synonym for the probable. Typicality reflects the result of historical contingency, which makes it unforeseeable although in hindsight recognizable. To be historical it cannot be probable or conform to an already mapped narrative. The unfolding narrative captures a process of "crystallizing the really typical" (Lukács 1983, 140). The predictable plots of certain conventions of realism do not yield the kind of historical engagement with social reality that meets the standard of realist fiction for Lukács. Instead they succumb to naturalism and its deterministic logic. Elsewhere, Lukács shifts the emphasis away from the capacity of individual characters to capture typicality altogether and argues instead that the whole must be typical: "The concrete totality of literary portrayal deals only with individuals and individual destinies, whose living interactions illuminate, complement and make each other comprehensible, the connection between such individuals being what makes the whole typical" (1980, 50).

Fredric Jameson grounds realism on the claim that it does not merely reproduce appearances but has a "binding relationship to the real itself, that is to say, to those realms of knowledge and praxis that had traditionally been differentiated from the realm of the aesthetic, with its disinterested judgments and its constitution as sheer appearance" (1988, 135). Knowledge and praxis, understanding the world and acting in it, are not necessarily modeled by characters in the novel but conveyed as a worldview through the novelist's total achievement. The reality created from realism is not imitation, and hence not a reality reproduced, so much as the explication of a dynamic model. Allusions to the visual and photographic (common metaphors of realism) are treated with deep suspicion as providing a false impression of transparency and immediacy. Thus Jameson credits Lukács with explaining how realism functions as a series of mediations rather than "the 'bad immediacy' of a photographic naturalism" (1988, 138). Furthermore, an understanding of realism's hybrid forms arises from the tension between assertions of what it is and what it is not, what Jameson has come to call the "antinomies of realism" that are part of his dialectical approach (2013, 2).

In his discussion of the war novel as a realist genre, Jameson comes closest to engaging the kind of insecurity explored here. Once again he identifies the novel's capacity to convey process over image as a function of realism. The difficulty of representing war, and indeed the genre's own haunted sense that its subject is unrepresentable, inhibits the novel of war from achieving a created totality (2013, 233). The eight narrative variants of war fiction that Jameson identifies are less interesting as a convincing list than as an example of a narrative model that makes sense only as it breaks apart. The point of the types is not that together they can make the whole cohere, but that the import of the high number of variations (and potentially more) somehow forestalls the escape to visual representation as a shorthand. For war "there is no correct or 'true,' photographically accurate rendering of such multidimensional realities" (Jameson 2013, 234). Writing cannot be photographically accurate, and photography cannot accommodate the multidimensionality that the best realist fiction is capable of conveying.

The effort to make space for stories and to keep the spectacular at bay provides an opening for the improbable to surface. In South Africa, protest fiction that displayed the spectacle of apartheid wrongs was the norm until the transition to democracy opened up more possibilities for fiction (Mda 2008, 42). Njabulo S. Ndebele (1994) addresses this shift in a manifesto of a new aesthetics of the "ordinary" that speaks against the spectacularization of suffering. The "rediscovery of the ordinary" aims to "break down the barriers of the obvious in order to reveal new possibilities of understanding and action" (1994, 52). Calling for more attention to the "interiority" of characters, Ndebele explains: "The spectacular documents; it indicts implicitly; it is demonstrative, preferring exteriority to interiority ... obliterating the details" (49). Furthermore, the spectacular disempowers its audience: "it confirms without necessarily offering a challenge. It is the literature of the powerless identifying the key factor responsible for their powerlessness. Nothing beyond this can be expected of it" (49). The "new possibilities for understanding and action" that Ndebele calls for through a fiction of the "ordinary" are stymied by the spectacle of wrongs.

Ndebele's intervention echoes the terms of Lukács's critique of naturalism, which he charged was a genre of documentation rather than narration. Description in naturalism drowns everything else out and inhibits a portrayal of characters as agents. The "dramatic element" that showcases characters in action in their particular environment and thus lends realism its historical insights cannot develop as the characters remain subordinated to that environment, one that is, moreover, prone to be viewed through the lens of "catastrophe" or crisis (Lukács 1971a, 118, 122). We find, therefore, a consistent thread of argument that warns against the limitations of "the reportage novel that takes its methods of depicting reality from eye-witness journalism" (Lukács 1980, 52) and advocates a kind of realism (the "ordinary") that engages with the density of everyday experience. The "complexity" of ordinary lives, the depth of affect and understanding, is easily overlooked by the framing of these lives within the context of unending crisis (Ndebele 1994, 53). Deep poverty persists even after the end of apartheid and creates an environment of prolonged insecurity that necessitates a fresh approach (Ndebele 1994, 54). If this type of realism aims to surprise, it surprises with "rediscovery," setting us back on course. The improbable registers a similar jolt, coming unexpectedly but making sense after all. In the examples that follow from works by Mda, Farah, and Akpan, two motifs prevail: a recurring comparison between journalism and fiction and an exploration of the real in their divergent discourses, and the depiction of children either as improbable characters or, more obliquely, as the inspiration of the adults' improbability or resilience.

Mda's improbable ordinary man

Mda's *Ways of Dying* evokes James's description of ensekirite as the "seemingly random political and criminal violence that ebbed and flowed in waves amid ongoing economic, social, and environmental decline" (James 2010, 8). Because, according to her observation, ensekirite is "experienced as vulnerability, anxiety, and a heightened sense of risk at a sensory level, especially by those who are most vulnerable," James comes to see it as the "embodied uncertainty generated by political, criminal, economic, and also spiritual ruptures that many individuals and groups continue to experience in Haiti" (2010, 8).[8] Out of this, the new emerges.

Even though the novel draws from real events and newspaper stories, *Ways of Dying* subverts what Lukács calls the "reportage novel," akin to "eye-witness journalism" (1980, 52). Mda has stated that "[e]very death Toloki mourns in my novel was a real death that I read about or I knew about personally because it affected family and friends" (2012, 382). The real, in the form of repeated atrocities against children or incidents of mass violence, is both highly traumatic and easily exploited for its sensational effects. Although

Mda engages the aftermaths of these horrors, he seeks to blunt the sensational treatment of them. The tension between a journalistic real and the real conveyed through imagined experience provides the novel with a space in which to explore the boundaries of the improbable.[9]

Set during the transition to democracy (between Nelson Mandela's release from prison and the election of 1994), *Ways of Dying* creates an exceptionally empathetic and resilient protagonist. Toloki, an impoverished homeless man (an ordinary man), does not flinch from confronting the extreme violence of his time and indeed facilitates a fuller account of it. He also reenergizes those who suffered the worse consequences of this violence, changing their orientation toward the future and helping them imagine new lives. This is "rediscovery."

In a reflection on the inspiration for the novel, Mda ties the work of the imagination to our response to trauma: "I knew that the brain was capable of creating magic to palliate the pain of the present. We draw within ourselves to comfort our sorrows and to heal our pain and we call it God. We are the originators of our own spirituality. Yes, I am a spiritual being, thanks to the power of imagination" (2012, 305). Locating resilience in introspection and creativity, he discusses imagination as a creative force that produces an individual, spiritual response to emotional pain. Laying claim to one's capacity for creativity and self-invention is fundamental to Mda's understanding of individual freedom. Because this capacity must be seized upon by the subject and is essentially self-directed, it places a significant degree of responsibility on individuals for realizing their freedom. At the same time, it calls upon the community to respond and accept these highly individualized visions of self in the effort to establish a secure community. This interaction between the individual and the community is complex and fraught with difficulty as different interests and exigencies interfere to render it precarious and threatened.

In *Ways of Dying*, Mda portrays such fragile self-invention as the lived reality of his characters and cushions it within the fiction of a collective narrator. The "we" who speak the novel as witnesses ("We know everything about everybody") buttress the wisdom of Toloki's sensibility, often melding into the protagonist's point of view as he takes on an increasingly large role as mourner of the dead (Mda 1995, 12). He begins as a "survival entrepreneur" (Barnard 2007, 152), inventing a "profession" so that he will not beg for a living (Mda 1995, 15). But his vocation acquires a larger platform: "He was a Professional Mourner who mourned for the nation" (Mda 1995, 166). "Ways of dying," we are told, are tragically the community's "ways of living" (1995, 98). Because this is a novel about overcoming limitations, "ways of living" must exceed the "ways of dying" after the deaths are properly mourned.

Journalists ready to report the sensational deaths in the townships are present from the opening scene, the funeral of Noria's five-year-old son, who was necklaced purportedly for betraying the movement. They hound the grieving Noria: "Newspaper reporters have been particularly keen to get close to her, to ask her silly questions such as what her views are on the sorry fact that her son was killed by his own people. They are keen to trap her into saying something damaging, so that they can have blazing headlines the next day" (Mda 1995, 9). Clearly an unfavorable portrayal, this passage emphasizes the ways in which the journalists obstruct Noria's voice, inhibiting her perspective on her experience. They seize on the shameful act of a black child killed by "his own people," which the collective narrator has also noted and explained that it complicates the telling of the truth (7). The event threatens to expose the community's "shame to the world" and thus has a silencing effect (7, 178). Yet what matters to Noria even more is another shocking truth: that her son was set on fire by his playmate, a four-year-old girl, and another child under the command of the Young Tigers, the youth wing of the "political movement" (189). The children do not understand their actions; exploited, they too become victims. Noria feels betrayed by the leaders in her community who refuse to apologize publicly and expect her to accept her son's guilt (177–78). These important details surface in the protected space of her private narration to Toloki.

Despite his critique of journalists, Mda leans on them at times to establish the facticity of the horrendous crimes he recounts. In referencing an instance of "mass rage" when ten men who had terrorized their community were brutally killed in revenge, he quotes directly from a newspaper account: "it was as if the killing had, in a mind-blowing instant, amputated a foul and festering limb from the soul of the community" (1995, 66). This comment recreates the triangulation of testimony as theorized by Boltanski. Distance and, consequently, the real are established by splitting off the voice of the reporter from the spectators of the event, foregrounding how they too are participants in their community's irruption of violence.

The novel's ending is emphatically child-centric. Renewal is signaled in the partnership of Toloki and Noria and their work in an orphanage. The scene is a celebratory outburst of the children's creativity, inspired by the figurines restored to Toloki and Noria from their childhood. Toloki's father, Jwara, had sculpted these figurines during intense fits of creativity inspired by Noria's beautiful singing voice. This artistic inheritance rather than the legacy of township violence dominates the ending of the novel. The figurines, little understood when Jwara sculpted them, reappear in the story 30 years later to inspire the children. Distanced from the emotional turmoil of their original creation, they are freed to be received as works of art. The story of the earlier rift among Jwara, Toloki, and Noria reflects the deep humanity of the villagers and the "complexity" that Ndebele wants readers to be resensitized to. In the past, artistic creativity emerged disruptively and with emotional and spiritual intensity to consume Jwara, taking him to his death, and set Toloki and Noria on their disparate journeys away from the village. It takes 30 years before Jwara's work can be freed from these painful associations and received as art.

The episode of Jwara's figurines is a story that has little to do with politics and comes to epitomize the independence of the aesthetic from the political, or what Jacques Rancière calls the "singularity of art." Modernist art "simultaneously establishes the autonomy of art and the identity of its forms with the forms that life uses to shape itself" (Rancière 2006, 23). For Rancière, this is an ideal for art *tout court.* In Mda, the aesthetic is lived and portrayed as part of the novel's real that eventually trumps the absolute destructive effects of insecurity because it holds within it humanity's freedom in an existential sense. The communal "we" records the emotionally turbulent events surrounding the creation of the figurines as a village story swept up by the events that consumed the larger, national canvas: the story of migration to the city. More conventionally, the real in Mda's novel is his "overview" of the "history of black South African urbanization over the last three decades" that Barnard tracks alongside the work of historians and sociologists (2007, 150). However, Mda tries to rescue the aesthetic realm's independence so that despite the long interlude of politics' disruption of the scene, the aesthetic reasserts itself in the children's innocent, decontextualized response to the figurines and their raw energy, monstrous and ugly (Barnard 2007, 158–59), which improbably becomes a source of joy. The continuity over different geographies and a fairly lengthy historical period (30 years) gives the novel a sweep that helps contextualize the recent violence, providing an outside and beyond to its consuming, centripetal momentum. This sweeping scale recalibrates the headline-grabbing events in the context of what the novel alone can present as momentous: the creation and legacy of Jwara's figurines.

Despite its extensive depiction of violence and social dysfunction, the optimism of Mda's novel and its openness to the future are unmistakable. The synergy of looking back and looking forward depends on the effectiveness of Mda's improbable protagonist. Yet, arguably, Noria too is improbable. Toloki's empathic, uncritical response to her narration of her loss of two sons, stories that contain improbable elements originating in the experience of trauma, stems directly from Toloki's own experiences coping with insecurity. When Noria tells him that she got pregnant without having intercourse, he reassures her: "I believe you, Noria. I believe you absolutely" (1995, 149). His story of becoming the professional mourner demonstrates his successful self-invention, but it is also not an end in itself. Through him, the deeper traumas of the stories of children and women in the settlements can be aired and recognized. Noria pleads with him: "You are a beautiful person, Toloki. That is why I want you to teach me how to live. And how to forgive" (151).

Space in the novel is mappable, as Barnard has shown, but chronology is more problematic. Noria's pregnancies both last fifteen months (Mda 1995, 150). The second pregnancy, which she thinks occurred without intercourse, is given an explanation unassimilable to Noria but plausible to the reader, who can intuit the truth about her experience. She was visited by men on a regular basis as if in a dream, and these men looked initially like "strangers" on top of her but in time resembled her deceased husband (149). These odd details point to a traumatic dissociation of the events of intercourse, which could be instances of rape or might indicate an involuntary return to her life as a prostitute. The extended duration of both of Noria's pregnancies is not explained away, however. It makes the most sense to consider them allegories for the difficulties of birthing the nation. The diachronic narrative is impeded, facing severe difficulties and indicating that the history making subjects are stymied. Toloki transforms the community's relationship to its times by empowering individuals to put their own meaning on events. Scenes of deaths and killings, such as those borrowed from newspaper accounts, are thus opposed in the novel to scenes in which Toloki invites Noria to fantasize that they are walking together through a garden, for example (Mda 1995, 112).

Toloki passes on his lessons of self-invention and together with Noria focuses our attention on a child-centered haven for which the future is open. Although unorthodox, Mda's novel is a reiteration of the allegory of the nation as family whereby South Africa during the transition reengineered its social bonds, reconnecting individuals to each other by exposing violence and injustice and abjuring them, while also enacting what Boris Boubacar Diop has called in the context of Rwanda "a resurrection of the living" (2006, 181). The raging war that threatens to tear the nation apart before it has even been properly constituted through the elections of 1994 is largely unacknowledged and needs its history (Mda 1995, 19).

A father's love

Farah has discussed his desire to present *Crossbones* as a corrective to lies told by journalists who gather information from sources without traveling to Somalia. In the period from 2000 till 2011 roughly, there was no way to verify the truth of most reporting on Somalia. Farah's fiction, therefore, provides an alternative narrative to unsettle the coherence of an ideological narrative in the international press (Levy 2012). He also repeats a commonplace gesture in the Europhone novel from Africa, which, aiming to set in motion a more historically nuanced discourse about Africa through the novel, has frequently defined its realist mode as a response to either ethnographic or journalistic accounts (Coundouriotis 1999, 13–15).

Reflecting back on the historical decade that spans time covered in the "Past Imperfect" trilogy, Farah explores in *Crossbones* the paradoxical sameness with a difference that Somalia's prolonged crisis has produced. The reader encounters once again the theme of the exile's return that organizes the trilogy, the returnee being the improbable figure. In *Crossbones*, however, the returnees' exilic bond to "their father's land" (2011, 35) is more tenuous than that of the returnees of the other novels.[10] The two brothers, Ahl and Malik, represent a cosmopolitan Somali diaspora and have no firsthand experience of Somalia. Born in Aden to a Chinese-Malay mother and Somali father, they are multilingual subjects, fluent in Chinese and Somali as well as English since they are now residents of the United States. Their context for understanding Somalia is both intimate, based on family and culture, and worldly, part of their broader experience of other continents. Malik is the son-in-law of Jeebleh (the protagonist of *Links*, 2004), and they arrive together in Mogadishu, with Jeebleh now playing the role of seasoned guide, drawing on the experience of his previous visit ten years ago. In *Crossbones*, Jeebleh revisits his allies from *Links*, and the novel rehearses an extended conversation about then and now, comparing the period at the height of the fighting in Mogadishu following the failed American intervention in 1993 and the novel's present, set in late 2006 as the US-supported Ethiopian invasion to oust the Islamists is imminent. The novel recounts the unfolding of the new Somali-Ethiopian war of 2006–2008, aiming to tie it to the longer history.

The theme of return affords a sense of continuity, a semblance of a stable point of reference for Somalia. The characters' intricate personal stories unfold within this setting of a decade's long insecurity, their details providing entry points into the nation's history that could be used to outline such a narrative and begin a project of reclamation of Somalia's national history from the discourse of emergency and dissolution. In Farah's view, the crisis begins in 1969 when Siad Barre becomes dictator rather than 1991, when his rule ends. Thus, the period of insecurity is significantly longer than the one assumed in the dissolution scenario that focuses on the fall of the regime. Barre's dictatorship left an indelible mark on Jeebleh and his close friend Bile, "intimates" who were raised in the same household, shared the experience of university, and then went to prison together as "political dissidents" (Farah 2011, 14). Jeebleh was released after ten years, whereas Bile spent 20 years in jail, most of it in solitary, a trauma that is a constant reference point in the trilogy (Farah 2004, 115). Somalia's invasion of the Ogaden (1977–78) similarly haunts the novel's present, inflecting the 2006–2008 conflict in ways that the United States is oblivious to despite its responsibility for supporting the Ethiopian invasion against the Islamist Shabaab.

In order to break the appearance of ahistoricity in the depiction of stagnation, Farah concludes his extended look at Somalia's dissolution by staging the assassination of Dajaal, who has come to represent skillful adaptation to the environment of insecurity. Instrumental to Jebleeh's safety and a symbol of how survival is possible, Dajaal becomes a problem for realism if he appears invulnerable. The ironies of the real come to the fore in a metafictional moment. Malik, a war correspondent, reflects on the meaninglessness of Dajaal's assassination: "I often think how, in fiction, death serves a purpose. I wish I knew the objective of such a real-life death" (2011, 288). Dajaal is a fictional character who dies in a novel, but he belongs in that novel's economy of the hard-core real, pertaining to war and violence.

A character who has endured from the first novel of the "Past Imperfect" trilogy, he is a former officer of the Somali army who fought in the Ogaden War and, during the period of the civil war, has run private security so effectively that Farah's other characters, those belonging to the soft realism of sentimental bonds, survive the dangers of Mogadishu despite their increasingly quixotic ventures in its uncertain landscape.

Antagonisms held over from the Ogaden War are the cause ultimately attributed to Dajaal's assassination. Farah's protagonists come to understand the death as a delayed act of vengeance, carried out because the 2006 invasion offered an opportunity to settle old scores (2011, 295–96). The new war is not so new, therefore, but a resurgence of the older conflict. The time of insecurity is marked by a prolonged waiting, where the irresolution of outstanding differences hovers over the future. Its extended temporality stretches the notion of emergency without attenuating the sense of crisis.

Dajaal's assassination, although foreshadowed by numerous failed attempts on his life, unsettles the reader's expectations about closure. Total dissolution has been held at bay, but will the tide turn now in what feels like the penultimate moment? The terrain of insecurity becomes unreadable just when we have become habituated through the "long space" of the trilogy. Moreover, because Dajaal had seemed so proficient at evading danger, it is hard for the other characters to intuit the kind of danger he failed to anticipate. Responding to their unease, those he helped claim him now as a person "loved." The debt of their own survival made Dajaal "not an employee." Bile calls him "family," although Cambara adds: "Except he wasn't family" (Farah 2011, 292–293). Thus, in death, Dajaal moves over to the soft realism of sentiment.

Such logic that extends affectively the claim of family to those who are not kin is one of the recurring motifs of potential social cohesion in Farah's work. It accelerates the pace of talk among "intimates," close friends and associates who are trusted and have shared histories, or "links," as Farah showed in the trilogy's first novel. Jeebleh, Bile, Cambara, and Malik spend a long time speculating as to why Dajaal was assassinated (2011, 295–96). Farah provokes readers—through the emphasis he places on his characters' conversation, their extensive but knowing speculation—to do the same and ask probing questions in order to break open the received narratives about Somalia. Thus, those discussing Dajaal's assassination do the work of fiction, giving purpose to his death by making it meaningful to the larger historical narrative being teased out of the condition of prolonged insecurity, the project that lies at the center of the novel. The sensational assassination has to be retrieved from the discourse of the news headline and placed in the richer narrative texture of fiction, where the threads connecting his death to a deeper past can be intuited and elaborated.

Farah's investigation of the mechanisms of Somali piracy in the novel yields a similar insight: that piracy succumbs to a logic of vengeance deferred. Ahl, the improbable returnee, intuits a discursive logic of finance revolving around the idea of debt that reflects a dynamic of deferred closure. On the war front, vengeance is habitually postponed with a knowing sense that opportunities for vengeance arise again in the long duration of insecurity. On the other hand, piracy leaves many unpaid bills for which Somalis can claim payment during this ongoing state of insecurity.

The improbable character motif plays a role in interrupting the suspended time that takes hold while waiting for the opportunity to exact vengeance. The improbable can open a different sense of potentiality for the future. Because the exiles' return provides the occasion to contextualize the stalled present within a longer historical frame, it intimates a deeper horizon into the future as well. Ahl functions as the novel's improbable figure because he arrives as a concerned father. He is described as "the director of a Minneapolis-based center tasked with researching matters Somali" (2011, 34), whereas Malik is a hardened war correspondent with extensive experience of insecure zones.[11] The two brothers embark on separate quests: Malik wants to learn how Somali piracy works and how it intersects with the activities of Shabaab, whereas Ahl is on a personal journey to retrieve his errant stepson, who was recruited into jihadism in Minneapolis and is missing somewhere among the pirates of Puntland. Thus, each brother also travels to different territory—Ahl to Puntland and Malik to Mogadishu.

The two figures, a father and a war correspondent, provide different ways of registering the real. Journalists are thought to bring expertise that presumably translates the local into intelligible terms for metropolitan audiences who might know enough not to be convinced by exoticizing stock narratives. Malik is ideally situated as an expatriate with the languages and local knowledge he needs, as well as access to the Western press. On the other hand, the father figure signals a different convention of the real in fiction. He locates for readers the interface between the private, familial, emotional world of characters and the outside world of things that matter: money, political influence, militarism, empire.

When Ahl leaves the purportedly safe space of family in Minneapolis for Puntland, he becomes a reference point for how the two relate: home and away, the United States and Somalia. He follows his stepson, Taxliil, who has already exposed the vulnerability of home to the dangers posed by a distant conflict. However, unlike Taxliil, who left with no intention to return, Ahl's purpose is to return with him, in the process establishing a corridor connecting the two places. The potential for family bonds to be read allegorically is ever present and functions in multiple ways. Malik and Ahl, as brothers of different sensibilities and deploying different methods, even traversing Somalia in distinct geographies, point to the fragmentation of the national. Somalia is repeatedly described as their "fatherland." As father figure to Taxliil, Ahl inevitably provokes readers to think about the authority of the fatherland, its inscription of identity even when it travels to distant geographies of exile. What are the expectations created by the fatherland? Why does Taxliil feel compelled to join the Islamists? These questions raise the problem of Taxliil's identity as an American teenager. What failure at home leads to this disaster? His abandonment by his biological father seems pertinent. An abusive man who left the family after raping Taxliil's babysitter, the father carries the legacy of violence and dysfunction with him from Somalia. Ahl is, therefore, on a mission to repair the bond to the fatherland that has gone awry, drawing in compensatory ways on his own surrogate fatherhood and love for the boy. The context for such filial bonds in the novel extends beyond Ahl and Taxliil as other surrogate father figures explain Somalia to their figurative sons and reconcile them to it: Jeebleh plays this role for Malik, Dajaal for Qasiir.

The figure of the loving father provides an improbable model for how to begin to dismantle terror. Farah is not interested in rehabilitating the patriarchal figure as such but wants to question the pull and authority of the fatherland as masculinized and violent. He often reverses gender expectations, as for example with Cambara's muscular interventions in *Knots* (2007) but also in *Crossbones*, in which it is Cambara who pulls Malik from the bombed vehicle. Characters who break the mold by going against type show in their responsiveness to love and their moral conscience that the terrain of insecurity is not dehumanizing to the degree feared. It does not leave us devoid of the possibilities of an ethical life.

The improbable in *Crossbones* is associated with a theme key to Farah's oeuvre: acting out of love or taking risks to save a person you love even when you have little likelihood of success. Ahl has no expertise to make him a credible actor in such a challenging environment, yet he succeeds. He arrives as an amateur and is contrasted repeatedly with his brother, who as a professional war journalist is supposed to be in his element in a place like Mogadishu. Thus, the novel's development of an improbable figure dismantles the superiority of expertise. To get his story, Malik must interview key players in piracy and Shabaab at a time when journalists are being relentlessly targeted.[12] Aware of his precarity, Malik bravely perseveres but fails to get information from the contacts he makes on his own. In fact, he antagonizes BigBeard, the Islamist responsible for the atrocity that unfolds in the novel's opening sequence. The reader has encountered BigBeard's depravity in this botched operation to "consecrate a safe house," the seizure of a private home as a military base for resistance to the Ethiopian invaders (2011, 4).[13] Having seen BigBeard's ruthlessness, readers brace for the worst when Malik decides to confront him directly. Farah allows Malik to walk away, surprising us, however, with Malik's delayed understanding of BigBeard's readiness to kill: "Whatever he expected, Malik did not think their conversation would end in a cul-de-sac of such naked threat" (250). He should have known better.

Operating separately in Puntland, Ahl pursues high-level contacts involved in piracy and human trafficking without the cool composure of his brother. Fearful and exceedingly anxious to the point of physical illness—wracked by emotion, in other words—Ahl examines his options:

"he has already formed a working relationship with a man who funds piracy [Fidno], a man who, for all he knows, is on first-name terms with the owners of the dhows in the human trafficking business. Is it too late to withdraw? More to the point, is there any other means by which he may pursue his aim, to locate his stepson?" (2011, 219). These are rhetorical questions that do not change Ahl's course. His doubts are expressed again: "Ahl thinks he is not suited for this kind of assignment the way Malik is" (258). Interviewing No-Name, who might have seen Taxliil among the human traffickers, Ahl is afraid and feels humiliated but insists on his parental claim. He corrects No-Name, telling him that Taxliil is his son, not nephew, "wondering if children have any notion what troubles one goes through for them" (263).[14] He exacts No-Name's promise to find Taxliil, which he is willing to do out of loyalty to Fidno (265). No-Name also promises to put Fidno, the key informant on the pirates, in touch with Malik.

All these intricacies of motivation and connection leave readers marveling at Ahl. Although under great stress, he is able to discern which communications and connections matter. Talk, spontaneous, conversational, and unpredictable, has impact. It can change circumstances and create a new reality. The effectiveness of Malik's professionalism, by contrast, is problematized. Malik becomes impatient with his brother, even condescending, dismissing Ahl's detailed account of his encounters and potential leads: "Malik senses that the more questions he asks, the more likely the trapdoor will open, and then he will drown in further irrelevancies" (2011, 152).[15] When Ahl shares information he received from Fidno, Malik thinks interviewing Fidno is "a development of the second-water grade, as far as diamond discovery goes, even if Ahl makes it sound as though he has uncovered a first-water-quality gem" (222). In particular, he does not trust Fidno's motives, because Fidno does not seek to be paid for the interview (223). Ahl, on the other hand, has overcome this hesitation because he has figured out the logic of deferred vengeance and compensation that links the economy of piracy to the ongoing conflict. In other words, he has begun to intuit the kind of deep understanding of Somalia's insecurity that Malik wants to attain but has not. Fidno will testify to expose the insurance companies and other corrupt financial institutions and middlemen who are syphoning off the lion's share of the ransom money and leaving the Somalis in the same destitute situation they were in before, with neither the integrity of their fishing waters nor the financial windfall of their brazen attempts to recoup that loss. Furthermore, Fidno wants to get back at Shabaab for killing YoungThing, the child recruit in the botched operation who is the brother of a friend (269).

Thus, Fidno's testimony is analogous to a bill for payment due. Crossbones signal danger, unlike links and knots, which both highlight the theme of connection in the trilogy. The point of crossing, arranged by Ahl so that Malik can get his scoop on piracy, is the transformative point, anticipated with great anxiety as potentially an appointment with death. When this crossing comes to pass, however, it illuminates matters and is not dangerous as anticipated. Critics condescendingly labeled this novel a suspense thriller (Levy 2012, 57), but the characterization misses the significance of the deliberately out-of-sync timing that marks Farah's intervention. He wants to distinguish his historical realism from journalism about Africa and genre fiction, types of discourse that share an affinity with each other and a sensationalizing tendency.

The repeated use of anticlimax throughout the trilogy grounds readers in the real, where truth is painstakingly constructed out of many testimonies and points of view. The attack on Malik's life does not coincide with the big reveal (his interview of Fidno) but comes after. Shabaab has been successfully targeting journalists, and Malik's life has been in danger from the beginning. The bomb that almost kills him, therefore, has nothing to do with Fidno or pirates. If anything, Fidno is an ally against Shabaab, a characterization against type since Somali pirates have been widely vilified.

Ahl painstakingly develops a rapport with Fidno, who comes to empathize with him as a father of a lost son. Fidno too had the opportunity to stand as a surrogate father, but YoungThing was killed by BigBeard. Ahl struggles to follow the unfamiliar logic of Fidno's conversation. He opens up to Fidno about Taxliil, pushed by his intuition rather than a reasoned strategy. In conversation with Fidno, "he senses Taxliil's presence stalking him and prowling the outer reaches of his conscience. When he infers that Taxliil wants him to trade his truth with this man, his resolve firms up" (2011, 217).[16] Accounting for networks of talk and exchange of information takes up a lot of Farah's novel. The prosaic and almost mechanical aspect of such descriptions leaves the reader perplexed with Farah's writing style. A telling example appears at the end of the novel, when information circulates in order to tie the loose ends of the plot:

> Cambara shares the latest news about Malik, who is still in no state to speak, much less comprehend what is going on, with Bile, who relays it to Xalan, so that she may pass it along eventually to Yusur. Xalan, for her part, tells Bile what she knows about Ahl and Taxliil so far and all that she has learned from the radio journalist in Djibouti. Cambara shares the latest news about Ahl with Jeebleh, who met her flight in Nairobi and took them by the waiting ambulance to the clinic, where Malik is now recovering after surgery. (2011, 384–85)

The plot develops as an unfolding series of communications between characters, paired in sequential conversations, who via phone, SMS messages, and e-mails stay connected and vitally involved in each other's lives against the backdrop of prolonged insecurity. The reader of Farah's trilogy is drawn into the scene as one more "intimate," someone already familiar with the long histories that connect the characters to each other, much like in real life, where circles of friends live in perpetual suspension over the details of one another's lives.

The efficacy of such communication becomes in Farah's world the strongest bulwark against the disintegrating forces of prolonged insecurity. When Cambara swoops in to pull Malik out of the wreckage of the IED explosion, her networks go into action to get him to a private clinic and then on a plane to Nairobi. But she also becomes the pivot point of all communications, the point of connection between the crossing stories of the two brothers' return to their fatherland. Informal networks are key, because they often bridge ideological divides. The national addiction to the stimulant khat, for example, creates chewing buddies who talk and share secrets. "The officer is my mate and we chew together" explains how a journalist friend knows why Ahl and Taxliil are detained at the airport in Djibouti on the way back to the United States (2011, 384). Similarly, the barrier of airport and immigration security looms imposingly but is breached through the ordinary habits of social intercourse that unfold alongside the high stakes effort to monitor the movement of individuals across national borders. Each brother's quest narrative illustrates the retrieval of the real from zones that have been thoroughly demonized by the media: the failed state, piracy, jihadism.

To invoke globalectics once more, the balance is righted when Farah dismantles the discourses that prioritize the expertise of the first world, which does not understand reality because it pretends to come from "nowhere" without acknowledging the situatedness that alone clarifies the historical forces at work. The search for Taxliil succeeds through a human network of care that bears no resemblance to humanitarianism in conventional terms. His return and the retrieval of the testimony about piracy allow Farah to suggest imaginatively what is possible in circumstances that are otherwise considered beyond the reach of reasoned action. The characters face serious consequences for their ventures into these dangerous places, but these consequences are rendered in a new economy of the plausible— realistically, as grave but not fatal. Living in a place marked by the effects of prolonged insecurity requires a flexible imagination that can recognize the implications of entanglements. Human situations are intricate and complex, and responses to insecurity nuanced.

The terrain of insecurity is shaped through memory, and it is perhaps not surprising that the consequences are most bleak for the resident Somalis who have the most memory. The deaths of Dajaal and his nephew Qasiir make it clear that in this country shaped by the prolonged insecurity of an almost thirty-year civil war, the old are being killed off. Dajaal and his nephew were witnesses to Operation Restore Hope, the failed American intervention in 1993. Their memory of the early years of the war is important for setting the record of how Somalia has evolved. However, this is also a dangerous, destabilizing memory, as it remains connected to a chain of unsettled scores. There are no political actors who can satisfy the demands for justice. Yet, as in the case of the explosion that almost takes Malik's life and kills Qasiir, the novel withholds the kind of information that would lend itself to the settling of scores. The reader never really knows who targeted them, or for that matter who assassinates Dajaal. Dajaal is stuck in the past, always aware that he fought in three wars (2011, 135, 158). A trajectory to a different future is hard to see in a life shaped by perpetual war. The present is all-consuming, and the best to be hoped for is a strategy of extrication from the present, afforded only to the returnees, the exiles that come back to the fatherland and have their place of exile to return to. The only one of the returnees whose sojourn in Somalia now seems permanent is Cambara, who is charged to nurse the fragile Bile, a symbol of a secular, cosmopolitan, and democratic Somalia whose political promise stalled at independence but is being kept on life support, a hopeful bill to sender, a deferred fulfillment. Bile, fragile as he is and has been since the beginning of *Links*, is not dead yet.

Farah gives a new vocabulary of insecurity. Two phrases stand out. Old man Dhoorre, the victim in the botched home invasion, tries to reassure YoungThing, the child recruit of Shabaab who enters the wrong house, by saying he "privileges peace, prioritizes peace," and is "not an enemy to your cause" (2011, 50). In the final confrontation, BigBeard asks Dhoorre why he is there, and his simple answer is: "Because I live here" (65). "Because I live here" echoes throughout the novel as the most basic statement of belonging, alluding neither to clan, nationality, or religion. Second, upon arrival in the Puntland city of Bosaso, Ahl is told that "everything here is ad hoc" (95). "Ad hoc" is an apt descriptor not of insecurity as such but of abandonment. Ahl reflects on this phrase describing it as "the heartlessness, the mindlessness of a community failing its responsibility toward itself; a feebleness of purpose; an inadequacy" (94). All these are variants of key words that represent what Ahl values: heart, mind (reason), community, responsibility, and purpose. It is Farah's improbable figure, the concerned father, who places these values within the setting of prolonged insecurity, reclaiming this terrain from sensational discourses and bringing it back to realism and its conventions of describing conflict.

Akpan's children

Children are frequently cast as the improbable characters in fictions of insecurity. Their ability to survive the horrors inflicted upon them by adults gestures toward the possibility of restoration. Child soldier narratives, as I argue in this book, often take the shape of recovery narratives whereby some semblance of restoring a lost childhood is put in motion. At another extreme, Farah's Raasta and Makka in *Links* are improbable children who not only retain their innocence in war-torn Mogadishu but also escape their abduction by a warlord unscathed. The complicated interventions on the girls' behalf have barely unfolded when they simply reappear unharmed.

Casting the children as allegorical figures for Somalia (Raasta as its poetic soul and Makka as its stymied development as its stymied development), Farah undercuts the logic of intervention. He suggests instead a course of engagement with local initiatives such as the Refuge, an NGO where the girls reside. In the Refuge, connections (links) among people are nurtured, providing a model for the nation that could emerge from the long history of conflict.

No one captures more effectively insecurity's compounding effects on children than Akpan in his collection of stories *Say You're One of Them* (2008). Unlike Ahl's loving quest to retrieve an errant youth, Akpan's stories show parents who frequently exacerbate or even cause their children's precarity. Yet the endings of his stories sometimes open a future for their young protagonists despite the spiraling crisis that seems on the verge of overwhelming them. In "My Parents' Bedroom," set during the Rwandan genocide, the girl narrator, Monique, captures this imperative succinctly just as her circumstances seem entirely hopeless, two paragraphs from the story's end: "We want to live; we don't want to die. I must be strong" (2008, 354). Tutsi soldiers of the Rwandan Patriotic Front (her mother's people) are coming to exact revenge against Hutus (her father's people), and she wonders: "If Papa couldn't spare Maman's life, would my mother's relatives spare mine?" (2008, 354). Hiding herself and her toddler brother from the mob, she escapes its murderous violence only to look back and witness the climactic tragedy of the orgiastic violence: the Tutsi army burns the house down, not realizing that inside are Tutsis hiding in the ceiling. Looking back is followed by: "We walk forward" (2008, 354). Set off on the road, the girl is now in motion, enacting the refugee's narrative of survival.

Two more stories in the collection end with children escaping with their lives toward uncertain futures and away from dangers that almost destroy them. In "An Ex-mas Feast," the dangers are due not only to the extreme poverty of Nairobi's shantytown, Kibera, but also to the emotional devastation these material conditions wreak on the fragile bonds of family. The love between the narrator, Jigana, and his sister, Maisha, is intense and affecting. Maisha turns to prostitution in part to raise her brother's school fees, giving him a future she forsakes for herself. He is unwilling to accept the terms of her sacrifice, and hence she keeps it hidden until the end when, ravaged by AIDS, she leaves the family after providing them with food and presents for Christmas. The scene is one of raw emotion, a final parting. All along the parents have preyed on the children and exploited them to feed their addictions. Their shame comes into the open in this scene, but it cannot forestall Maisha and Jigana's younger sister from following Maisha into prostitution. Jigana, torn apart by the prospect of losing Maisha and ashamed that her condition is a result of her efforts to help him, destroys the school supplies she has gotten him, breaking the pens, "the ink spurting into my palms like blue blood" (2008, 34). The place where Maisha's trunk had been is "like a newly dug grave" over which he weeps (34). The emotional pain leads Jigana to flee, and thus the story ends: "I hid among a group of retreating kids and slipped away. I ran through traffic, scaled the road divider, and disappeared into Nairobi. My last memory of my family was of the twins burping and giggling" (35).

Arguably, the melodramatic outbursts of emotion and the depiction of urban squalor identify "An Ex-mas Feast" as a naturalist text. Yet it is clear that Akpan does not mean Jigana's escape as a descent deeper into a predetermined fate. It is not the last move in an inevitable plot that consigns him to a Kenyan lumpenproletariat with no hope.[17] The shift in geography from Kibera over the wall and into Nairobi hints (improbably) at a new freedom and possibly even rising fortunes, accessing something bigger and less hopeless. It is posited as Jigana's escape out of the naturalistic setting he had been trapped in. It is also an emotional divorce from the dysfunctional family (or, read allegorically, the postcolonial nation) that threatens to consume him. Familial roles trap children in a situation where their obedience is demanded whereas the protection owed them is absent. The parents' formulaic adherence to familial convention is evident in the mother's sentimental fixation on the family Bible and its record of a family tree (2008, 18). Jigana's flight into metropolitan Nairobi repeats (perhaps parodically) an established pattern of flight to urban centers that is an embrace of individuation (Slaughter 2004, 36). Jigana is taking charge of his future, and although being a street kid in Nairobi might not make him secure, obeying the adults in his family has been most dangerous so far. Asserting his autonomy is the only way into a viable future.

Akpan offers neither reassurances nor hints of trouble in the story's ending. Indeed, he seems to elide the allegory implied by Jigana's slippage into Nairobi, a metropolitan center that represents the globalized world and from whose privileges the failed postcolonial space of Kibera is walled off. Akpan ends the story with Jigana's last memory of his family, the giggling toddler twins, dissonant sounds of glee against a background of family bonds coming undone. The resonance of this glee hangs in the air as the only predictor of what the new will bring. Is it a warning of sorts about the promises of globalization, a mere mirage of riches? It is impossible to know, but Jigana would certainly be doomed if he does not jump over the wall.

In "Fattening for Gabon," readers are confronted again with the traumatic separation of siblings. The environment of extreme insecurity populated by adults who prey on children brings about an unbearable circumstance: in order to survive, the more able sibling abandons the younger, weaker one. Once more, escape presents the possibility of a future though the story had seemed to be moving inexorably toward death. The escape is an improbable reversal of fortune where the witness who survives gets to tell his singular story. Unlike the hints of optimism in Jigana's memory of his giggling twin siblings, Kotchikpa's separation leaves him off kilter: "I ran and I ran, though I knew I would never outrun my sister's wailing" (2008, 172). Kotchikpa had to push his reluctant sister out of the way in order to escape the dark concrete room in which they were confined while awaiting their passage to Gabon by a child trafficking ring. Unable to navigate the emotional manipulations of the adults with her child's understanding, Yewa distrusts her brother and refuses to obey him as he urges her to jump out of the window.

Throughout the story, Yewa's shrillness and raw emotional outbursts punctuate the twists and turns of the plans being shaped against her and Kotchikpa. Her tantrums make her a force to contend with. Although a burden to her older brother, who worries about her well-being and assumes the responsibility of saving them both, Yewa helps Kotchikpa by rocking the boat and exposing the inconsistencies in the adults' promises to them, which then enables him to see their evil intent. Akpan develops Yewa's unruliness as a feature of her immaturity; she is also impetuous, temperamental, unable to accommodate other people's points of view, stubborn, and easily distracted. Kotchikpa shares few of her childlike qualities and behaves more like a parent should, bearing the responsibility to protect her until he cannot. The adults fail miserably to fulfill their roles as protectors and nurturers of the children's development, and the readers' hope for the uncle's good intentions and the sincerity of family bonds is shattered. The uncle's belated *prise de conscience* and his resistance to the child traffickers, who he was responsible for engaging, redeem him in the eyes of the children. But his change of heart worsens their situation, making it more precarious. After he is killed, the children are left truly alone and in great peril at the hands of the traffickers.

Such danger and precarity make Kotchikpa's choice understandable and permit readers to feel the relief of his escape to a degree even though the story makes clear that its consequences burden Kotchikpa. There is no language of aftermath or of trauma therapy. There is no spoken "it was not your fault." The story leaves readers feeling the weight Kotchikpa carries. What kind of possibility, if any, does Akpan open up with Kotchipka's escape? The improbable figure does not resolve its hesitant impulse toward the future by making a more comfortable memory of the past. The figure remains singular, seared by the knowledge of having fallen short in the effort to survive and of being marked by the past's unassimilability. As Kotchikpa turns toward the future, the momentum forward is unmistakable, and memory follows.

Conclusion

This exploration of how a notion of the improbable figure might open up a sense of the future in novels that depict states of prolonged and acute insecurity aims to revitalize the understanding of a historical realism that both offers a critical assessment of the present and situates its key figures as active agents in determining that reality. The paradigm of emergency and intervention, too, often casts the subjects of such narratives as suffering objects of pity, reduced to a kind of incapacity that seems insurmountable unless the emergency they are in is resolved. If realism is theorized through metaphors of documentation and reporting, problematized here through the persistent attention to journalism within the novels, it fails to account for the ways in which contemporary African writers are drawing on the inventedness of the fictional realm to produce an alternative ambiance of the real.

In *Ways of Dying*, readers are faced with a cascade of extreme acts of violence and the likelihood of a society coming undone just as it is emerging as the democracy it has long aspired to become. Events in the novel redirect this momentum without shortchanging the attention due to the acute suffering of the people. Mda depicts creativity and the imagination as the deep sources of the people's resilience. In his work, Farah is intent on showing over and over how his characters communicate with each other, giving all the minute details of their ordinary conversation and the means through which they carry it out, because his characters must be recognizable even if their circumstances are distant. The improbable figure, Ahl, emerges as a surprise, pushed by experience and circumstance to do something that the discourse of insecurity has cast as impossible: to penetrate Shabaab and retrieve and return a young recruit to Minneapolis. For Farah, opening the corridor between the two places is key. He is creating an imagination of how that is possible, how ordinary actors, motivated by universal emotions, can achieve a connection to realms cut off by the distancing of the emergency paradigm. In the end, father and son are held up by Homeland Security, delaying their return to the United States. The novel opens a corridor of connection between two distant places but unsettles the meaning of return, signaling that a reciprocal quest journey might need to be initiated into the United States. Finally, Akpan's children, allegorical figures of the continent's poor, come out of the most extreme subjugation because they are astute readers of their environment, adaptable, and motivated to live. The resilience of these child survivors, who emerge from trauma with their moral compass intact, provides the building block for a usable memory that could open the past to constructive investigation. Thus, in these works we find a forward-looking historical realism that opens the future by promising a wiser receptivity to the past.

Notes

1 The Iraqi army made a significant effort to reenlist soldiers who had left because of the fear of ISIS. Upward of 6,000 soldiers had reenlisted by the end of September 2014, including not only deserters but also soldiers honorably discharged by their commanders (Semple 2014).

2 Our reference point does not have to be French realism exclusively. Writing on Elizabeth Gaskell, Elaine Freedgood notes that plots depicting the poor are predictable because the realist novel as a genre sees the poor as limited. Gaskell seeks to disrupt this predictability by leaving realism and resorting to melodrama (Freedgood 2014, 211).

3 Hitchcock's examples literalize the "long space" as a feature of trilogies and tetralogies, a feature of form. Below I treat the third novel of Farah's trilogy "Past Imperfect," *Crossbones*.

4 Arango's journalism gestures to such a sensibility of the real. His newspaper feature is accompanied by an online video that warns of its graphic content. The improbable happy ending is thus couched in a construction of the real that feels like a throwback to the period before the war.

5 A clarifying discussion of the difficulties of disentangling free indirect discourse from focalization more broadly can be found in Hortstkotte and Pedri, 2011.

6 Uncertainty about the duration of intervention bleeds into uncertainty over the nature of the intervention and its goals. Doctors Without Borders, for example, is vigilant about maintaining this distinction. It seeks to intervene when it identifies "a state of rupture and through it the imperative for action: something must be done and done quickly. Practitioners frequently uncover problems that antedate the emergency and are understood in retrospect to have been precipitating factors. In this sense, disaster—not development—lies at the heart of the organization" (Redfield, 2013, 14).

7 Redfield discusses emergency in terms of the biopolitical and the state of exception (2013, 18–20).

8 Although James traces the long history of such insecurity from Haiti's independence in 1804 forward (2010, 8–13), the reign of terror accelerated during the necropolitical regime of the Duvalier dictatorships, 1957–86. The international community lent its tacit support as the Duvaliers allowed the Haitian economy to provide cheap labor for the textile industry reaping profits in the global North (James, 2010, 11).

9 Critics have puzzled over the novel's contradictory tone—social realism on the one hand, fantasy on the other—calling it "implausible," although Gail Fincham describes this as Bakhtinian "heteroglossia" that purposefully exposes social contradiction (2012, 22–23).

10 In *Links*, Jeebleh had been thrown into exile after serving time as a political prisoner during Siad Barre's dictatorship. In *Knots*, Cambara leaves the safety of Canada to reclaim her ancestral home from the warlord who has occupied it. Thus, Jeebleh and Cambara have suffered personally the consequences of the reign of insecurity.

11 Malik, "a freelance journalist based in New York, has come along too, intending to write articles about the ancestral land he has never seen" (Farah, 2011, 11).

12 One of Farah's goals in the novel is to document the targeting of journalists by Shabaab during the mid-2000s. The sources he lists for his novel reflect his engagement with news accounts of such killings (2011, 387–388).

13 In this episode, BigBeard forces one of his child soldiers, YoungThing, to kill the elderly man who occupies the house and then orders one of his other fighters to kill the boy.

14 He corrects Fidno as well, who refers to Taxliil as Ahl's nephew: "My nephew—why nephew? He is my son." Fidno replies: "Makes no difference. Nephew, son, stepson." Ahl knows differently, but chooses not to insist. The silence allows him to follow Fidno's logic to see where it will lead.

15 Ahl, however, looks up to Malik, recognizing his own lack of experience: "Ahl thinks he is not suited for this kind of assignment the way Malik is" (Farah, 2011, 258).

16 Ahl also has premonitions and begins to see signs of Taxliil's return, wondering, for example, if a bird on his windshield is an "epiphany": "He feels that things are falling into place" (2011, 276).

17 Akpan writes against type here. The urban street youth of Meja Mwangi's *Kill*

Me Quick (1973), for example, occupy a readily recognizable naturalistic universe that holds no hope for them. Fully engulfed in the squalor of the urban slum, they can only express their resistance by turning to crime. Akpan's insistence on preserving the innocence and sincerity of the victimized children sets a very different tone.

Works cited

Akpan, Uwem. *Say You're One of Them*. New York: Back Bay, 2008.

Arango, Tim. "Escaping Death in Northern Iraq." *New York Times*. 3 September 2014. http://www.nytimes.com/2014/09/04/world/middleeast/surviving-isis-massacre-iraq-video.html?src=xps.

Bakhtin, M. M. *The Dialogic Imagination: Four Essays*. Edited by Michael Holquist, translated by Caryl Emerson and Michael Holquist. Austin: University of Texas Press, 1981.

Balzac, Honoré de. *Le Colonel Chabert Suivi De Honorine Et De L'interdiction (1832)*. Paris: Garnier, 1964.

Barnard, Rita. *Apartheid and Beyond: South African Writers and the Politics of Place*. Oxford: Oxford University Press, 2007. DOI: 10.1093/acprof:oso/9780195112863. 001.0001.

Barnett, Michael, and Thomas G. Weiss, eds. *Humanitarianism in Question: Politics, Power, Ethics*. Ithaca: Cornell University Press, 2008. www.jstor.org/stable/10. 7591/j.ctt7v7ms.

Boltanski, Luc. *Distant Suffering: Morality, Media, and Politics*. Translated by Graham Bruchell. Cambridge: Cambridge University Press, 1999.

Calhoun, Craig. "A World of Emergencies: Fear, Intervention, and the Limits of Cosmopolitan Order." *Canadian Review of Sociology and Anthropology* 41, no. 4 (2004): 373–395. doi.org/10.1111/j.1755-618X.2004.tb00783.x.

Calhoun, Craig. "The Imperative to Reduce Suffering: Charity, Progress, and Emergencies in the Field of Humanitarian Action." In *Humanitarianism in Question: Politics, Power, Ethics*, edited by Michael Barnett and Thomas G. Weiss, 73–97. Ithaca: Cornell University Press, 2008. www.jstor.org/stable/10.7591/j.ctt7v7ms.

Chouliaraki, Lilie. *The Ironic Spectator: Solidarity in the Age of Post-Humanitarianism*. Cambridge: Polity, 2013.

Coundouriotis, Eleni. *Claiming History: Colonialism, Ethnography and the Novel*. New York: Columbia University Press, 1999.

Coundouriotis, Eleni. "The Child Soldier Narrative and the Problem of Arrested Historicization." *Journal of Human Rights* 9, no. 2 (2010): 191–206. doi.org/10. 1080/14754831003761696.

Farah, Nuruddin. *Links*. New York: Riverhead, 2004.

Farah, Nuruddin. *Knots*. New York: Riverhead, 2007.

Farah, Nuruddin. *Crossbones*. New York: Riverhead, 2011.

Fassin, Didier, and Richard Rechtman. *The Empire of Trauma: An Inquiry into the Condition of Victimhood*. Translated by Rachel Gomme. Princeton: Princeton University Press, 2009.

Fearon, James D. "The Rise of Emergency Relief Aid." In *Humanitarianism in Question: Politics, Power, Ethics*, edited by Michael Barnett and Thomas G. Weiss, 49–72. Ithaca: Cornell University Press, 2008. www.jstor.org/stable/10. 7591/j.ctt7v7ms.

Fincham, Gail. *Dance of Life: The Novels of Zakes Mda in Post-Apartheid South Africa.* Athens, OH: Ohio University Press, 2012. www.jstor.org/stable/j. cttlj7x979.

Freedgood, Elaine. "The Novelist and Her Poor." *Novel: A Forum on Fiction* 47, no. 2 (2014): 210–223. doi.org/10.1215/00295132-2647158.

Hitchcock, Peter. *The Long Space: Transnationalism and Postcolonial Form.* Stanford: Stanford University Press, 2010.

Hortstkotte, Silke, and Nancy Pedri. "Focalization in Graphic Narrative." *Narrative* 19, no. 3 (2011): 330–357. doi: 10.1353/nar.2011.0021.

James, Erica Caple. "The Political Economy of 'Trauma' in Haiti in the Democratic Era of Insecurity." *Culture, Medicine, Psychiatry* 28 (June 2004): 127–149. doi.org/10.1023/B:MEDI.0000034407.39471.d4.

James, Erica Caple. *Democratic Insecurities: Violence, Trauma and Intervention in Haiti.* Berkeley: University of California Press, 2010.

Jameson, Fredric. *The Ideologies of Theory: Essays 1971–1986.* Vol 2. Minneapolis: University of Minnesota Press, 1988.

Jameson, Fredric. *The Antinomies of Realism.* London: Verso, 2013.

Levi, Primo. *Survival in Auschwitz.* Translated by Stuart Woolf. New York: Touchstone, 1996.

Levy, Michele. "Nuruddin Farah. *Crossbones.*" *World Literature Today* 86, no. 4 (July–August 2012): 56–57.

Lukács, Georg. *Studies in European Realism.* New York: Grosset and Dunlap, 1964.

Lukács, Georg. "Narrate or Describe." In *Writer and Critic and Other Essays,* 110–148. New York: Grosset and Dunlap, 1971a.

Lukács, Georg. *The Theory of the Novel.* Translated by Anna Bostock. Cambridge: MIT Press, 1971b.

Lukács, Georg. *Essays on Realism.* Edited by Rodney Livingstone, translated by David Fernbach. Cambridge: MIT Press, 1980.

Lukács, Georg. *The Historical Novel.* Preface by Fredric Jameson, translated by Hannah and Stanley Mitchell. Lincoln: University of Nebraska, 1983.

Mda, Zakes. *Ways of Dying.* New York: Picador, 1995.

Mda, Zakes. *Sometimes There Is a Void: Memoirs of an Outsider.* New York: Farrar, Straus and Giroux, 2008.

Mwangi, Meja. *Kill Me Quick.* London: Heinemann, 1973.

Ndebele, Njabulo S. *South African Literature and Culture: Rediscovery of the Ordinary.* Introduction by Graham Pechey. Manchester: Manchester University Press, 1994.

Ngũgĩ Wa Thiong'o. *Globalectics: Theory and the Politics of Knowing.* New York: Columbia University Press, 2012.

"Nuruddin Farah: *Crossbones,* A Reading and Conversation with Peter Hitchcock." Center for Place, Culture and Politics, The City University of New York, 1 February 2012. Web, http://vimeo.com/37250776.

Rancière, Jacques. *The Politics of Aesthetics.* New York: Continuum, 2006.

Redfield, Peter. *Life in Crisis: The Ethical Journey of Doctors Without Borders.* Berkeley: University of California Press, 2013.

Rushdie, Salman. "Magic in Service of Truth." *New York Times Book Review,* 18 May 2014. http://www.nytimes.com/2014/04/21/books/review/gabriel-garcia-marquezs-work-was-rooted-in-the-real.html?ref=review.

Semple, Kirk. "Iraq Army Woos Deserters back to War on ISIS." *New York Times*, 28 September 2014. http://www.nytimes.com/2014/09/29/world/middleeast/iraq-army-woos-deserters-back-to-war-on-isis.html?src=xps.

Slaughter, Joseph R. "Master Plans: Designing (National) Allegories of Urban Space and Metropolitan Subjects for Postcolonial Kenya." *Research in African Literatures* 35, no. 1 (2004): 30–51. DOI: 10.2979/RAL.2004.35.1.30.

Stephens, Sharon, ed. *Children and the Politics of Culture*. Princeton: Princeton University Press, 1995.

United Nations General Assembly. *Convention on the Rights of the Child*. 20 November 1989.

5 The refugee experience and human rights narrative

Whether they are fictional or real-life accounts, narratives that seek to capture the experience of refugees pivot on a tension between mobility and stasis. At stake in this tension is the identity of the refugee and the extent of autonomy and agency accorded to them in the experience of displacement. Moreover, this tension between mobility and stasis foregrounds the incommensurability of place and time in such narratives. Whereas narrative exegesis generally draws the meaning of the diachronic from its associations with specific settings, refugee narratives are structured around a radical rupture of time from place. Such stories create a topos (or literary invention of place) that occupies the diachronic alone and repeatedly rehearses the experience of flight. In this constant movement, the refugee is portrayed as acting to save their life.

However paradoxical this may seem, given the precarity of the civilian in flight, the story of flight is central to the imaginary of the refugee who must hold onto a sense of agency and of movement towards a destiny. By narrativizing the experience, the author creates a subject who persuasively stands for a rights claimant. Thus, refugee narratives contribute to the broader project of sorting how human rights concerns shape narrative form: the stories dramatize the claims to human rights by going beyond a representation of the wrong and creating a compelling portrait of the claimant. Moreover, as iterations of human rights narratives that attempt to counter the dehumanization of rights abuse, such stories compensate for the refugees' loss of agency.

While narrating the refugee in stasis, we toggle between different terms. The figure becomes precarious all over again in the place of uncertain refuge and as they become dependent on various external determinations, most crucially whether they meet the legal criteria for refugee status or are designated instead, for example, as a migrant without asylum rights.[1] A term holding a more existential than legal meaning emerges in the literature as well: exile, with its evocation of both homelessness and the aspiration of a return, perhaps captures best the experiential uncertainty of the stasis during extended in-between time. Exile, moreover, seeks to maintain connection to what has been lost through memory. Thus, it also foregrounds the temporality of narrative: the place that the exile yearns for is a place of the past. Such restoration is not only a matter of a physical return but a turning back in time to the past before the dislocation. Refugees, therefore, express their exilic condition through memory, maintaining a sense of identity even as a return is either unlikely, or undesirable as too dangerous.[2] Moreover, they exhibit "a passion for history," pertaining specifically to their story of flight through which they keep the thread of connection to the past (Malkki 2002, 359). The narrative of flight retains its relevance, showing how the refugee in stasis holds on to an agentic identity with the potential to redress the condition of exile.

In what follows, I trace the central role of the story of flight in our representations of the refugee and then turn to evocations of the exilic condition of displaced persons to show how they keep alive the story of flight during the invariably long periods of limbo that follow. These are highly traumatic histories whose memory is frequently resisted or feared by refugee populations (Agier 2011, 165). Thus, the tension between remembering and forgetting is acute and bears, furthermore, on the difficult toggle between the terms refugee and migrant, which we might distinguish in part by how prominently war features in each narrative.

In flight

The most dramatic stories of refugee experience are the stories of flight. Yet, the consequences of flight shape the political reality of refugee experience as one of stasis. Stuck in camps (sometimes for generations as we have seen with the experience of Palestinians expelled in 1948), refugees are marked by their struggle to circumvent the limitations stemming from their loss of mobility and autonomy (Peteet 2005, 99). Nonetheless, stories told about refugee experiences invariably emphasize the original story of flight rather than the story of immobility. For example, in an explanation of his collaboration with Sudanese refugee Valentino Achak Deng, Dave Eggers talks about the challenges he faced in his attempt to fill out Deng's story so that he could account not only for Deng's dramatic flights from his village and then from camp to camp, but also for the much longer period Deng spent in refugee camps. In Deng's oral account, "whole years would be skipped because 'nothing of note' had happened" (quoted in Dawes 2007, 209). The challenge of handling this skewed relationship between narrative and real time determined in large part Eggers's choice to use fiction rather than nonfiction. Fiction allowed him to devise an ingenuous overlaying of the traumatic elements of Deng's experience of resettlement in the US with the tension between the flight and immobility of his refugee experience in Africa (Eggers 2007).

This skewing in favor of the stories of flight provokes us to think about its purpose and how it shapes representations of the refugee. Hope is kept alive, even in the most desperate situations, by holding on to an idea of autonomy; the refugee constructs themself as a figure who can walk out of their circumstances and toward a restored normalcy.[3] The photographic record of refugees in flight captures this intentionality very well. An image published by the American Jewish World Service on 20 June 2017, for example, shows a line of women walking at a slight angle to the viewer's right, heads slightly turned to look into the camera. The women have a clear direction on a marked road that continues beyond where the photographer stands. Thus, the image captures the determination and intentionality of the figures.[4] Moreover, such photographs contrast with other representational strategies that use aerial images showing individual figures as dots in a mass movement where the elements overwhelm the fleeing humanity. Roland Barthes commented on such representations as showing "eternal essences of refugees" (1972, 96). Such a mass will be forever walking, going nowhere, in Barthes's estimation. They are stalled in flight, part of the landscape, and removed from history. Consequently, images that by contrast show recognizable figures on a smaller scale convey more powerfully the symbolic potential of walking. The image of a refugee walking purposefully to a new destiny resonates with the effort to capture agentic individuals in flight. Moreover, stories of flight can also offer an imagined return to the experience of flight after it is over that needs to be understood outside the frame of traumatic repetition. The circumstances of the flight justify the human rights claims of the displaced person, portraying them as an agent responding to an emergency. This displaced figure is recalled repeatedly to fight back against the humiliating conditions of refugee existence in camps.

Propelled to move by events beyond one's individual control, the refugee confronts an unrelenting pressure to act and make choices that determine survival. A story that depicts an actor making such momentous decisions and struggling contrasts sharply with the living-death motif of the experience of entrapment in a camp, memorably depicted by Primo Levi through the figures of the "musselmans, the men in decay" in Auschwitz (Levi 1996, 89). Levi's discussion has become a flashpoint of theoretical thinking on camps and biopolitics, and the figure of the "Muselmann" has been taken up in particular by Giorgio Agamben in his work on witness (1999). The risk that a humanitarian camp might recall a concentration camp, especially by evoking the abandonment of our fellow human beings, becomes palpable when logics of incarceration creep into the governance of refugee camps and war overwhelms places of refuge with exigencies of violence and death (Agier 2011, 184).

The refugee narrative depicts flight as a sequence of events with a certain duration over time. The spatially delimited camp or reception center is then imbued with the refugees' desire for a continued or renewed mobility. This desire for renewed mobility comes into focus powerfully in the refugee encampment known as the Jungle of Calais. "A place of refuge for the world's exiles," the Jungle was viewed by its occupants as a point of transit even though leaving it was exceedingly difficult: "it was home to thousands of disparate, desperate people. It was their unequivocal choice against the stagnation and impotency that characterizes most reception centers in Europe" (Santur 2018, 60). This contrast between official and unofficial (unsanctioned by the host state) places of refuge centers on the idea that the place of refuge is not about arrival but departure: it is created by migrants as a staging ground for leaving.[5] Reconceived by the effort to move beyond them, places of stasis and limbo exceed their limits.

A paradigmatic text depicting refugee flight is Marie Béatrice Umutesi's account of walking two thousand kilometers across Zaire in the aftermath of the 1994 genocide in Rwanda. The text merits close attention as it elucidates several key elements of narratives of flight. In *Surviving the Slaughter* (2004), the mental state of a refugee in flight expresses itself as a series of refusals vital to her survival. At the time of her stay in the camps of Kivu, Umutesi reflects:

> A refugee suffers, not only from having been torn from her land, her house, her work and her country, but also from having to beg to survive. For someone who has had work that allowed them to live decently, it is difficult to accept someone else deciding for her what she should eat and how much. It is even more difficult to spend the entire day sitting around with nothing to do but wait for the distribution of aid. Feeling useless is the worst thing imaginable. To forget their uselessness, the refugees threw themselves headlong into drink and debauchery. Alcohol and sex became their major pasttimes. (Umutesi 2004, 82–83).

Umutesi is one of the refugees, but she distances herself from the condition of refugee as described here in order to avoid despair. It is "they" who feel useless and descend into debauchery. Indeed, Michel Agier corroborates Umutesi's impression of the psychic danger and loss of purpose when he speaks generally of camps: "the problem of idleness dominates life in the camps. This problem, closely correlated to the feeling of abandonment, affects everyone, but more directly those who had a recognized, more or less official, job before the exodus" (2002, 329). Elsewhere in her narrative, Umutesi is more inclusive, representing Rwandans as "we." At Tingi Tingi, for example, she speaks of "we" who suffered through "Hell" before humanitarian aid arrived at the camp (2004, 143). What makes the passage above different, therefore, is that it registers her refusal to succumb to the effects of "uselessness." She tells us that it is "difficult to accept" the loss of purposefulness.

She discovers purpose, however, in writing and thus, during the periods of stasis in the camps, she begins to record her experience: "I made a habit of writing so that people could know and break their silence, but also to stop my own pain. I often wept while I wrote, but when I had finished I felt comforted" (Umutesi 2004, 78). Umutesi expresses a strong testimonial impulse and her narrative has been recognized as exemplary. René Lemarchand notes that her "wrenching account surpasses all others" that documented the flight of Hutu refugees into Zaire: "[Umutesi] is unsparingly honest about the scenes of apocalypse she witnessed in the course of her grueling trek .... Hers is the voice of hundreds of thousands who never lived to tell their story ...." (2005, 93–94).[6] She poignantly captures the stories of those who perished in the flight to Kivu so that they will not be forgotten: "I described the suffering of Muhawe and the other children, who, like him, were starving and whose graves lined the long road into exile" (Umutesi 2004, 78). This is not "testimony as event," whereby the act of giving testimony reconstitutes the refugee into a political subject (Agier 2011, 162). For Umutesi, testimony is a private act of writing that helps her cope with the deaths she experiences and, more enduringly, the effort to record events for readers in the future, beyond the refugee camp. It is writing for history, as she does again, a decade later, when she references the same events to explain the challenges of reconciliation in Rwanda (Umutesi 2006).

The power of the imagination to call forth the image of "the long road into exile" is highly motivating and inspiring. The "road" is both a real place, tragically evoked with reference to the children's graves that line it, and an imaginary topos. It suggests a destination (exile) and points to the refugees' capacity for struggle as well as a promise of arrival. Thus, trapped in the camp where she feels the paralysis of "uselessness" closing in on her, Umutesi resists by holding in the imagination the tragic scenes of struggle on the road. Furthermore, this writing enables her to break the silence in other ways. It inspires her to speak out in the camps where she takes on an activist's role, most significantly during her stay at Tingi Tingi (Umutesi 2004, 147–148).

As she flees from camp to camp, in and out of the forest, Umutesi admits: "It was at times like this that I hated the international community, which had abandoned us at the moment that we most needed them. They knew that some of us had survived the rebels in the forest, but they seemed in no hurry to come to our aid" (Umutesi 2004, 145). By addressing the international community, Umutesi speaks as a rights claimant on behalf of herself and her community, knowing full well that such claims are made on the basis of the story of flight. The Convention Relating to the Status of Refugees addresses the displacement of the individual "outside the country of his nationality," adding that the refugee must be "unable or, owing to such fear, is unwilling to avail himself of the protection of that country" (United Nations 1951). This condition of being "outside" begs the question "how come?" and thus invites the telling of a story to ground the refugee's claim for protection. Lying outside the official testimonial practices that are part of the camp's governmental actions, Umutesi's account exemplifies the extended timeline of exodus and deracination that is set in motion by armed conflict. The story of flight, however, has a function that goes beyond proving the claim to legal refugee status. It has an enduring power to hold at bay the dehumanizing aspects of the refugee experience of dependence by characterizing the refugee as heroic and agentic. It also holds at bay the "typological approach" of assigning homogenized identities to refugees (Malkki 2002, 357). To counter such tendencies, for example, the United Nations High Commissioner for Refugees (UNHCR) highlights stories of individual refugees on its website (UNHCR 2020). Similarly, Umutesi fills in as much background as she can on individual refugees.

As noted, Umutesi deepens our sense that the refugee narrative rests on a series of refusals which characterize agency. During her flight from the camps at Tingi Tingi, Umutesi encounters a girl dying by the side of the road. This figure of the abject is shocking: with unseeing eyes wide-open, excrement-stained clothing, flies swarming around her, and insects crawling on her face, the girl brings into focus the extent of the refugees' abandonment by the international community (Umutesi 2004, 165). The girl's condition provokes Umutesi to protest against the empty promises of human rights protections. The international community, she writes, had "abandoned us once again and let us wander in the forest like wild beasts ... allow [ing] this young girl of sixteen to collapse on the road like a dog, food for the ants of the equatorial forest" (166).

Umutesi pours out her anger, an eloquent defense of the humanity of these subjects, to contextualize her act of refusal: from this point onward, she turns away when she smells "rotting flesh" (Umutesi 2004, 166). Thus, she uncouples "seeing" from testimony: "Afterwards I held my nose and looked to the other side until we had passed by" (166). She makes a conscious choice not to look at the abject because it will destroy her ability to keep moving, to stay on the road. The scene also signals to the reader that the subject of her testimony is not the graphic account of the horror. The refusal to look at death is analogous to the refusal to accept the condition of uselessness, which is also related to Umutesi's other significant refusals: first, the refusal to marry or to create an alliance with a man who might protect her during her trek (Umutesi 2004, 201–202, 220), and second, the refusal of repatriation to post-genocide Rwanda where as a Hutu she feels unsafe (224).[7] These refusals together show that the refugee holds on to the prerogative of choosing a destiny.

Umutesi aims to recast the refugee story as a story of war where the protagonists are not armed combatants but women and children fleeing for their lives. Buchi Emecheta laid the groundwork for such depiction of war in *Destination Biafra* where what she calls "women's war" is the story of women heroically saving children while fleeing from combatants (1983, 208). Although their experience is harrowing, Emecheta creates an idealized portrait of resilience and cooperation among refugees. Brought together by chance and unaware of the social differences that separate them, the women in the novel struggle as one. In a similar fashion, Umutesi gives witness to the heroic cooperative effort to save the weakest children. Like Emecheta, she also tells the stories of the deaths of children in a manner that stresses their personhood. The death of one of Umutesi's "adopted" children, Zuzu, best demonstrates the collective effort to buck the inevitable. Zuzu collapses several times by the side of the road and the group of children accompanying Umutesi return to find her and carry her further, repeatedly defying the odds to which Zuzu inevitably succumbs. Umutesi refuses that inevitability to the last, recounting Zuzu's passing as "She [Zuzu] could *do* no more" (Umutesi 2004, 193, emphasis added). In this episode, the dying child is not a passive victim.

Umutesi's posture of refusal affords us an illuminating glance back to Hannah Arendt. In "We Refugees," Arendt focuses on the ambivalence of the refugee's refusals. Writing at a time after World War II when we see the "historical emergence of 'the refugee' as an epistemic object" (Malkki 2002, 357), Arendt says of German Jewish refugees: "If we are saved we feel humiliated, and if we are helped we feel degraded. We fight like madmen for private existences with individual destinies ..." (Arendt 1994,114). The refusal of a collective destiny as "refugees" creates for Arendt ironies that come close to a refusal of history. She lucidly identifies the impulse of the refugee to take on antithesis, to hold onto the idea of an individual destiny even when it seems almost to require distorting the past: "in order to build a new life, one has first to improve on the old one" (Arendt 1994, 114). Having lost everything and starting anew, the refugee continuously bucks her invisibility (115).

A refugee dreams of arrival: arrival to a safe place where a future might be possible. However, arrival or resettlement, is fraught with danger, which can prevent the narrative of flight from belonging to the past. We have already alluded to how Eggers finds a creative solution to render the long years of encampment, but he also portrays the dangers of resettlement, an aspect of the refugee narrative that we do not have in Umutesi. In *What is the What* (2006), Deng confronts new forms of precarity as a victim of crime in the United States, whereas his effort to build an individual destiny is thwarted by tragic events stemming from the lasting trauma of Sudan's civil war, which follows him into exile. Deng loses the woman he loves, a resettled refugee like himself who is murdered by another survivor of the war. Throughout these difficult experiences of new violence, he yearns to tell all the Americans he meets the story of his flight as if it can somehow prevent the new dangers he faces, and also perhaps to convince himself that he will survive these new devastating losses.

Resettlement, therefore, forces new truths to the surface but also returns us to the centrality of the narrative of flight. We see this as well in *Every Year, Every Day, I am Walking*, a production of the South African Magnet Theatre (2012). The play dramatizes the connection between a refugee's refusals and memory. A mother (Ma) and her two daughters (Ernestine and Aggie) suffer an attack that destroys their village somewhere in West Africa (the play was created in 2006 and does not name the war it depicts). Their house is burned down and Ernestine dies in the fire. The mother witnesses the death but Aggie does not and hence retains the hope of reuniting with Ernestine throughout their long flight to South Africa. Aggie sustains her spirit by writing letters to her sister, which she entrusts to their mother. After their arrival in South Africa, most likely a permanent place of exile, Aggie accidentally discovers the stash of unsent letters. The repressed memory of Ernestine's death surfaces and shatters Aggie's magical thinking. Instead of accepting the truth, however, Aggie attempts to flee again. Refusal to accept the death could allow her to retain the agentic identity of someone who chooses her destiny, captured metaphorically here in her renewed flight. The healing turn in the play portrays Aggie reconnecting spiritually with Ernestine when she recalls the story Ernestine used to tell her about migrating elephants (animals that importantly symbolize free movement across borders): "The elephant could walk anywhere" (2012, 53). In a tribute to her sister, she speaks to the audience, declaring: "Every year. Every day. I am walking. Every year, every day, I am walking ... walking with you" (Magnet Theater 2012, 51). Recast now as metaphor, walking sustains hope and a sense of agency as it also enables an acceptance of loss. The "you" here is presumably Ernestine. Aggie, coming to terms with her sister's death, now holds her in memory. However, "you" also opens up the possibility of solidarity with a larger public.

The powerful symbolism of walking, its ability to recall us to freedom despite the depiction of harrowing conditions in testimonial accounts, is in stark contrast to narratives that depict refugees or migrants who surrender their autonomy as passengers in trucks or boats. Surrendering one's ability to "Rise Up and Walk" (to evoke Maathai once more) is tantamount to death. Ghassan Kanafani's classic novella of Palestinian refugees, *Men in the Sun* (1978), is an important precursor to African texts that treat this theme. Kanafani depicts three men's attempt to escape the dehumanizing experience of living in a refugee camp by entrusting their fate to a trafficker. Waiting in the refugee camp is deadening but planning an escape where you surrender your autonomy brings tragic consequences. The walking figure remains elusive, more aspirational than real.

Ten years after the nakbah, or catastrophe of Palestinian expulsions, Abu Qais, Assad, and Marwan decide independently of each other to flee from the camps across Iraq and into Kuwait. As Abu Qais tells himself: "In the last ten years you have done nothing but wait. You have needed ten big hungry years to be convinced that you have lost your trees, your house, your youth, and your whole village" (Kanafani 1978, 13). Psychic survival requires a flight towards a destination holding the promise of a life resembling normal. It is a tenuous promise, however: "If I arrive. If I arrive," as Abu Qais notes (14). The narrator profiles each of the three men in turn, telling us what they lost in the nakbah, who they were before, and who they became after. What they thought was temporary refuge has no end in sight and despair pushes each of these men to propel himself of his own will into flight a second time. Kanafani puts emphasis on the vicissitudes of history and the unpredictability of events. The three men come together by chance on the Iraq-Kuwait border as they negotiate their passage into Kuwait. They agree on the same smuggler, another Palestinian, Abul Khaizuran. Kanafani renders Abul Khaizuran a symbol of Palestine's wounded national pride, left with little but delusional scenaria for its restoration. A Palestinian fighter who suffered a castrating wound in the conflict and who refuses to accept his lost manhood, Abul Khaizuran promises more than what is possible. His improbable plan to ferry the three men inside his water truck's empty tank fails and the men succumb to the extreme heat.

Abul Khaizuran's ability to convince the refugees to go along with his risky plan foregrounds the desperation of the group and opens up the unsettling possibility of the refugees' exploitation by a fellow Palestinian. Yet the relation is not simple. Kanafani makes evident that the magnitude of Abul Khaizuran's trauma makes him more like the refugees than unlike them. He too fled earlier from the hospital where he was being treated for his unbearable wound and we learn: "It was as though his flight could bring things back to normal again" (1978, 38). The same impulse drives all the men. Flight is hope and thus Abul Khaizuran knows how to convince the others to hope in him. The refugees' trust in him brings the situation close to "normal" again as these four disparate individuals forge a common destiny. Various delays and contingencies during the journey mess up Abul Khaizuran's timing and the unbearable heat inside the water tank takes the refugees beyond what they can endure.

Such deadly passages have occurred repeatedly in history. Two Guinean teenagers who sought passage in the cargo hold of a Sabena airplane and perished in that unlivable space in 1999 have become iconic figures and catalysts for scholarly discussion of the plight of African migrants. The teenagers wrote a poignant letter, found with their bodies, in which they asked for Europe's hospitality in terms that articulated perfectly the humanitarian logic of responsiveness to suffering (Fassin 2012, 256).[8] The irony of their deaths exposed the emptiness of this humanitarian logic. No such poignant words are imagined by Kanafani. Instead, the closing lines of the story repeat Abul Khaizuran's unsympathetic question to the dead men: "why didn't you knock on the walls of the tank?" (Kanafani 1978, 56). His words, a form of blaming the victim, reveal his failure to see his fate as connected to theirs. By placing Palestinians in a relation of greed and betrayal, Kanafani ties the fate of continued statelessness to an impotent nationalism. The impasse is most appalling when Abul Khaizuran dumps the bodies of the three men near a rubbish heap. The abandonment is complete as there is no promise that these refugees' death will be remembered.[9] Although striking a different tone, the Guinean boys and *Men in the Sun* both illustrate how, in its failure, the story of flight implicates the reader as someone who has not done enough.

Such stories seek to caution about the magical thinking driving people to reach some other place. Thus, they arguably put the responsibility back on the migrants in order to push them into an alternative trajectory that they need to imagine for themselves and aspire to. Although, such cautionary tales treat the impulse to migrate empathetically, they warn that its promise of arrival is a mirage. Moussa Touré's film drama, *La Pirogue* (2013) tells such a story eloquently: the voyage to Spain on the open seas in a traditional, wooden fishing boat is harrowing, but most of the migrants make it. This arrival, however, is ironic. They reach Spain only to be sent back to Senegal in a mockery of their superhuman effort to survive the journey.[10] Touré tells the story of economic migrants and not individuals fleeing war. Given the opening scene of the film with its staging of a traditional wrestling match, the migrants clearly feel their masculinity is in crisis (there is only one woman passenger on the pirogue, who is a stowaway). Caught in the decades' old unresolved tension between tradition and modernity, the men justify their decisions to migrate with different flawed iterations of their masculinity. Thus, Touré's film exhibits another key dimension of the African migrant narrative's debt to Kanafani, which similarly centers on ideas of injured manhood.

Humanitarian narratives, as I have argued elsewhere, are naturalist narratives that conform to a logic of necessity driven by environmental conditions of war and emergency (2014, 10–11). The challenge is to go beyond the humanitarian frame and see that the figure in flight is not acting out a determined naturalist narrative but instead holds some historical particularity unique to their circumstance that we as readers are called to attend to. This renewed availability to history results from breaking or challenging the frame through which we understand refugee experience and, as we shall see in what follows, it motivates the narrative of the exile.

Exile and proleptic temporality

The radical rupture of time from place that marks the narrative of flight persists in the second narrative paradigm of refugee experience—that of exile. A condition of exile signals both an arrival to a place of refuge and a circumstance of homelessness. The exilic consciousness, moreover, holds on to a temporality from the place left behind; it does not belong in the now of the place of arrival. Thus, often used in humanitarian discourse as an umbrella term to group displaced persons who have not yet received a determination of their legal status, the term exile underscores the experience of traumatic rupture from home, and its temporality emanates from there, from the home that has been lost.

In their fieldwork, Agier (2008) and Malkki (1995) both refer to refugees in camps as exiles. Furthermore, Agier clarifies a shift in the term so that we understand contemporary exiles are not the same type of exiles as the "political exiles of the 1930s, 1940s, and 1950s ..." (2008, 24). More polemically, he stresses the exiles' difference from migrants:

Exodus in war is not a simple migration from one place to another. It is best to make clear right away that refugees are not migrants. Not only have they not chosen to be on the move, but their exile actually prolongs the violence .... The original suffering, formed by the emotional personal experience of destruction of places, goods and human beings, is then deepened in the course of a trajectory of wandering, a wounding existence (2008, 23–24).

Leaving aside for the moment Agier's too easy characterization of migration as voluntary, the insistence that war constitutes the core narrative and is at the origin of all refugee experience, creating "an existential community," is an important concept. Whereas there are many pressing reasons a) to insist that migration stems from extreme physical insecurity and b) to dispel the idea that it is chosen freely and therefore migrants can be disciplined for it, we also find a hesitance to come to terms with war experiences that makes the refugees' stories harder to access. If you give migrants some of the features of refugees, the refugees' particularity (their war experience) recedes further from view. This problem is exacerbated when the two paradigms of displacement are closely aligned. Therefore, Agier's directive that we understand the narratives of refugees as war narratives is timely.

"Existential," for Agier, indicates that exile is demarcated by a particular sensibility of precarity based on (and not somehow beyond) historical experience. He places the exile in the context of what he has called the "existential community" of exodus for which historical retrospection becomes a means of political re-subjectification. Agier's work yields a bold, sweeping theory of refugees as the world's "undesirables" situated "on the margins of the world," as his titles indicate (2011, 2008). His topic is primarily refugee camps and other forms of mass resettlement of large populations displaced by conflict in places generally far from Europe and the United States. Although Agier tends to homogenize refugees in broad generalizations, he opens up an important aspect of the refugee experience that has wide applicability to scholars in the humanities: he identifies the refugees' multiple engagements with history through an array of narrative, testimonial, and documentary practices. The historical impulse is equally important to the experience of the refugee in flight, as Umutesi's example has shown.

Existence means survival, the affirmation of life. Memory, therefore, sets the contours of this sense of the existential, and the narrative of displacement (the story of war that these individuals share) becomes an imaginary placeholder from where the "existential community" gains coherence, repeating in stasis (what Agier calls the stage of "confinement") the rupture of time from place we find in the narrative of flight:

Different forms of testimony ... may become a vector in the existential community of refugees finding its voice and socialization. This recognition—a *cultural* one, to be precise—based on narration of the experiences of war, exodus and refuge, would give back to the refugees and displaced the humanity that massacres, destitution, assistance and illegality have successively taken away from them. (Agier 2008, 74).

The refugee figure cannot be evoked without reference to the violent rupture from place that occurs in the context of armed conflict. Recognition, gained by articulating the narrative of rupture, "give[s] back" (although Agier states this conditionally) and hence makes explicit a hope for restoration (not of place but of existence or humanity) that remains, even in the best-case scenario, incomplete. When testimony becomes a "vector" through the community, it constitutes a new socialization, demonstrating how narrative, by establishing a sequence over time (the most rudimentary function of narrative), can make something historically in the now. Testimony offers a kind of belonging that substitutes for the loss of place, whose restoration (ultimately a matter that must be resolved politically) is not imminent and might never happen at all.

Typically, the exilic sensibility is associated with the irreparable loss of a particular place. However, such a return physically to the same place is not something that most refugees want or can imagine. The rupture is irreparable and the sense of persistent danger inhibits such longings. It is still true, however, that the exilic consciousness occupies a compensatory, second order existence that longs for wholeness. This idea functions as a broad metaphor for modernity, but there is good reason to hesitate and instead hew closer to the exile's desire to be restored to history, which lies at the core of their testimonial effort.

As noted, the recognition of the refugee as an exile presumes a narrative that gives historical visibility to particular "existential communities." Time becomes a topos in narratives of flight.[11] Characterizing the refugee as an exile prompts us to remember the war that brought on the exodus. It also pushes back against the homogenizing of refugees, which sees them as similarly adrift and unbelonging because of their placelessness. The story of exodus itself offers a place of belonging. Thus, Malkki speaks of refugees' "passion for history" as the strong motivation to explain the events of their exodus.

However, in his fieldnotes, Agier also observes a desire among refugees to forget out of fear of what the past can stir up. Although testimony "*may* become a vector" that gives the community visibility, it may also not emerge at all. The memory of the war is feared psychically as a destabilizing trauma that inhibits coping; it is feared politically out of worry that the conflict will be rekindled in the place of refuge (Agier 2011, 165–167). Recognizing how such fear complicates the work of exilic remembrance allows us to understand at least in part why refugee narratives can be unsettling and, even as Said argued, resistant to humanistic reading (2000, 174). Agier, of course, is positing a humanistic reading of refugees, but he and Said share an insistence on a historical approach. The difference is that Said navigates the politics of representation anxiously, distrusting most gestures at universalizing humanity because they hijack the point of view of those cast out. It is worth lingering for a moment, however, on where Agier and Said converge: the issue of the historical nature of this experience.

As a theorist of the exilic consciousness, Said warns against a too easy slippage into generalizations about the modern condition. Indeed, by offering a posture of refusal, Said expresses something similar to Umutesi's cumulative refusals over the course of her flight that helped her retain the singularity of her effort to survive. Said toggles between the terms refugee and exile, aiming to see the one through the other and thereby break down the distinction: "The word 'refugee' has become a political one, suggesting large herds of innocent and bewildered people requiring urgent international assistance, whereas 'exile' carries with it … a touch of solitude and spirituality" (2000, 181). Although the exile appears as someone whose suffering can almost be redeeming, the "refugee" haunts the exile, disrupting any easy assimilation of the figure. Therefore, the exile carries the experience of traumatic displacement as a defining remainder so that "its essential sadness can never be surmounted" (173). Gesturing toward Arendt's "We Refugees," Said reiterates that not even professional achievement and success in the place of resettlement can mute the sorrow: "The achievements of exile are permanently undermined by the loss of something left behind forever" (2000, 173). The insistence on this historical loss is what Lucy Stonebridge has called Said's "refusal to concede the political experience of mass displacement to literary humanism" (Stonebridge 2018, 12).

Said complicates the passage of the real into story. To unmoor us as readers, he stresses the scale of the subject: "that exile is irremediably secular and unbearably historical; that it is produced by human beings for other human beings; and that, like death but without death's ultimate mercy, it has torn millions of people from the nourishment of tradition, family, and geography" (2000, 174). The emphasis on scale does not distance the events from us, but draws us into the circle of their implications to find our complicity, which is located precisely in our tendency to draw the figure of the exile into a "'good for us'" narrative (174).[12] To redress this tendency, we must engage with the historical nature of the phenomenon ("produced by human beings for other human beings") where the real does not fit comfortably into story.

Thus, we have three articulations of the refugee in relation to historical narration: Malkki speaks of the refugees' "passion for history"; Agier sees the repetitions of testimony over time transforming the act of retrospection into a "vector" that mobilizes a new political community; and finally, Said sees the history of flight and refugee exodus as the haunting trace of the historical in the exile. Narratives of exile depict realities difficult to assimilate, experiences that are mute and that resist our desire to coopt them as humanistically uplifting. If the passage from refugee to exile also maps onto a passage from voicelessness to a particularly (peculiarly) privileged form of utterance for some (e.g. the exiled writer such as Umutesi), the narrative of the experience of dislocation returns us to the reality of violent rupture and irreparable loss in such a way that it conveys the distance between us and the events, and discomfits us rather than uplift us. There should be no "good for us" take away, or else this would be a failure of reading. It is incumbent upon us to do the work of contextualization that illuminates the particularity of what we read in the frame of its historical circumstance.

Umutesi, whose work is central to my exploration of the narrative of flight, demonstrates how the refugee and the exile lie in a continuum. Her harrowing account immerses us in a very difficult to assimilate history that is also under threat of erasure. Umutesi wrote her memoir while living in exile in Belgium, but her story of flight is an inconvenient narrative that disrupts a widely held understanding of events disseminated by the politically powerful about the Hutu refugees who fled into Zaire immediately after the genocide (Lemarchand 2005, 99). These refugees were largely perceived as fleeing génocidaires, whereas Umutesi shows them as civilians. Her survival permits her dissident voice, which she deploys to create a "vector" through the suffering of those with whom she shared her experience of flight. Her exile is politically resistant and demonstrates the powerful alignment of refugee and exile.

In the context of Rwanda's history, moreover, there is another, quite different exilic experience, one more widely recognized than the flight of Hutu civilians into Zaire in the aftermath of the genocide. Exile is central, of course, to the Tutsi experience of persecution, which is marked by repeated flights from Rwanda beginning in 1959. For the Tutsi, this narrative has been conventionally rendered to express the imperative of a return and restoration. Their survival was not a given but had to be fought for, giving rise to the Rwandan Patriotic Front. Scholastique Mukasonga takes a completely different tack in narrating the Tutsi history of exile, however. Her story, an unfamiliar one for those who do not know Rwanda's post-independence history well, casts Tutsi exile as a problem of internal exile. Like Umutesi's story of Hutu civilians, Scholastique recasts the narrative of Tutsi exile to provide a new look at historical experience.

The story of internal displacement of Tutsis within Rwanda's borders constitutes an important contextual gesture for understanding the genocide overall. It is crucial for seeing the events of April to July 1994 as a genocide because they establish a sequence of actions that demarcated and dehumanized the Tutsi as an ethnic group over decades. These actions are especially important because they included physical displacement and containment—signature precursors to genocide that help us identify the crime. It might seem unnecessary to defend the mass killings of 1994 as a genocide, yet, as the proceedings of the International Tribunal for Rwanda demonstrated, meeting the legal standard of genocide was surprisingly challenging (Wilson 2011, 178–179).

Mukasonga has made multiple facets of this history leading up to the genocide her subject as a writer. Framing this work as a refugee narrative allows us to compare Mukasonga to Umutesi despite the political divide that frequently situates them in different conversations about the genocide. Umutesi is more clearly focused on flight and Mukasonga stresses exile, but together they show the ways that such narratives, capturing disparate, even "opposing" sides of the narrative of conflict, can bring a discomfiting historical awareness to the reader, necessary before we can envision a political solution to the challenges of reconciliation.

In *Cockroaches* (2016), Mukasonga insistently describes her family's experience of forced, internal displacement as exile and prompts us to confront the existential dimensions highlighted by Agier. Moreover, like Umutesi, Mukasonga makes her narrative difficult, disrupting assumptions about the temporality of events and historical closure.[13] Together, the two writers' texts afford a fuller picture of the multi-directionality of the conflict's impact. Mukasonga's aim to unsettle her reader is manifest in her repeated gestures to take us further back in history or to reorient us geographically. For example, her novel, *Our Lady of the Nile* (2014, originally *Notre Dame du Nil* 2012), differs in its representational strategy than the celebrated works of the *Rwanda: écrire par devoir de mémoire* project, which yielded such acclaimed novels as Boubacar Boris Diop's *Murambi, le livre des ossements* (2000) and Tierno Monémbo's *L'Aîné des orphelins* (2000). Looking at the aftermath and working backwards to reconstruct the events, the authors of the memory project sought to document the genocide from an African perspective in order to redress the dominance of a global north discourse about it.[14] Instead, Mukasonga writes a novel set decades before the genocide, seeking to uncover its political and historical causes in, what seems like, an unlikely place: a Catholic school for girls around the time of independence. Yet, in literary terms, this setting makes a recognizable gesture. Mukasonga has chosen the paradigmatic setting for telling the story of transition from colonialism to independence (the school), put it in explicitly gendered terms that open up the novel to allegories of the nation while also prefiguring the violence against women that played a central role in the genocide.

As noted, her autobiographical work *Cockroaches* (2016, originally *Inyenzi, ou Les Cafards*, 2006) centers explicitly on the theme of exile as internal displacement, thus creating a geographical disorientation in the reader. Mukasonga aims to contextualize and broaden the scope, and to thus make the genocide less available to simplified narratives. The text focuses on Nyamata, a town where one of the largest single massacres of the genocide occurred. The church where thousands perished is today one of the important genocide memorials. However, Mukasonga gives readers less familiar with Rwanda's history a new picture of Nyamata by recasting it as a place of exile, marked decades before the genocide by the violence against Tutsis. From Magi, her hometown in the Butare province, Mukasonga was expelled to Nyamata with the other Tutsi survivors of the ethnic cleansing of 1959: "They decided who could stay and who was to be expelled. As it happened all the Tutsis whose houses had burned were to be banished.

Maybe they wanted to be sure there were no stray Hutus among the exiles" (2016, 18). The path of the family's exodus took them over the border into Burundi and then back into Rwanda, thus figuratively breaking the bond with their nation and reentering Rwanda as refugees. Once in Nyamata, they realized that Tutsis from other parts of Rwanda had also been banished to Nyamata (21).

The displaced were crowded in a school, living communally with make-shift kitchens and shelters made of "four stakes and a straw roof" in the school yard (2016, 21). Food was distributed to them ("the refugees") by soldiers (22). Most importantly, they felt exiled to a different country and assumed they would return home soon: "We would go back home again very soon, back to Rwanda, because no one thought of Nyamata as Rwanda" (23–24). Instead, the authorities decided to move people into the neighboring communities and out of the school. To force this, they canceled the refugees' food rations and gave each family a machete to clear the bush and start to build a life and community from scratch. Mukasonga also recollects that "Gitwe [the place they were sent to] was a very straight road through the brush, leading nowhere" (27). As the refugees head down a road to "nowhere," the placelessness that defines exilic sensibility sets in. But Gitwe, like Nyamata before, was to them "a temporary encampment" (28). They continued to hold onto the conviction that they would return, although the reader realizes the particular meaning of their precarity: during those long years they were only waiting for the final assault against them.

Thus, the limbo of exile has a devastating iteration in Mukasonga. In retrospect, it appears as a long wait leading up to the genocide. It is the completion of the action that began with the original break-up of the community in Butare and thus a particularly hopeless limbo. The "margins of the world" to which Mukasonga and her family were pushed to were not geographically distant nor were they outside the borders of the state from which she held her citizenship. Yet this is the segregation and banishment that set the stage for genocide because of its peculiar invisibility. Mukasonga's book can turn us into particularly anxious readers of Agier, who is grappling with conceptualizing the problem of millions of refugees confined (hence segregated and banished) in camps and other precarious spaces (in the underbelly of cities, for example) who could (and have, as Umutesi narrates regarding the Hutu refugees in Zaire) become targets of mass killing.

Mukasonga speaks warmly of the people in Bagesera (the province where Gitwe was located) who were poor but not unwelcoming, but she does not stop referring to her family and the others as "the refugees" and this period as one of "internal exile." Moreover, Mukasonga rereads the history of this region by seeing, in the various violent episodes and the hostile political climate, ironic foreshadowing of the genocide itself. Thus, speaking of the attacks in 1963, she describes the survivors in light of what was to happen in 1994: "The helicopters went back and forth over the houses. My parents and big brother had disappeared. I never found out where they'd hidden [in 1963], maybe on Rebero Hill, where *some thirty years later*, the last surviving inhabitants of Gitwe and Gitagata would resist to the end ..." (2016, 43, emphasis added). The events are connected, and the timeline of the genocide extended—not three months but 30 years, punctuated by repeated episodes of displacement. This temporality of repeating events creates a morass. But, in this stalling, Mukasonga also works against the reader's negative anticipation and makes the lives of her family gain as much fullness as possible, bucking the sense that their deaths trump all meaning. At the same time, however, it is hard not to be aware of the sense of being trapped, since we know already that all this leads up to the genocide.

Soon after the events of 1963, Mukasonga's family moved again, this time to Gitagata, into an abandoned home of a Tutsi who had fled into exile in Burundi (2016, 47). Then, in 1973, she left for Burundi accompanied by her brother André. Poignantly, she tells us they were the ones the family chose to survive (99–100). Although the distance is short and it takes only one night to reach Burundi, Mukasonga renders this flight as a secret and dangerous escape across a border that is typical of war refugee narratives. The terrain is inhospitable, full of wildlife ("howls, birds taking flight, pounding hooves"). She must force herself through the bush and "its dense thickets" full of thorns. There is no path as such and they arrive once again in the middle of nowhere: "As far as the eye could see, there was nothing but brambles" (2006, 102–103). This exile to safety provides her opportunity, building on the efforts her father had made to ensure his children were educated.

Most poignantly, the narrative of exile in Mukasonga makes explicit the exile's burden of survivor's guilt. Mukasonga's skillful (dis)orientation of the reader creates suspense in the last sequence of the novel, which narrates her return after the genocide. Already knowing the worst and thus full of ambivalence over what she might find or what she should be looking for, she discovers the total destruction of the community of Gitagata and hardly a trace of her family's home. A chance encounter with a Hutu neighbor is revelatory, however, and brings her narrative into crisis.

This is a man whom she had met as her parents' guest on a rare return visit in 1986. The occasion was her sister's wedding and the man was invited because he was a neighbor. Mukasonga presses him to recognize her and give her an account of what happened. For a fleeting moment, he voices an admission: "Yes, that's Cosma's daughter [Mukasonga], now that I see her, I can certainly ask for her forgiveness ..." (2006, 163). But this admission does not hold. The man expresses various denials without elaborating about what he needs forgiveness for. The intimacy and happenstance occurrence of such a momentous encounter, its coming into focus for a fleeting second only to be denied and recanted, captures poignantly the fragility of the truth of events. The effort to establish what happened, the sequence and detail of events, is never fully accomplished and the stories that we end up with are incomplete.

We might accept such partial accounting as inevitable, but Mukasonga brings us tantalizingly close to the possibility of a fuller account, which she withdraws just at the moment it becomes discernible. This teasing possibility—that we could know but won't because those who hold some important truths withhold them purposefully—leaves one feeling that the conflict is ongoing, playing out in a contest over memory. The most likely closure, forgetting, works against history. Thus, the literary narrative offered by Mukasonga works against the pressure of this forgetting. Her narrative illustrates the forgetting at work in the form of discreet actions taking place during her post-genocide visit. Active forgetting, the suppression of intimate details that locate particular people in particular places, constitutes an episode in her retrospective account.

As a narrator, Mukasonga accomplishes something astonishing with the force (and surprise) with which she brings the tantalizing possibility of concrete truth to her reader and the dramatic withdrawal of this possibility. Moreover, the withdrawal is rendered as a named person's deliberate action such as we now recognize probably happens frequently in postconflict societies. Most importantly, the withdrawal of truth underscores the exilic condition and its existential suffering. The not-knowing, the absolute separation from home which the exilic condition imposes, the silence with which the survivor must live, all contribute to a psychic placelessness. The melancholic, mournful tone of Mukasonga's prose holds in place this lack. Its beauty is not compensatory, not a "good for us" story, but a painful reminder that we cannot have certainty. At the same time, our distance can motivate repeated efforts at historical accounting and demand political solutions.

Notes

1 Internally displaced persons also challenge the legal determinations. The 1969 Refugee Convention agreed to by the Organization of African Unity expanded the definition of refugee to include internally displaced persons. The UNHCR has followed OAU Convention in its interventions in Africa, but distinctions between these two types of displaced persons persist globally (Gatrell 2013, 244).

2 More recently, historian Peter Gatrell has affirmed this idea, agreeing with Malkki that refugees have sought meaning in history: "refugees have helped to fashion themselves by recourse to history" and found ways to mobilize their understanding of their history to act collectively (2013, 12). Gatrell, furthermore, notes the "general absence of refugees in historical scholarship". This "invisibility," he says, "reflects a belief ... that refugees emerged only fleetingly on the stage of history before being restored to a more settled experience" (11). The gap between patterns of representation of refugees and their experience also becomes apparent here in these preconceptions.

3 An example of the inspirational power of the walking figure is Wangari Maathai, who was awarded the Nobel Peace Prize for leading the Greenbelt movement in

Kenya. She describes how she thought of herself as a walking figure in order to continue struggling in face of great odds: "I have never stopped to strategize about my next steps. I often just keep walking along ... My slogan was 'Rise Up and Walk'" (2007, 286–287).

4 https://ajws.org/blog/4700-new-refugees-every-day/ accessed on 13 September 2019. The composition of such images is not recent. In the African context, it echoes iconic images from the Biafran War in which refugees (usually groups of families including men) are repeatedly portrayed walking in a line, carrying children and whatever goods they can, toward the camera. See for example photos from the Associated Press archive, including http://www.apimages.com/metadata/Index/Associated-Press-International-News-Nigeria-BIA-/136e25de8de4da11af9f0014c2589dfb/20/0. Furthermore, the work of photographer Hosam Katan from Aleppo, Syria, in 2014, underscores the wide dissemination of the motif of a figure in flight. In these images, Katan repeatedly captures figures running or walking straight into the camera as if they will exit the scene of war (2018).

5 Hassan Ghedi Santur (2018) shows that the Jungle of Calais is a point of departure rather than arrival, and is understood, therefore, as the place of opportunity for further mobility (to migrate to Britain). This trajectory is apparent in his profile of a Somali refugee (Ahmed) who has endured a five month flight from Hargeisa to arrive in Calais and fails multiple times to find stowage in a truck to cross into Britain.

6 Lemarchand (2005) details the importance of the history that Umutesi makes accessible to us through her testimony as it upends the accepted narrative about Hutu refugees in Zaire that emphasizes the presence of Hutu génocidaires in the refugee population and elides the tragic story of hundreds of thousands of Hutu civilians who fled Rwanda fearing the retaliatory actions of the RPF.

7 Lemarchand explains how the prospects of return turned to "illusion" for many of the refugees (Lemarchand 2005, 96) and credits Umutesi's account for showing that the claim that only génocidaires stayed back from repatriation was disinformation to justify Rwanda's intrusion into Zaire (2005, 94).

8 Simon Gikandi (2001) sees in this same letter a profound historical contradiction: "the boys quest was for a modern life in a European sense of the world; their risky journey from Africa was an attempt to escape both poverty and alterity; it was predicated on the belief that their salvation could only come from Europe, which only two generations earlier black nationalists ... had declared to be the major threat to the prosperity and well-being of Africa" (630–631).

9 In *After the Last Sky* (1999), Edward W. Said reads Abul Khaizuran's futile complaint to the dead men ("why didn't you knock on the walls of the tank?") as a manifestation of the political diffidence of Palestinians who are too accommodating to their plight. Thus, he reads Kanafani as a call to action.

10 Mahriana Rofheart (2014) examines this cautionary attitude across different media of cultural production in contemporary Senegal. The study offers important insights that go against assumptions of a humanitarian logic sympathetic to the migrants' motivation to leave. Thus, Rofheart places emphasis on the harm done by global cultural paradigms that encourage neoliberal individual self-fashioning and the myth of the global north as a place where such achievement is attainable for all.

11 Lyndsey Stonebridge connects placelessness specifically to the experience of "non-sovereignty" or "statelessness." Thus it coincides with the loss of rights since rights come from citizenship (2018, 14–15). In the discussion that follows, I don't stress statelessness because normative assumptions about the state require different nuance in the case of postcolonial African states.

12 In a widely cited passage, Said puts it thus: "At most the literature of exile objectifies an anguish and a predicament most people rarely experience firsthand; but to think of the exile as beneficially humanistic is to banalize its mutilations, the losses it inflicts on those who suffer them, the muteness with which it responds to any attempts to understand it as 'good for us'" (Said 2000, 174).

13 Born three years apart (Mukasonga in 1956 and Umutesi in 1959), the two writers belong to the same generation and share a similar educational background. Umutesi remains in exile in Brussels, and writes as a dissident Rwandan. Mukasonga was in exile during the genocide and splits her time between France and Rwanda.

14 Nicki Hitchcott explains the memory project's origins and its aim to write back to western responses to the genocide (2009, 152).

Works Cited

Agamben, Giorgio. *Remnants of Auschwitz: The Witness and the Archive*. Translated by Daniel Heller Roazen. Brooklyn, NY: Zone Books, 1999.

Agier, Michel. "Between War and City: Towards an Urban Anthropology of Refugee Camps." *Ethnography* 3, no. 3 (2002): 317–341. www.jstor.org/stable/24048113.

Agier, Michel. *On the Margins of the World: The Refugee Experience Today*. Translated by David Fernbach. Cambridge, UK: Polity, 2008.

Agier, Michel. *Managing the Undesirables: Refugee Camps and Humanitarian Government*. Translated by David Fernbach. Cambridge, UK: Polity, 2011.

Arendt, Hannah. "We Refugees." In *Altogether Elsewhere: Writers on Exile*, edited by Marc Robinson, 110–119. Boston: Faber and Faber, 1994.

Barthes, Roland. *Mythologies*. Translated by Annette Levers, New York: Hill and Wang, 1972.

Coundouriotis, Eleni. *The People's Right to the Novel: War Fiction in the Postcolony*. New York: Fordham University Press, 2014.

Dawes, James. *That the World May Know: Bearing Witness to Atrocity*. Cambridge, MA: Harvard University Press, 2007. www.jstor.org/stable/j.ctt13x0m08.

Eggers, David. *What is the What*. New York: Vintage, 2006.

Eggers, David. "It Was Just Boys Walking." *The Guardian*, 25 May 2007, 2007. http://www.theguardian.com/books/2007/may/26/featuresreviews.guardianreview29.

Emecheta, Buchi. *Destination Biafra*. Glasgow: Fontana, 1983.

Fassin, Didier. *Humanitarian Reason: A Moral History of the Present*. Berkeley: University of California Press, 2012.

Gatrell, Peter. *The Making of the Modern Refugee*. Oxford: Oxford University Press, 2013. DOI: 10.1093/acprof:oso/9780199674169.001.0001.

Gikandi, Simon. "Globalization and the Claims of Postcoloniality." *South Atlantic Quarterly 100*, no. 3(2001): 627–658.

Hitchcott, Nicki. "A Global African Commemoration—*Rwanda: Écrire par devoir de mémoire*." *Forum for Modern Language Studies* 45, no. 2(2009): 151–161. DOI: 10.1093/fmls/cqp003.

Kanafani, Ghassan. *Men in the Sun*. Translated by Hilary Kilpatrick. London: Heinemann, 1978.

Lemarchand, René. "Bearing Witness to Mass Murder." *African Studies Review* 48, no. 3(2005): 93–101. DOI: https://doi.org/10.1353/arw.2006.0025.

Levi, Primo. *Survival in Auschwitz.* Translated by Stuart Woolf. New York: Touchstone, 1996.

Maathai, Wangari. *Unbowed: A Memoir.* New York: Anchor Books, 2007.

Magnet Theatre. "Every Year, Every Day, I am Walking." In *The Magnet Theatre 'Migration' Plays,* compiled by Jennie Reznek, 9–54. Mowbray, SA: Junkets Publisher, 2012.

Malkki, Liisa H. *Purity and Exile: Violence, Memory, and National Cosmology among Hutu Refugees in Tanzania.* Chicago: University of Chicago Press, 1995.

Malkki, Liisa H. "News from Nowhere: Mass Displacement and Globalized 'Problems of Organization.'" *Ethnography* 3, no. 3(2002): 351–360. DOI: 10.1177/ 146613802401092797.

Mukasonga, Scholastique. *Our Lady of the Nile.* Translated by Melanie Mauthner. Brooklyn, NY: Archipelago Books, 2014.

Mukasonga, Scholastique. *Cockroaches.* Translated by Jordan Stump. Brooklyn, NY: Archipelago Books, 2016.

Peteet, Julie. *Landscape of Hope and Despair: Palestinian Refugee Camps.* Philadelphia: University of Pennsylvania Press, 2005.

Rofheart, Mahriana. *Shifting Perceptions of Migration in Senegalese Literature, Film, and Social Media.* Lanham, MD: Lexington Books, 2014.

Said, Edward W. *After the Last Sky: Palestinian Lives.* Photographs by Jean Mohr. New York: Columbia University Press, 1999.

Said, Edward W. *Reflections on Exile and Other Essays.* Cambridge, MA: Harvard University Press, 2000.

Santur, Hassan Ghedi. "Maps of Exile." In *Mediterranean,* edited by Bhakti Shringarpure, Michael Bronner, Veruska Cantelli, Michael Busch, Jessica Rohan, Melissa Smyth, Jason Huettner, Gareth Davies, and Noam Scheindlin, 59–87. Storrs, CT: Warscapes, 2018.

Stonebridge, Lyndsey. *Placeless People: Writing, Rights, and Refugees.* Oxford: Oxford University Press, 2018. DOI: 10.1093/oso/9780198797005.001.0001.

Touré, Moussa, director. *La Pirogue.* Story by Abasse Ndione. K-Films Amérique, 2013.

Umutesi, Marie Béatrice. *Surviving the Slaughter: The Ordeal of a Rwandan Refugee in Zaire.* Translated by Julia Emerson. Madison: University of Wisconsin Press, 2004.

Umutesi, Marie Béatrice. "Is Reconciliation between Hutus and Tutsis Possible?" *Journal of International Affairs* 60, no. 1(Fall/Winter 2006): 157–171. www.jstor. org/stable/24358018.

UNHCR. "Special Features." Accessed 8 May 2020, 2020. https://www.unhcr.org/ en-us/special-features.html.

United Nations. *Convention and Protocol Relating to the Status of Refugees.* Accessed 24 June 2020, 1951. https://www.unhcr.org/en-us/1951-refugee-convention.html.

Wilson, Richard A. *Writing History in International Criminal Trials.* New York: Cambridge University Press, 2011. DOI: 10.1017/CBO9780511973505.

6 "You only have your word"
Rape and testimony

Introduction

Describing the aftermath of her sexual assault in Tahrir Square in Cairo on 11 February 2011, CBS reporter Lara Logan placed the emphasis on the victim's narrative: "With sexual violence, you only have your word. The physical wounds heal. You don't carry around the evidence the way you would if you had lost your leg or your arm in Afghanistan" (Stelter 2011). For Logan, the absence of a visible wound threatens to erase her story. It signals the anxiety that her words perhaps will not be enough, and thus foregrounds the added work her words must do to make the crime perpetrated against her real to others.

A similar problem that highlights the evidentiary burden carried by words arises in the legal context where the sexual assault complainant's testimony has unique significance because it carries most of the burden of proof on the issue of consent.[1] Some of this burden can shift to witnesses, but never entirely. While Logan's attack was in public, her account emphasizes her isolation during it: surrounded by her attackers, Logan lost contact with her colleagues, though they remained on the scene and tried to defend her. The intimate nature of the attack makes her perspective essential, not merely to prove that she was attacked—her colleagues can testify to that—but in order to ascertain the nature of the harm done to her.

This chapter explores the entanglement of three contradictory premises about the narrative testimony of rape, which arise from the definitional burden that this testimony must carry. These premises are explored through the frames of legal theory, visual theory, and narrative texts—both testimony and fiction. Examples are drawn in large part from the Rwandan genocide, where the correlation of narrative testimony to the production of images has shaped a rich vein of philosophical inquiry into the nature of witnessing whose relation to the law has not been fully explored.

Logan's claim that "you only have your word" captures the first of these contradictory premises. A victim's words are highlighted in the sense that they stand alone as both accusation and evidence of the nature of the harm done. In the legal setting, as Kirsten Campbell has shown, the complainant-witness "embodies the wrong before the court," opening up the complexities of how legal memory constitutes evidence (2002, 166). Logan's statement alerts us, however, to the potential weakness of words: it is all she has, she tells us. The sexual assault victim's testimony is weakened by the absence of other types of corroborative evidence, especially that which can be rendered visually—both literally with the exhibition of a physical wound or image and metaphorically as in the recreation of the event. The law has conventionally relied on a "realist" model that assumes memory is a reproduction of reality (165). Legal memory is constituted by the charges, the evidence collected by the prosecution, and the "procedural and evidentiary rules of a hearing" (155). Yet in the prosecution of rape, the vacillating definitional parameters of the crime reveal a dissonance between the visual and the narrative. This dissonance presents a challenge to the realist model of legal memory, which has conditioned us to think of legal memory as a reproduction of the event to be corroborated by other types of evidence in order to show that it is something more than a powerful story. In the prosecution of rape, we encounter a special emphasis on narrative testimony that brings into crisis the aspects of the realist model that call up metaphorically a visual representation of the harm done.

The second set of contradictory premises pertains to the competing definitions of rape as a war crime that put our propensity to think visually in a new context. In its prosecution of Jean-Paul Akayesu, the International Criminal Tribunal for Rwanda (ICTR) introduced a new definition of rape, referred to as a "conceptual definition," in order to combat the limitations of the conventional "mechanical definition" that relies on an explicit account of penetration and a high degree of specificity of anatomical detail. By contrast, the conceptual definition places emphasis on the whole person and the dignity of the victim, thereby permitting testimony that is less graphic and addresses the psychological damage done by the crime. This conceptual definition better captures the victim's manner of talking about her experience than the mechanical definition, which places an emphasis on what happened in order to create a picture of the crime in consonance with realist legal memory. The mechanical definition dehumanizes what are highly personal traumatic narratives to fit the convention of a realist legal memory.[2] The conceptual definition, on the other hand, does work that is compatible with Campbell's unpacking of legal memory into distinct types and validates the need to acknowledge that the realist model is not the only one at play.[3] Despite this innovation, the ICTR reverted to the mechanical definition in subsequent trials, as did the International Criminal Tribunal for Yugoslavia (ICTY) because the conceptual definition was perceived as confusing (Campbell 2007, 415–416).

This legal tangle (two definitions of the crime, multiple models of legal memory) exposes a third tension, the tension between the expectation to give an explicit account of the crime and the hesitation of women to provide that account even as they are willing to testify on their own terms. Complainants' resistance to giving a mechanical description comes either from fear that doing so is injurious and traumatic to them, or from the sense that these details are less relevant than the psychological harm they experienced. Campbell's contrast between the legal memories of the defense and the prosecution captures this tension. The defense, according to Campbell, treats the complainant's memory as a state of mind, "an opinion or belief," and therefore as a "labile mental representation." The prosecution, on the other hand, sees the complainant's testimony as an "accurate account of the event" that is not the same as a "photographic image," but is rather an account which "captures the experience" and is hence "truthful" (2002, 166–167).

In both instances, Campbell makes reference to the visual (the unstable labile mental representation contrasted to the truthful even though not photographic image) as the contested standard for measuring the persuasiveness of testimony. Such references to the visual suggest that we need to bring into play in this discussion theories about the visual representation of rape that can provide a way to think about the demand for explicitness in testimony, even though, as we shall see, they simultaneously exhibit contradictory impulses to reveal and to hide. Ariella Azoulay suggests that we search for photographs of rape in the extant photographic archive not by seeking explicit images but by interpreting the images of historical events and identifying the moments before and after rape may have occurred (2012, 235–237). This interpretive, conjectural practice is only possible if we go from victims' testimony back to the visual record and see it with new eyes. Azoulay, therefore, brings up the contradiction of a historical record that simultaneously silences and reveals.

The tangle that this essay identifies has to do with the requirement of explicitness in evidence and our reliance on visual metaphors to understand what explicitness means. Legal theorists grapple with the many ways the law attempts to iron out ambiguity and stabilize narrative meaning, if only for the instrumental purposes of arriving at a verdict. The conceptual definition of rape attempts to tackle the ways in which the criterion of explicitness hampers the victims of rape by denigrating the value of their oblique testimony. Just as visual theory can destabilize the photographic archive and alert us to the residual evidence of rape as a war crime, the conceptual definition can help us understand testimony with a fresh perspective. Testimonial narratives are more likely to use a conceptual definition of rape and thus serve as a counterpoint to the law's tendency to revert to the mechanical definition.

Legal, visual, and narrative frames

As articulated by the ICTR, the conceptual definition drew an analogy between torture and rape:

The Chamber considers that rape is a form of aggression and that the central elements of the crime of rape cannot be captured in a mechanical description of objects and body parts. The Convention against Torture and Other Cruel, Inhuman and Degrading Treatment or Punishment does not catalogue specific acts in its definition of torture, focusing rather on the conceptual frame work of state sanctioned violence. This approach is more useful in international law. Like torture, rape is used for such purposes as intimidation, degradation, humiliation, discrimination, punishment, control or destruction of a person. Like torture, rape is a violation of personal dignity, and rape in fact constitutes torture when inflicted by or at the instigation of or with the consent or acquiescence of a public official or other person acting in an official capacity (Prosecutor v. Jean-Paul Akayesu, 1998, 597).

To highlight this change, legal scholar Anne-Marie de Brouwer commented that "describing the body parts involved is not done for any other crimes: for instance, murder or torture is not defined as 'blood flows,' 'arms being chopped off,' etc." (2005, 108). This change entails a shift from a focus on the perpetrator's action (penetration) to the victim's experience ("a violation of personal dignity"). If rape is visualized as a series of specific types of penetration, the effect is to fragment the victim's identity and foreground the injured body in place of the whole person. The shift to a conceptual definition illustrates instead how the injury is to the whole person. The Akayesu Judgment also specified that "[s]exual violence is not limited to physical invasion of the human body and may include acts which do not involve penetration or even sexual contact."[4]

The conceptual definition opens the possibility for a much broader range of testimonial narratives, helping us to recognize the full significance of laconic or oblique references to sexual assault. If we cease to have the expectation that the authenticity of rape testimony depends on its illustration of the "mechanical," we can begin to move away from the inhibiting assumption that rape delegitimizes speech, effectively silencing the victim (Hengehold 2000, 189, 194). In testimony given to Yolande Mukagasana, a survivor of the genocide, rape victims gave ample details about the peripheral circumstances surrounding their rape, although they made reference to the assault without elaboration. They might specify that they were repeatedly violated and refer to the number of men that assaulted them, but they rarely gave details about the rapes themselves (Mujawayo and Belhaddad, 2004; Mukagasana 2001, 146). They would also affirm that they either witnessed the rapes of other women or were aware that other women were raped alongside them. Victoire M., for example, is haunted by being the only survivor among the women: "Aucune fille avec laquelle j'ai été violée n'est plus en vie" ["None of the girls with whom I was raped are still alive."][5] Moreover, the women's narratives hold onto the circumstantial details, illustrating how rape as a systematic practice was integral to the implementation of the genocide. Thus Clémence K. makes the routine of rape a central focus of her testimony to Mukagasana:

> J'avais dix-sept ans. J'ai été encerclée et l'on m'a assise de force au sol. Les gens riaient et me demandaient où était ma famille. Je ne répondais pas, je cachais ma poitrine de mes bras. Finalement, l'un d'eux m'a emmenée et enfermée, toujours nue, dans une pièce sombre. Le jour, il allait travailler, c'est-à-dire tuer, piller, violer, humilier ... [.] Le soir il me battait et me violait.

> I was seventeen years old. I was surrounded and they made me sit on the ground by force. The people laughed and asked me where my family was. I did not answer them, and hid my face in my arms. Finally, one of them took me away and locked me up, and kept me continuously naked in a dark room. In the daytime, he went to work, that is to say to kill, pillage, rape and humiliate ... [.] At night he beat and raped me. (Mukagasana 2001, 103, author's translation)

Clémence emphasizes her humiliation more than her physical pain, which must have been considerable.

Many women begin their testimony by stating their age at the time of the attack, a poignant detail not just because some were young like Clémence K. but because it places us in the chronology of a life interrupted, much like an obituary would. This chronology has more than one key moment, however, as Mukagasana places the age of each witness at the time of the testimony in the heading that introduces their narrative. The moment from which retrospection becomes possible creates the possibility for a new period in the women's lives, the one after the act of testifying. Thus, it is not only the assault that demarcates a before and after, but the testimony does so as well in a potentially empowering way. Moreover, reading these testimonies does not give the impression that the incidents of rape were skipped over because they are not described mechanically. Instead our attention is drawn to how the event of rape is situated in history, how it reveals the intersection of a particular life and a historical event.[6]

The emergent legal discourse has the potential to undermine the importance of explicitness by putting emphasis instead on the victim's experience of "intimidation, degradation, humiliation, discrimination, punishment, control or destruction of a person."[7] A different kind of explicitness is highlighted, one which requires that we recognize the victim's testimony as addressing the violence done to her whole person. Esther Mujawayo, who like Mukagasana, is a survivor and has worked as a counselor to rape victims, refers to the survivors' suffering both from the violence of the attack and the guilt that they survived their families precisely because they were raped (Mujawayo and Belhaddad 2004, 197). Perhaps because she self-identifies as an exile, Mujawayo is especially harsh in her critique of the post-genocide regime's treatment of rape survivors, accusing it not only of silencing the victims, but also of allowing them to succumb to AIDS in large numbers (17). The aftermath of the rape is tantamount to being subjected to a slow death sentence, both mentally and physically (81). The silencing of survivors of rape after the genocide is deeply ironic as it duplicates the original violence against them, which was intended to destroy their capacity to speak.

The safe havens created for these women tend not only to their physical needs (and those of their children) but also provide them with an appropriately supportive context and sympathetic audience—a feminized sphere—in which to testify to their experience. Mujawayo works with refugees in Germany, and Mukagasana has supported a group of widows in Rwanda. Both note repeatedly that women who maintained their silence agree to tell them their stories because they know them in their capacity as female survivors of the genocide. Furthermore, Mujawayo associates the premise of a sympathetic space as a frame for her own testimony. This invites the reader to provide a safe space for her account of the most traumatic incident of her experience: the drowning of her adoptive daughter, Rachel, in human waste, which she had never been able to talk about before writing her book (Mujawayo and Belhaddad 2004, 260). Kathryn Abrams and Irene Kacandes refer to a "space" for women within which their experience, even when they have been egregiously violated, may be treated less sensationally and spectacularly, scaling back on the register of horror to allow for it to be expressed (2008, 13, 22).

Literary depictions of rape have a greater imaginative range of expression, but they too treat the degree of explicitness as a problem. Depictions of rape in imaginative literature (novels, short stories, etc.) are often indirect and allusive; we might only know that rape has occurred by reading between the lines. Playing with this habit of reading, J. M. Coetzee, for example, makes Lurie's rape of Melanie in *Disgrace* simultaneously a matter of certainty and of the reader's conjecture. In the same novel, Lucy refuses to testify to the police, but she does talk to her father about her rape without discussing its mechanics (2000, 25, 156).[8] The Zimbabwean novelist Yvonne Vera similarly addresses the issue of explicitness by depicting rape in detail without ever being literal.[9] In *Without a Name*, Mazvita's rape by a freedom fighter is described as metaphor. The action could be accounted for literally by describing Mazvita being pursued across a field, caught, brought down, and assaulted. Instead we read that the land, the key symbol of the freedom struggle, pulls her down. The land links synecdochically the (largely denied) gender violence to the militarized, hyper-masculine freedom struggle (2002b, 29–30). Moreover, in her last novel, *The Stone Virgins*, sexual assault takes the form of a macabre dance between attacker and victim in the presence of the victim's sister's decapitated corpse (2002a, 75). Such indirection allows Vera paradoxically to draw out these scenes of assault, giving a fuller account of their emotional toll.

A literary reading of a text in which the account of rape is rendered obliquely permits the recovery of the unrepresented event because this reconstitution takes place against the backdrop of its original censoring (in the silence of the first reading) and hence is suitably framed, acceptable as that which bears the mark of its prohibition. The caution that leads us initially to read along the grain of the indirect reference to rape stems from the anxiety that a more explicit narrative is potentially pornographic. This unease reflects the influence of patriarchal authority and its framing of rape. Reading against the grain of this obliqueness does not mean filling in the mechanical details. It means reading perhaps more literally and against the habit of interpolating a visual scene for signs of what the obliqueness itself tells us and how it sensitizes us to the conceptual dimension of the crime of rape.

Even before the Rwandan genocide, African women's war experience was defined by rape. Buchi Emecheta's novel of the Nigerian Civil War, *Destination Biafra* (1983), prefigures the real life testimonies that have emerged from Rwanda, exploring the problems that arise from the lack of authority given to women's testimony. A groundbreaking feminist narrative about war, the novel depicts its protagonist, Debbie, as an intrepid record keeper—not unlike Marie Béatrice Umutesi who, in her memoir, *Surviving the Slaughter: The Ordeal of a Rwandan Refugee in Zaire* (2004), narrates her flight out of Rwanda and across Zaire (today the Democratic Republic of Congo) DRC, drawing attention to her record-keeping during the journey. Umutesi is motivated to survive in order to testify to her experience (2004, 78). Similarly, Debbie (Umutesi's fictional precursor) is an educated woman on the run in the middle of a war, who is cast as a witness but also as a survivor of rape. Emecheta turns the struggle to be heard into an element of the plot and narrates Debbie's efforts to gain testimonial authority. After an unsatisfactory experience giving testimony at a humanitarian event in London, however, she gives up on her personal narrative and adopts instead the impersonal voice of the people's historian.[10] The historical work to which Debbie devotes her energies is a text the reader does not have and remains a hypothetical text. Instead we have Emecheta's third person, realist novel about Debbie, which opens up a space for future testimonial narratives by creating an expectation for them. Umutesi, for example, can now step into that narrative space and be more readily believed.

Philosopher Susan Brison, writing about her own experience of rape and the process of reconstituting the self after, makes a point that echoes Emecheta's novel:

> In order to construct self-narratives we need not only the words with which to tell our stories, but also an audience able and willing to hear us and to understand our words as we intend them. This aspect of remaking a self in the aftermath of trauma highlights the dependency of the self on others and helps to explain why it is so difficult for survivors to recover when others are unwilling to listen to what they endured. (2002, 51)

Brison seeks to shift at least some of the emphasis away from the difficulty of finding the language to speak and onto the problem of the audience and its willingness to "understand our words as we intend them" (2002, 51). This requires empathetic listening and an understanding that the story of the harm done is not tantamount to the story of bodily injury. Brison is also addressing the semantic situation: how can we avoid mishearing, how can we be receptive to the words? She points to a reader's willingness or unwillingness, but as literary scholars we might be more skeptical about how intention shapes reading.

Witness narratives are configured in a "complex circuit between what the witness feels that she can tell; what (she believes) others can hear; and what, once others have heard, they can apprehend and repeat" (Abrams and Kacandes 2008, 20). In *Destination Biafra*, Emecheta creates a protagonist who, like Brison, has largely overcome any difficulty with finding her words, but learns that her words are not heard as she intended them (243). Taking our cue from Azoulay's (2008, 217) interrogation of the absence of images of rape, we might ask about this misrecognition: why do we dismiss what we read as something other than the testimony of rape? Brison's *Aftermath* contains the testimony of the impact of the crime defined conceptually as affecting the whole self (2002, 38–39). Arguably, we often already have what we claim is absent. Emecheta handles this situation in a metanarrative fashion by framing a woman's rape-centric narrative of war with Debbie's exploration of her authorial difficulties.

Emecheta and Brison each point away from explicit depictions of rape, considering such depictions as either detracting from the credibility of the accounts or distracting from the graver implications of the harm.[11] As I noted above, oblique accounts do not require that we fill in the mechanical details, but instead that we read against the habit of interpolating a visual scene and for signs of what the obliqueness itself tells us, or how it sensitizes us to the conceptual dimension of the crime of rape. These testimonial narratives (fiction and non-fiction) are thus cautionary examples for those who rely on visual, literal, or explicit evidence in the legal context. At the same time, however, the visual should not be identified exclusively with the literal or realist. A fuller engagement with Azoulay's visual theory considerably complicates the use of photographs in the courtroom without, however, arguing against their use. To her, the writing of history rather than the examination of the legal context is more pertinent, but this chapter initiates a discussion of how Azoulay's theory might intervene in legal practices by sensitizing us to other ways in which photographs speak about historical events.

As previously noted, Azoulay explores the implications of an "implicit prohibition on showing any images of rape" because they are perceived as pornographic. The photographs we do not have, she argues, are photographs which would be analogous to those documenting other human rights abuses (2008, 270). In the Akayesu Judgment, photographic evidence is discussed only in reference to the crime of genocide, and not in reference to rape. The British photographer Simon Cox gave evidence at the trial, showing his photographs of bodies strewn with Tutsi identification cards.[12] Presumably some of these bodies may have been of women who had been raped, providing the kind of conjecture that Azoulay proposes we speculate about. Azoulay suggests how to read the existing photographic record and theorizes on the implications of the absence of explicit rape photographs in that record. This absence, she argues, has a direct influence on how we talk about rape (2008, 253–255). While victims of rape are not silent and have sought to testify to the crimes against them, historical narratives of the same events silence these occurrences (Azoulay 2012, 232–235). Rape as a crime is downplayed by being viewed as occurring in isolated circumstances, rather than systematically or extensively, and by being recorded in histories in passing or in footnotes. As de Brouwer and Sandra Ka Hon Chu have put it, rape has been treated as "collateral damage inconsequential to the larger considerations of wartime politics or justified as an inevitable consequence of war" (2009, 18).

Lifted from its peripheral status by its recognition as a crime against humanity, rape has a legal standing that should solicit more serious attention by historians. Here, Azoulay's concerns about the visual archive become central and take shape through what she explains as the ontology of the photograph. The photograph captures a dynamic among the photographer, the photographed, and the viewer instead of being a static image framed by the photographer's intention (2008, 105). Azoulay explains that the "photographic image produced in an encounter, then, invariably contains more and less than that which anybody intends to inscribe within it: more and less than that which one of the parties of the encounter at the moment of photography is capable of framing" (2012, 220). The photograph speaks beyond intention by recording any number of circumstantial and spontaneous elements that are there for us to see long after the event. The viewer is compelled not only to observe everything in the photograph, but to ask questions about what is included by accident as well as, more controversially, what might have been left out of the photograph and could have been included. Similar to the definitions of testimony that stress its circular, hesitant, and accidental structure, Azoulay's ontology of the photograph destabilizes not only our belief that it is shaped through the intentionality of the photographer but also our sense of what it is that we recognize in the image (2012, 18). The photograph exposes more than it was intended to reveal and makes us as viewers more aware of our dependence on context. We need to bring to the photograph a certain historical understanding in order to unlock its full meaning.

What does Azoulay's visual theory teach us about the discourse of rape? Moving back and forth between the visual and the discursive, Azoulay acknowledges that the anxiety over the images' reception (the fear that they will be received as pornography) drives the prohibition on photographs of rape and she suggests that this implicit prohibition may contribute to the disabling of the discourse about rape, obscuring women's words even further. Azoulay encourages us to confront the fact that we do not really know what a photograph of rape might look like and that we need to assume that it does not need to be made, but already exists. We might discover it by reexamining the existing photographic archive for the traces of rape in photographs in which so far we have not recognized rape (2012, 232–235).

The excess of meaning revealed to the viewer in another place and another time from when the photograph was taken has the potential to be highly destabilizing, reframing the photograph in a new way that casts aside our concern with identifying the intentions of the photographer. If the analogy between what Azoulay calls the prohibition of the rape photograph and the silencing of the rape account holds, then it is arguable that a work of fiction such as Emecheta's (a third-person, omniscient narrative) can reconstitute the relationship between the character and the reader in a way that positions the narrator's voice not as a surrogate for the author, but as a surrogate for the viewer or reader, who is reconstituting, or reframing the picture in which the character was disabled, curtailed, censored. The text registers the act of censorship and cannot make up for its lacunae by making the account of rape available in an alternative form. What it does instead is provide a proliferation of detail that needs to be interpreted because there is something at stake for the reader in understanding Debbie's experience. Emecheta's novel, which deploys all of realism's conventions but was still deemed unconvincing by her readers, should not be understood as constructing the narrative of "women's war."[13] The novel's effort is not centered on its realism as such. Instead, it attempts to bring us to a point where reading in a feminist way seems like a moral imperative for ourselves and the precondition from which the narrative of rape can be freed from its own erasure.

Representing sexual violence and the Rwandan genocide

This section considers how a particular figure, the impaled woman, has shaped the discourse about rape in the Rwandan genocide. She is a static image repeated frequently and because she is dead, she is an absent witness, to be spoken about or for. The term absent witness echoes Dori Laub's characterization of the Holocaust as an "event without a witness" (Felman and Laub 1992, 75). Laub explains that: "[W]hat precisely made a Holocaust out of the event is the unique way in which, during its historical occurrence, the event produced no witnesses. Not only, in effect, did the Nazis try to exterminate the physical witnesses of their crime; but the inherently incomprehensible and deceptive psychological structure of the event precluded its own witnessing, even by its very victims" (80). In an analogous fashion, the victims of rape in Rwanda were either silenced by being killed or silenced through their trauma. The figure I am calling the absent witness, moreover, makes reference to the genocide memorials and thus presents us with an opportunity to examine how a visual representation affects the ways in which rape is talked about. As we shall see, she is not silent in fact. She is either given voice in novelistic accounts that try to recreate her perspective, or appears in testimony from the genocide as a survivor who can speak of her ordeal, countering the assumption that such assault necessarily causes death.

Originating in the memorial at Nyamata Church with the exhibited corpse of a victim known as Thérèse Mukandori, the figure of the impaled woman has been referenced repeatedly in testimony, fictional accounts of the genocide, historical works, and in the debates over Rwanda's controversial practice of exhibiting remains at its genocide memorials in the early years following the genocide.[14] In the testimony collected by Mukagasana discussed above, rape with an object constitutes a rare instance where a mechanical detail surfaces. Cécile M. remembers hearing (between fainting spells as she is being raped by multiple men) one of her attackers saying: "Moi, au lieu de me salir, je préfère lui introduire ce morceau de bois" [I, in order not to soil myself, prefer to invade her with a piece of wood] (Mukagasana 2001, 148). In this passage, Cécile's point of view is disembodied; she refers to herself being spoken about. The mechanical detail allows no coherent subject position from the victim's point of view. Moreover, as Cécile's testimony shows, not all victims of this crime died, although the figure that circulates is one of a victim who died of the attack. At the ICTR and in the documents of various nongovernmental organizations (NGOs), ample evidence was provided that women were frequently raped with objects. In the prosecution of Akayesu, the witness identified as "KK" gave extensive testimony where she "described the Interahamwes forcing a piece of wood into the woman's sexual organs while she was still breathing, before she died."[15] In "Shattered Lives," the 1996 Human Rights Watch (HRW) report that first exposed the extent of sexual violence in the Rwandan genocide, there are multiple testimonies of survivors who were raped with sticks and other objects.[16]

Such atrocities are referred to in the novels written about the genocide as a type of action characteristic of the sexual violence of a historical event that saw very extensive sexual violence overall. Thus in Tierno Monénembo's *The Oldest Orphan*, the protagonist remembers hearing of the "[i]mpaling of pregnant women and the carving up of the dying" (2004, 87). Faustin resents being unfairly considered a génocidaire (a perpetrator of the genocide), held accountable as if he "thrust a stake up Mrs. Mukandori's vagina (whose impaled mummy image went around the world)" (Monénembo 2004, 43). The allusion to this crime circulates as a specific visual detail about "how" (the "mechanics"). In Boubacar Boris Diop's *Murambi: The Book of Bones*, the reader follows the protagonist, Cornelius, on his visit to the Nyamata Church where he sees the corpse of a woman with "her head pushed back and the scream extracted from her by the pain ... frozen on her still grimacing face. Her magnificent tresses were disheveled, and her legs wide apart. A stake—of wood or of iron ... had remained lodged in her vagina"(Diop 2006, 73). The reader is able to identify this victim as Theresa, a character from earlier in the novel, because of her distinctive hair style. The reader's ability to identify the victim that Cornelius sees only as an anonymous body contributes to the many ways in which Diop complicates the issue of guilt in his novel. It also shows Diop struggling to find a way to register the subjectivity and personhood of the victim while also holding onto the image of the manner of her death.

Diop's and Monénembo's novels were written as part of "Rwanda: écrire par devoir de mémoire" [Rwanda: writing out of a duty to remember], which brought ten African writers to Rwanda in 1998 in order to inspire an African literary response to the genocide (Hitchcott 2009, 151).[17] Both of the other novels that were written for this program, Monique Ilboudou's *Murekatete* (2000, 65) and Koulsy Lamko's *La Phalène des collines* (2002, 22, 30, 45) refer to the impaled woman. Indeed, Lamko's text takes her as its protagonist. Another work from this project, Véronique Tadjo's non-fiction account, *In the Shadow of Imana: Travels in the Heart of Rwanda*, describes her own encounter with Mukandori's impaled corpse at Nyamata (2002, 11). As we saw, Diop's novelistic account of a similar scene recreates Theresa's life to humanize the figure of Mukandori. Tadjo's more journalistic style builds on a contrast between brief identifying details. She writes:

> Site of genocide. / Plus or minus 35,000 dead. / A woman bound hand and foot. / Mukandori. Aged twenty-five. Exhumed in 1997... . She has been raped. A pickaxe has been forced into her vagina. She died from a machete blow to the nape of her neck. You can see the groove left by the impact. She still has a blanket over her shoulders but the material is now encrusted into the skin. (2002, 11)

In Tadjo's text, these details situate Mukandori's interrupted life in the context of the larger massacre at Nyamata Church. By drawing attention to the exhumation, Tadjo marks a moment of rebirth of sorts, when Mukandori, revealed once more, comes back into our consciousness, pressing us with the details of her story (Tadjo 2002, 11). The description of the rape is elicited from the forensic description. The writer's attention strays, however, as she notes the encrusted blanket, directing the reader to the moment of her (that is the author's) witness of Mukandori's corpse, rather than the rape and murder that preceded. In other words, this passage struggles to balance the restitution of the narrative of the crime against the gruesome presence of the corpse that spectacularizes it.

By noting the encrusted blanket, Tadjo makes an ambiguous move, tending more towards a reminder that death is on display rather than keeping us focused on the forensic task of collecting evidence to indict an atrocity. Sara Guyer calls the practice of exhibiting the dead a commemoration of "death-in-general" that repeats genocide's logic of "impersonality" (2009, 155, 163). "Only testimony," she reminds us, "turns the bones from transhistorical icons of death into the markers of a historical event (159)."[18] The detail of the encrusted blanket crystallizes a difference between two types of reference to the impaled woman. The first asks us to reexamine this particular practice of memorializing the victims of rape. The other takes the visual figure of the impaled woman as permission to narrate the atrocity retrospectively.

The repetition of the image of impaling and its rise to an iconic status needs analysis. As noted before, it presents us with an instance where the visual tells not only that a rape occurred but also how it happened. The presence of the wooden stick, the way it is positioned in relation to the body, and its proxy role but also its instrumentality as a weapon that kills in the act of raping, provides an explicitness that approximates the status of the censored photograph. In fact, the wooden stick reveals one aspect of the logic behind the implicit prohibition on photographs of rape: it facilitates the censorship of the image of the rapist. In the image of the impaled victim, the stick lends itself as a proxy, a metonymic substitute for the rapist. The figure of the impaled woman intact with the weapon between her legs represents the crime, calling forth the presence of the perpetrator. Since survivors of rape were often told that they could walk away because they had already been killed, it makes sense that this symbolic figure refers to the two crimes as entangled (HRW). Echoing this reality, Diop ends his novel by expressing his protagonist's "most ardent desire ... for the resurrection of the living" (2006, 181). The genocide sites, as witnessed by the authors who participated in "Rwanda: écrire par devoir de mémoire," function to keep alive the memory of the crimes rather than to memorialize the victims (Guyer 2009, 160–161). They accentuate the symbolic work of the figure of the impaled woman, circulating an image of death and a manner of killing that connote the obliteration of a person and a people, and recall the identity of the hateful perpetrator via the proxy of his weapon.

To get at the contrast between the texts that refer the questions pertaining to the symbolic meaning of the impaled woman to the memorials as practice and those that use the memorials as a prompt for writing history, we can compare Lamko's *La Phalène des collines* and Gil Courtemanche's *Sunday at the Pool in Kigali* (2003). Both use fiction to undertake a controversial approach to the memory of the dead. Lamko, drawing from the oral and the fantastic, creates a heroine who is Mukandori's spirit after death in the form of a butterfly that flies out of her decomposing body. Her voice is irreverent, angry, cynical, and funny at times. She complains about the disrespect for the dead, their deep desire to be put in the earth rather than be displayed without dignity. Then she turns her attention to those who visit the memorial, mocking their prudery and their prurient interest. Finally, she escapes from the space of the memorial and follows those who had come to visit it out into contemporary Rwanda, providing biting observations about what she sees (Lamko 2002, 13–14, 24–25, 21, 48). Lamko has committed himself to living in Rwanda (he is originally from Chad) and has spoken about the need to nurture the voices of survivors. At the same time, he is wary of disempowering victims by speaking for them (Kalisa 2006, 517–21).

Courtemanche, on the other hand, provides a fictional journalistic investigation of what the genocide must have been like, and thus something more like a realistic account. The predictable course of events presented in his novel includes the rape and impaling of the character Georgina (2003, 98–99). One can think of Courtemanche's method as an allusion to what Achille Mbembe calls an "aesthetics of vulgarity" that indicts how the powerful turn the people into the abject through their violence (Härting 2008, 61, 64). It is particularly interesting how impaling fits in the narrative sequence of gang rape that Courtemanche imagines. The rape is recounted by one of the perpetrators who expresses in cruel and mocking language Georgina's resistance, which leads the men to rape her with a stick. They then turn to her husband, they force him to rape her, and they subsequently kill him. This mechanical detail and the shocking scene it brings to life are organized around the logic of a sadistic cause and effect sequence that momentarily seems as if it might derail because of Georgina's resistance. It does not, however, as the victim is totally overwhelmed. The analogy between torture and rape becomes apparent here. In the end, the perpetrators assert their absolute control over the cause and effect sequence, obliterating Georgina and her husband (Courtemanche, 2003, 98–99).

The critique of Courtemanche's poetics addresses the extent to which he works back from the known fact that women were raped with objects to show how it must have happened, creating a pornographic scene (Härting 2008, 66). We could also pay attention, however, to the emphasis on the first person account, to the "I" of the perpetrator, and hence to the way Courtemanche exposes the violent work that language does during the genocide. Georgina's direct speech is absent despite the fact that her resistance is noted (Courtemanche 2003, 98–99). Although readers may be wary of Courtemanche's emphasis on the recreation of the scene, he makes us vividly aware of the need for a language to respond to the perpetrator. Furthermore, the novel alerts us to the dangers of the realist legal memory, which insists on an explicit narrative. By comparison, Lamko in his novel puts in motion an angry, combative response by the victim, making for a sharp contrast with Courtemanche's aesthetic choices.

Jean-Philippe Stassen's graphic novel of the genocide, *Deogratias: A Tale of Rwanda* (2006), further complicates the question of how the visual and the language that accompanies it should correlate. The figure of the impaled and decapitated female victim, Venetia, surfaces as a mute image. In the panel with her image, which shows a bottle between her bloodied legs, the only accompanying word is the name of the perpetrator, Deogratias (Stassen 2006, 74). No further explanation is given. This naming of the perpetrator exposes the proxy function of the weapon. It makes explicit what the image tries to convey, whereas naming the perpetrator, who is known to the reader, shocks us out of our identification with the protagonist. Deogratias is the Hutu friend of Venetia's daughters, now turned génocidaire. His guilt leads him to madness and by the end of the novel, he is delusional, believing that he has turned into a dog like the ones he saw eating corpses (Stassen 2006, 76–77). This metamorphosis is powerfully rendered by Stassen's drawings, where Deogratias's figure contorts into the form of an ugly dog and reverts partly back to his human form when he encounters others. The drawings capture the intensity of the psychic drama and perform work traditional to the novel in order to explore the protagonist's state of mind.

Venetia's identity is important to Stassen's message. She is the mother of Deogratias's love interest; her other daughter is his actual lover. Venetia is a sexually empowered woman who has turned men's interest in her to her advantage. A typical figure of urban African fiction, she is a single mother who resorts to prostitution and manages to manipulate her circumstance to her advantage for the sake of her children. She also forms a relationship with a Belgian Catholic priest, who is presumably the father of one of her daughters. He might have saved her except that Venetia went back to her village in order to find her daughters, and met her death upon returning. Venetia succumbs to the genocidal violence and becomes the symbolic figure of the impaled woman. Both daughters are also raped and killed, but we have no image of these acts; they are merely reported (Stassen 2006, 15, 19, 39, 42, 57–58, 61). In the economy of a graphic novel and its pared down traffic between words and images, Venetia was already an allegorical figure before her death, symbolizing Rwanda's uneasy modernity and the messiness of its colonial history. Her collaboration with the Belgians and her position at the intersection of religion, sex, morality, and exploitation, turn her killing and decapitation into the kind of crime that makes symbolic sense as an exorcism of the negative legacy of colonialism (Stassen 2006, 60).[19] Sex, in particular, stands as metonymy for the impulse that drives the colonial enterprise, a trope that has a longstanding rhetorical history in colonial literature.[20] Whites are everywhere in this novel, clearly implicated in the racial logic that made the genocide possible and even complicit in the killing. Deogratias's ensuing madness is not only punishment for his actions but a consequence of a protracted and complicated history of abjection.

If we are ready to accept that the impaled woman is a symbolic figure in a political allegory, we have gone very far from the originating impulse behind the dissemination of this figure as a symbol of real crimes. But before we dismiss Stassen's allegorical treatment as disrespectful of the real experience of actual victims, we need to think of his work as a response to the memorializing practice. What we see in Stassen is an appropriation of an explicit image that has already circulated and is available as a vehicle for the representation of rape in terms of its mechanical definition. This appropriation permits the meaning of rape to acquire the shape given to it by the observer. The observer's point of view makes us uncomfortable because of the prohibition against explicit treatments of rape discussed earlier. The teller of the story in Stassen's text is not the silenced victim, as in Lamko's novel who, we should note, also turns into an observer/commentator when she is transformed into the butterfly. What we are seeing is the mythologizing of the figure of the impaled woman as a way of writing the narrative of good versus evil political power in contemporary Rwanda.

The explicitness of the image paradoxically facilitates the allegorization of the figure, leaving us with the question of whether this takes us too far from the problem of narrating the historical experience of women. Stassen's allegorizing is historical in intent. By using a visual imaginary to depict Deogratias's madness, Stassen depicts the all-consuming nature of the genocide's consequences. Whereas one may want to challenge Stassen's assertions, he does present a radically different historical thesis from that of Rwanda's post-genocide regime, one whose articulation is facilitated by his appropriation and recasting of the figure of the impaled woman as the death of a Rwanda that had been shaped by its colonial history and the Rwandans' continued entanglement in its ideology.

Conclusion

But if explicitness leads to allegorizing, how do we recapture the testimonial? Allegory has taken us far from the historical experience of the victims. Attempts to render these experiences realistically, such as the effort undertaken at the ICTR, have failed to make these experiences speak. Valuing the "conceptual" definition of rape rather than the "mechanical" is crucial to bringing us back to the testimonial legal memory.

What we see in novels about the genocide is a response to the manner of official commemoration and an echoing of the elevation of this particular crime to iconic status. This method of commemoration is conventional in the sense that it calls forth the mechanical rather than the conceptual definition of rape, and in fact, depends quite heavily on it, because its emphasis is on what the perpetrator did. It is a discourse about political power with women as its symbolic trophy. It is an unusual instance because it allows for rape to circulate as an image, which asserts unequivocally that women who suffered this kind of rape died. This is convenient because these women represent the definitively silenced victims of rape as opposed to the survivors and their children, who are shunned by society.[21]

The revisionist impulse that gave shape to the shift towards a conceptual definition of rape must do more to address the monolithic presentation of rape victims as dead. Between 250,000 and 500,000 women were raped in Rwanda between April and July of 1994, and survivors have not fared well, leading the United Nations to pass a resolution in 2004 declaring the rape survivors as the group that is most vulnerable and in need in post conflict Rwanda (de Brouwer and Chu 2009, 11). Several projects have now sought to collect testimony of rape survivors, and listening to these testimonies seems more urgent than ever as time passes and denial is creeping in (de Brouwer and Chu 2009, 17). As the Holocaust showed us, the event became believable only when it was "testified to by the eventual victors" (Abrams and Kacandes 2008, 16). We need to backtrack and expand the frame through which we understand what happened. The survivors' testimonies inevitably unsettle and destabilize other narratives, but the historical narratives of the genocide must accommodate them. The rejection of the survivors of rape and their children brands them as the shameful signs of an unclean historical record that the victors' version of history aims to purge. But purging is precisely what the genocide also attempted to do. Restoring the survivors' point of view to the historical record alongside that of other voices establishes the richer and fuller archive, indispensable for the writing of the genocide's history. Whereas the historical project is inevitably different from the legal one, this is a case where legal thinking, however tentative, spearheads a significant reconsideration of what rape testimony addresses and how it is received.

Notes

1 There is wide consensus that the definition of rape hinges on showing the alleged victim's lack of consent: see Campbell 2002: 149, 158–159; and Drew 1992, 470, 479. However, for rape in conflict situations, consent is not a very useful concept at trial. Instead, the "specificity of the harm" must be compared "to other harms under humanitarian law" (Campbell 2007, 411, 418–419). Kirsten Campbell thus advocates a shift away from the emphasis on consent and its focus on the complainant, and for a greater emphasis instead on the "context and conduct of the defendant" in order to examine the wrong perpetrated (2007, 430). I flesh out the implications of this distinction in the body of the chapter.

2 The shift from a mechanical to a conceptual definition is also beginning in the United States where the Federal Bureau of Investigation (FBI) has come under criticism for using an eighty-year-old definition of rape— "the carnal knowledge of a female, forcibly and against her will"—in its statistical tracking of the frequency of sexual assaults, and has been called upon to widen its definition to include "sexual assault cases that involve anal or oral penetration or penetration with an object, cases where the victims are drugged or under the influence of alcohol or cases with male victims" (Goode 2011).

3 These types are divided according to whether the memory is from the perspective of the witness, the defense or the prosecution. Campbell calls the witness's memory "testimonial memory," concluding that it is not just the "description of an act; [it] embodies the wrong before the court" (2002, 166).

4 Prosecutor v. Jean-Paul Akayesu, 1998, supra note 11, ¶ 688. Such non-physically invasive acts included, for example, women being forced to remain nude.

5 Author's translation. Sometimes the women were removed to the forest or taken to someone's house to be raped, but often they were raped and humiliated in the open (Mukagasana 2001, 147).

6 There is one exception to this habitual avoidance of mechanical details: evidence regarding rape with objects and death by impalement through the vagina. The last section of this article provides a detailed discussion of this point.

7 Prosecutor v. Jean-Paul Akayesu, 1998, supra note 5, ¶ 597.

8 Two women are raped in the novel: Melanie is raped by Lurie, and Lurie's

daughter, Lucy, is raped by a number of African assailants who invade her property.

9 Two of Yvonne Vera's novels treat rape in this fashion: *The Stone Virgins* (2002a) and *Without a Name* (2002b).

10 Emecheta shows that the problem is not producing the testimony, but having it heard the way Debbie intended it. When Debbie testifies, she has trouble making her audience believe that she is recounting her own experience. A privileged Nigerian, she is deemed an unlikely victim of a crime that is considered as the affliction of the poor. She seeks to testify as a victim of rape, but the humanitarian framework authorizes her to speak weakly in that capacity (Coundouriotis 2014, 149–150).

11 Debbie in Emecheta's novel turns away from personal testimony, avoiding the narration of her assaults (1983: 241–43). Brison explains that when she spoke about her assault she described herself as "a victim of an attempted murder," thus avoiding reference to rape (2002, 3).

12 Prosecutor v. Jean-Paul Akayesu, 1998, ¶¶ 116, 161.

13 "Women's War" is the title of the chapter that contains the novel's climactic episode (1983, 206). Debbie characterizes her experience as a "war for her womanhood" (174).

14 For a description of what the Nyamata Memorial looked like when the authors that are discussed visited in 1998, see Cazenave and Célérier 2011, 84, 92.

15 Prosecutor v. Jean-Paul Akayesu, 1998, ¶ 429.

16 HRW, 1996, *Shattered Lives: Sexual Violence during the Rwandan Genocide and its Aftermath* (hereafter, "Shattered Lives"). In the testimony of Perpetue, we have another instance of the victim herself describing such an act: "The two were complaining they were feeling tired from all the killing. Then, one of them sharpened the end of the stick of a hoe. They held open my legs and pushed the stick into me. I was screaming. They did it three times until I was bleeding everywhere." Id. ¶ 139. Once again we see how rape with an object provides the exceptional instance in which we find a mechanical detail given by the victim herself. Before she gets to this detail in her testimony, Perpetue has enumerated her multiple other rapes without giving any mechanical details. Id. ¶¶ 137–42. In the same report, Human Rights Watch notes that the assumption that women would not talk about rape "is patently false. Rwandan women will talk, but only under certain conditions," such as the opportunity to speak to a female investigator. Id. ¶ 91.

17 Although invited, Zimbabwean novelist Chenjerai Hove refused to participate in the project because he felt it did not serve the purpose of reconciliation. Hove found that Rwanda offered an "overdose of reality, which would leave the writer with nothing more to write because there is nothing more to create" (Mda 2018, 110). Moreover, he objected to the display of the dead saying "The Rwanda government is fighting barbarity with another form of barbarity" (quoted in Mda 2018, 110).

18 Guyer discusses the exhibit at the Nyamata memorial, but makes an error here. She discusses at length the anonymity of Mukandori, "an unknown woman who was raped and murdered," even though her identity is widely referred to in the literature about Nyamata (2009, 164).

19 This comes close to the thesis of one of the more influential historical studies of the genocide, Mahmood Mamdani's *When Victims Become Killers: Colonialism, Nativism, and the Genocide in Rwanda*(2001).

20 A good example is the energy that animates H. Rider Haggard, *King Solomon's Mines* (1885). See also H. Rider Haggard, *She* (1886), where Africa is feminized and made ready for conquest.

21 For how children of rape have fared in post-genocide Rwanda, see Weitsman 2008, 561. In her description of the systematic rape during the genocide, Weitsman also refers to "a multitude of rapes with foreign objects" and describes rape as the "prelude to death. Some women were penetrated with tools of all sorts—spears, gun barrels, bottles, or the stamens of banana trees" (573).

Works cited

Abrams, Kathryn, and Irene Kacandes. "Introduction: Witness." *Women's Studies Quarterly* 36, nos. 1–2 (Spring/Summer 2008): 13–27. DOI: 10.1353/wsq.0.0043.

Azoulay, Ariella. *Civil Imagination: A Political Ontology of Photography.* Translated by Louise Bethlehem. London: Verso, 2012.

Azoulay, Ariella. *The Civil Contract of Photography.* Translated by Rela Mazali and Ruvik Danieli. Brooklyn: Zone, 2008.

Brison, Susan J. *Aftermath: Violence and the Remaking of a Self.* Princeton: Princeton University Press, 2002.

Campbell, Kirsten. "Legal Memories: Sexual Assault, Memory, and International Humanitarian Law." *Signs: Journal of Women in Culture and Society* 28, no. 1 (2002): 149–178. doi.org/10.1086/340908.

Campbell, Kirsten. "The Gender of Transitional Justice: Law, Sexual Violence and the International Criminal Tribunal for the Former Yugoslavia." *International Journal of Transitional Justice* 1 (2007): 411–432. DOI: 10.1093/ijtj/ijm033.

Cazenave, Odile, and Patricia Célérier. *Contemporary Francophone African Writers and the Burden of Commitment.* Charlottesville: University of Virginia Press, 2011.

Coetzee, J. M. *Disgrace.* New York: Viking, 2000.

Coundouriotis, Eleni. *The People's Right to the Novel: War Fiction in the Postcolony.* New York: Fordham University Press, 2014.

Courtemanche, Gil. *A Sunday at the Pool in Kigali.* Translated by Patricia Claxton. Edinburgh: Canongate, 2003.

de Brouwer, Anne-Marie L. M. *Supranational Criminal Prosecution of Sexual Violence: The ICC and the Practice of the ICTY and the ICTR.* Cambridge, UK: Intersentia, 2005.

de Brouwer, Anne-Marie, and Sandra Ka Hon Chu, eds. *The Men Who Killed Me: Rwandan Survivors of Sexual Violence.* Madeira Park, BC: Douglas and McIntyre, 2009.

Diop, Boubacar Boris. *Murambi: The Book of Bones.* Translated by Fiona Mc Laughlin. Bloomington: Indiana University Press, 2006.

Drew, Paul. "Contested Evidence in Courtroom Cross-Examination: The Case of a Trial for Rape." In *Talk at Work: Interaction in Institutional Settings,* edited by Paul Drew and John Heritage, 470–520. Cambridge: Cambridge University Press, 1992.

Emecheta, Buchi. *Destination Biafra.* Glasgow: William Collins Sons, 1983.

Goode, Erica. 2011. *"Rape Definition Too Narrow in Federal Statistics, Critics Say." New York Times,* 28 September 2011. https://www.nytimes.com/2011/09/29/us/federal-rules-on-rape-statistics-criticized.html?searchResultPosition=3.

Guyer, Sara. "Rwanda's Bones." *Boundary 2* 36, no. 2 (2009): 155–175. doi.org/10.1215/01903659-2009-009.

Haggard, H. Rider. *She*. London: Penguin, 2001 (first published 1886).

Haggard, H. Rider. *King Solomon's Mines*. London: Penguin, 2007 (first published 1885).

Härting, Heike. "Global Humanitarianism, Race, and the Spectacle of the African Corpse in Current Western Representations of the Rwandan Genocide." *Comparative Studies of South Asia, Africa and the Middle East* 28, no. 1 (2008): 61–77. doi.org/10.1215/1089201x-2007-056.

Hengehold, Laura. "Remapping the Event: Institutional Discourses and the Trauma of Rape." *Signs: Journal of Women in Culture and Society* 26, no. 1 (2000): 189–214. www.jstor.org/stable/3175384.

Hitchcott, Nicki. "A Global African Commemoration—Rwanda: écrire par devoir de mémoire," *Forum for Modern Language Studies* 45, no. 2 (2009): 151–161. doi.org/10.1093/fmls/cqp003.

HRW. *Shattered Lives: Sexual Violence during the Rwandan Genocide and its Aftermath*. (September 1996). http://www.hrw.org/legacy/reports/1996/Rwanda.htm.

Ilboudo, Monique. *Murekatete: roman*. Bamako: Le Figuier / Lille: Fest'Africa, 2000.

Kalisa, Marie Chantal. "Theatre and the Rwandan Genocide." *Peace Review: A Journal of Social Justice* 18, no. 4 (2006): 515–521. doi.org/10.1080/10402650601030476.

Lamko, Koulsy. *La Phalène des collines: roman*. Paris: Serpent à plumes, 2002.

Laub, Dori. "An Event Without a Witness: Truth, Testimony and Survival." In *Testimony: Crises of Witnessing in Literature*, co-authored by Shoshana Felman and Dori Laub, 75–92. New York: Routledge, 1992.

Mamdani, Mahmood. *When Victims Become Killers: Colonialism, Nativism, and the Genocide in Rwanda*. Princeton: Princeton University Press, 2001.

Mda, Zakes. *Justify the Enemy: Becoming Human in South Africa*. Edited by J. U. Jacobs. Pietermaritzburg: University of KwaZulu-Natal Press, 2018.

Monénembo, Tierno. *The Oldest Orphan*. Translated by Monique Fleury Nagem. Lincoln: University of Nebraska Press, 2004.

Mujawayo, Esther, and Souâd Belhaddad. *SurVivantes: Rwanda, Dix Ans Après le Génocide*. La Tour-d'Aigues: Éditions de l'Aube, 2004.

Mukagasana, Yolande. *Les Blessures du Silence: témoignages du génocide au Rwanda*. Paris: Actes Sud/Médecins Sans Frontières, 2001.

Prosecutor v. Jean-Paul Akayesu. 1998. Case No. ICTR-96-4-T, Judgment, ¶ 597 (2 Sept.). pdf.

Stassen, Jean-Philippe. *Deogratias: A Tale of Rwanda*. Translated by Alexis Siegel. New York: First Second, 2006.

Stelter, Brian. 2011. *"CBS Reporter Recounts a "Merciless" Assault."* *New York Times*, 28 April 2011. https://www.nytimes.com/2011/04/29/business/media/29logan.html?searchResultPosition=15.

Tadjo, Véronique. *The Shadow of Imana: Travels in the Heart of Rwanda*. Translated by Véronique Wakerley. Oxford: Heinemann, 2002.

Umutesi, Marie Béatrice. *Surviving the Slaughter: The Ordeal of a Rwandan Refugee in Zaire*. Translated by Julia Emerson. Madison: University of Wisconsin Press, 2004.

Vera, Yvonne. *The Stone Virgins.* New York: Farrar, Straus and Giroux, 2002a.

Vera, Yvonne. *Without a Name and Under the Tongue.* New York: Farrar, Straus and Giroux, 2002b.

Weitsman, Patricia A. "The Politics of Identity and Sexual Violence: A Review of Bosnia and Rwanda." *Human Rights Quarterly* 30, no. 3 (2008): 561–578. DOI: 10. 1353/hrq.0.0024.

7 Torture and textuality

Guantánamo Diary as postcolonial text

Mohamedou Ould Slahi's *Guantánamo Diary* speaks to us with devastating insight from inside the torture chamber and remaps the boundaries of what has been treated in literature as a spectacularized scene—a prohibited place laid bare to view. Slahi's writerly predicament calls to mind J. M. Coetzee's reading of Alex La Guma's paean to the antiapartheid fighter in *In the Fog of the Seasons' End*, in which Coetzee alerts us to the importance of the novelist's entrance "into the dark chamber" of the prison cell. Breaking this barrier, the novelist gestures towards demystifying state secrets (1992, 361). Moreover, it is appropriate to locate Slahi's book explicitly in the temporality of the postcolonial, the resistant writing-back taking place in a crisis of legitimacy brought on by the aftermath of empire, and to place it alongside such prison memoirs as Wole Soyinka's *The Man Died* (1972) and Ngũgĩ wa Thiong'o's *Detained* (1981). However, Slahi's 2015 text, redactions, edits and all, makes seeing less important as a metaphor for witnessing torture than the "dark chamber" paradigm might imply and foregrounds instead a resistant interiority that, in an almost novelistic manner, depends on character development and dialogue.[1] Slahi provokes us to rethink the textuality of narratives of torture—their dependence on written language and a reader's response—to bring to light the abuses of secret rendition, detention, and torture. We might ask, therefore, how does foregrounding the textuality of *Guantánamo Diary*—the many ways in which Slahi conveys his awareness of writing a "book" and announces the power of the written word to overcome the limitations of his confinement—affect our understanding of the relationship between the narrative account and real events that encompass not only his own individual plight but the broader history of the "war on terror?" Moreover, what does this question of textuality reveal about the temporality of the postcolonial and its interruptive force?

What follows, therefore, is an exploration of textuality in *Guantánamo Diary* that takes up three questions in turn: what is the impact of writing an account of torture on our understanding of the literary? What are the stakes of postcoloniality in this text, especially in the context of human rights' appearance as colonial mimicry? And finally, how does the emphasis in this reading of *Guantánamo Diary* on textuality and postcoloniality recast the robust critiques by United States intellectuals of the war on terror, especially Judith Butler's reflections on indefinite detention?

Narrative as reconstructed experience

Attempts to theorize the particular textuality of narratives of torture frequently tackle the problematic border between imaginative literature and documentary account. For Barbara Harlow, the political stakes in accounts of torture and detention pose a challenge to the entire architecture of literary study. The scholarly field tends to segregate political literature into a confined space apart as a special case, enacting a second silencing similar to the blacking out of the torture site (Harlow 1992, 8–9). Moreover, Harlow's attention to textual form is particularly provocative for thinking about Slahi's account. Reading human rights reports such as *Nunca Mas* (the 1986 report of the Argentine National Commission on the Disappeared), she proposes that such texts make a literary argument about form and demand a role for literary reading in the sphere of politics: "*Nunca Mas* proposes … the reinstatement of the literary, of writing and reading—as discipline and practice—as an active, transitive, sociopolitical force" (Harlow 1992, 248). The phrase, "reinstatement of the literary," addresses literature's displacement as a form of silencing that the written reports about torture forcefully reverse. The claim that literature is a "discipline" and a "practice" announces a role for the literary beyond the realms of the academy and culture. It also exposes these spheres as more porous. Harlow suggests, therefore, that the degree to which the borders separating the academy from the political appear hardened in place should alert us to the counterforces upholding these divides (1992, 4).

Following Harlow, we can draw the parallel between *Nunca Mas* and *Guantánamo Diary* even more forcefully when we consider the key role of the *habeas corpus* petition in undergirding both texts. Slahi presents his entire narrative as an elaboration of his petition. Indeed, he recognizes that his demand to know "WHY AM I HERE?" (which he places directly to his interrogators) amounts to a "Petition for a Writ of Habeas Corpus" and he presents this recognition as a key moment of retrospective storytelling—made during his detention but after the episodes of torture were over (2015, 63). Harlow emphasizes the importance of such "reconstruction" of events in narratives of torture as pushback against official attempts to stamp out the memory of the occurrence (1992, 8–10).[2] Reconstructing his experience, Slahi thus explains that he learned later from his lawyers what the legal term for his demand is and elaborates in detail how he put together his intuited understanding of what is just with the proper legal term:

> Obviously the phrase makes no sense to the average, mortal man like me. The average person would just say, "Why the hell are you locking me up?" I'm not a lawyer, but common sense dictates that after three

years of interrogating me and depriving me of my liberty, the government at least owes me an explanation why it's doing so. What exactly is my crime? (63)

This question posed (or reconstructed) in a narrative text and its demand for accountability stake particular claims for writing as a medium. Speaking of *Nunca Mas* and the demand for accountability for disappeared persons that it presents, Harlow concludes: "The signification of a habeas corpus writ or of *Nunca Mas*, what they demand, is not nostalgia for a 'lost presence' (in the Derridean sense), nor vengeance (of a psychoanalytic or oedipal kind), nor even the restoration of a traditional family structure; rather, it is the instantiation of another kind of writing altogether" (1992, 248). The idea that the narrative of torture demands the "instantiation of another kind of writing altogether" guides the present reading of *Guantánamo Diary* and its focus on the memoir's textuality, its self-awareness as writing, and its location in a postcolonial temporality. These features are crucial to bringing to the fore Slahi's subjectivity and the stakes in the denial of his legal personhood.

Originally published while Slahi was still a detainee (after an arduous ten-year process to gain clearance for publication), *Guantánamo Diary* problematizes the function of narrative closure as it confronts the possibility of indefinite detention. Problems of temporality abound and are evident in the text's disjunctions, stalling, reversals, and lack of temporal orientation. Larry Siems edited the manuscript with an eye toward retrieving a chronological, narrative through-line, which importantly underscores the unresolved endpoint of a linear account. In his introduction to the 2015 text, Siems notes that chronology is a problem in the manuscript and explains that he reworked some of it "incorporat[ing] the appended flashbacks within the main narrative" (xii). Siems also provides "A Timeline of Detention" to help the reader, signaling in yet another way that the sequential chronology of a diary form is not clearly conveyed in the manuscript.

Although these conditions of publication changed when the second "restored" edition of the text was published in 2017, a year after Slahi's release, the continued censorship of the original manuscript created new challenges for assembling the unredacted text. Slahi and Siems worked closely together to restore the redacted sections without access to the original. This process, Siems admits, entailed new writing (for the 2017 edition) "to reconstruct the scenes that the censored text obscured." Siems calls this a process of "restoration and reparation, as of an ancient building or damaged painting" (2017, xi).[3] As we see below, retrospection and reconstruction are key elements of a prison narrative's gestures of resistance. The lived experience of a difficult temporality remains throughout both versions and is best contextualized in terms of the stalled temporality of the postcolonial.

At the same time, *Guantánamo Diary* belongs to a recognizable vein of human rights narration: accounts of torture constitute a paradigmatic genre in human rights in which we find that the harm done, aimed at destroying subjectivity and voice, finds a response that redresses voicelessness through a testimonial account of the harm (Slaughter 1997, 407, 413). Accounts of torture are both politically necessary and difficult to execute because of the challenges they present to realistic documentation. Whereas the narrative of torture responds to an imperative to bear witness and depict the kind of abuse it is calling out, it must at the same time remain wary of creating conditions to occasion inappropriate responses, such as "erotic fascination" with the exposure of the body on display.[4] Such narration is a form of resistant documentation that counters explicitly the prohibition (frequently inscribed in the law) of creating a visual record related to torture. Black sites, dark chambers—detention centers and prisons—are kept at the limits of representation so that their existence can be denied (Coetzee 1992, 361).

Although Coetzee calls for literature to "demystify the torture chamber" by exposing it to view and shattering state secrecy, he recognizes that how the writer renders the state-censored scene matters (358). Whereas he sees the political necessity of such imaginative engagement with the scene of torture, he notes that the difficulty is one of narrative authority: "The true challenge is: how not to play the game by the rules of the state, how to establish one's own authority, how to imagine torture and death on one's own terms" (364). Claiming (and reconstructing) from one's own point of view a scene aimed at destroying subjectivity presents deeply political aesthetic dilemmas. The writer must succeed in creating a convincing, resistant voice that exposes the failure of torture without diminishing its devastating effects.

To establish an authoritative and resistant point of view, torture narratives (*Guantánamo Diary* included) frequently focus on the surroundings or setting. These details of setting function as the torture victim's breach of the taboo against representation of the inner sanctum of the state. The importance of place or location to the torture narrative is, therefore, central and serves as an anchor for its orientation towards realism and documentation. Thus, the term "diary" in Slahi's title (which was the publisher's choice as the manuscript had no title) is intended to signal the text's authenticity as a document from inside the torture chamber. It does not allude to the organization of the text—it tells us instead that the chronicle comes from that place, Guantánamo. What we read in *Guantánamo Diary* is a reconstruction of events from within the prison but after the torture, and not an in-the-present, accretive account implied by the diary format. Slahi insists throughout that he is writing a "book," thus clearly signaling the public nature of the document and his desire to find an audience of readers.[5] The text, therefore, exhibits an intentionality that exceeds the first order task of documenting daily experience. More than once, the narrator addresses the reader directly as "Dear Reader" (Slahi 2015, 232, 244). A text that refers to itself as such, *Guantánamo Diary* signals its literariness despite its subject matter. Thus, it belongs to the tradition of prison narratives that Harlow explicates. The text's emphasis on setting—a distinctive feature of torture narratives, as noted—is rendered frequently through the experience of disorientation and blocked senses (blindfolds, etc). Thus, the torture (the acts of abuse) transforms into an extension of the environment, allowing the narrator's authority over the description of setting to take over the narration of the torture.

The seriousness with which Slahi takes the writer's role has not been enough to establish his ownership of his own story. His authority is fragile to this day and his story vulnerable to appropriation by other writers who seek to recast it as a human rights story that reinforces the moral authority of the concerned spectator. The Pulitzer Prize for distinguished feature writing in 2020 went to Ben Taub's story for the *New Yorker*, "Guantánamo's Darkest Secret." Taub recaps Slahi's background, how he became a terror suspect through circumstantial evidence, and the horrors of his experience in rendition and detention. He hews close to Slahi's own narrative, quoting from *Guantánamo Diary*, but refers to the text as Slahi's "diary" in lower case, describing it also as a body of letters sent to his lawyers from detention. By insistently referencing the "diary," Taub diminishes the status of Slahi's writing. *Guantánamo Diary* is an internationally acclaimed, widely read and translated, best-selling book. Taub does not offer significant new facts about Slahi's experience. Instead, he recreates the "heart of darkness" motif to implicate his American readers in the lie that has been Guantánamo. Repeating the pattern of revelation and concealment explained in Chapter 2 (on "Congo Cases"), Taub exposes the "dark secret" of Slahi's innocence and the information that this was evident to those who detained him despite the fact that we already know as much. It is not the revelation of the facts that is at stake for Taub as much as the effective re-creation of the exposé, so that the readers can experience their *prise de conscience* anew, this time without acknowledging Slahi's voice of protest but taking in Taub's involved narration with its emphasis on discovery.

In a letter to his lawyer dated 9 November 2006 (thus after the completion of his manuscript), Slahi dismisses his lawyer's request that he write "everything I told my interrogators" as impossible. In his typically punchy tone, he writes: "Are you out of your mind? How can I render uninterrupted interrogation that has been lasting the last 7 years?" (2015, xvi).[6] And to prevent this statement from creating too comfortable a ground for the reader in liberal, moral outrage as they contemplate the implications of seven years of "uninterrupted interrogation," he continues: "That's like asking Charlie Sheen how many women he dated" (2015, xvi). This popular reference is not meant to detract from the seriousness of his circumstance, but to disrupt the availability of the scene of interrogation and torture so that its subject remains Slahi's alone to explicate. The Charlie Sheen reference keeps us from sentimentalizing Slahi's suffering and casts his interrogators as vulgarly promiscuous in their coercive questioning. Slahi does not want to be defined by his abjection, nor does he want it to serve the purpose of a moral cleansing for his liberal interlocutors. Furthermore, his dismissal of the lawyer's request to tell "everything" is framed in terms of a question about the plausible degree of realism of such an account. The expectation of completeness addresses a standard of authenticity that is based on a particular understanding of the real as documentation: the sincerity of the narrator is demonstrated by providing exhaustive detail, what Thomas W. Laqueur has explained as humanitarian narrative's (the narrative of human suffering) "reliance on detail as the sign of truth" (1989, 177). In the letter, Slahi defines in his own terms what constitutes a full account: "Yet I provided you everything (almost) in my book, which the government denies you the access to" (2015, xvii). This statement makes clear both that he conceived himself as writing a "book" and that his intention is testimonial: to give a full account, to narrate "everything (almost)." Furthermore, rather than address the impossibility of an absolutely complete account, "everything (almost)" signals that Slahi deliberately withholds some information. He discusses withholding information from his interrogators several times and asserts the prerogative to shield friends and family: "questioning involves a lot of stuff nobody wants to talk about, like your friends and your private life. Especially when the suspicions are about things like terrorism, the government is very rude. In the interrogation, you always avoid talking about your friends and your private, intimate life" (2015, 93). Despite the duress he was under, Slahi understands that interrogation is transactional and remains tactical throughout. As author of a "book," it is his prerogative to withhold some information, and this gesture pushes against the censorship of parts of his text by the US government. At the same time, Slahi demonstrates his awareness of his own book's textuality, its non-coincidence with the real, and its ambition to go beyond documentation to create a subject that speaks from the zone of exception, upending the assumptions that those occupying such a space have been forced to surrender their voice and point of view.

Writing as a postcolonial African subject

Guantánamo Diary is a paradigm shifting text that calls for a decentering of our discourse on the war on terror to take a postcolonial perspective into account. Yogita Goyal reflects on the postcoloniality of Slahi's text but locates its temporality in the extended tradition of the slave narrative. Thus, she reads forward from the nineteenth-century genre of the slave narrative (alluded to by Slahi himself when he draws an analogy between rendition and the capture of Africans sold in the slave trade) to the reality of Slahi as a citizen of a postcolonial nation with compromised sovereignty (2017, 75). Contra Goyal, who aims at connecting US and postcolonial narrative forms, the emphasis in this chapter is on pulling away from hegemonic academic discussion of US narrative forms in order to hear Slahi's resistant voice and its postcolonial inflection more clearly. The relevant history concerns colonialism and imperialist interventions in Africa, which undermined national sovereignty on the continent. The history of an African diaspora marked by the trauma of the middle passage confines Slahi to the trajectory imposed on him. Moreover, references to breaking the chains of slavery have different connotations in African liberation discourse. They were often standard rhetoric in speeches by nationalist leaders such as Jomo Kenyatta. Kenyatta made these allusions in order to push back against the tide of disillusionment with the postcolonial state; thus, he referenced the achievement of independence as an absolute break with subjugation to shore up his political influence. The universalizing language of freedom from slavery was used intentionally to obscure the troubling ways in which precarity and insecurity persisted because of neocolonial corruption (Coundouriotis 2014, 41–43). Therefore, Slahi's use of this imagery is ironic because it underscores how things have not changed; the predicament of disillusion endures.

Slahi writes self-consciously as a Mauritanian national denied his rights. Located within a temporality of the postcolonial, he places emphasis on how the trajectory of rendition (as he is forcibly moved from one place to another) implicates Mauritania, a weak, postcolonial nation, as a willing instrument of the United States. He shares a widely held postcolonial sensibility of lack of trust in his own government, and an awareness that the poverty of Mauritania and the weakness of its sovereignty originate in its colonial history. He explains, for example: "You could clearly tell that the country had no sovereignty: this was still colonialization in its ugliest face," and "kidnapping me in my own house in my country and giving me to the U.S .... that is not OK .... Don't get me wrong, though: I don't blame the U.S. as much as I do my own government." (2015, 85, 126) He obsessively comes back to this profound sense of betrayal by his country: "My country turned me over" (166). He remarks bitterly on the irony that his rendition to Jordan from Mauritania occurred on 28 November 2001 when 28 November commemorates Mauritanian independence from France in 1960. On such a day:

> the independent and sovereign Republic of Mauritania turned over one of its own citizens on a premise. To its everlasting shame, the Mauritanian government not only broke the constitution, which forbids extradition of Mauritanian criminals to other countries, but also extradited an innocent citizen and exposed him to the random American justice (132).

This passage is bitter and full of accusation, but it also clearly demarcates what could have been or should be a reassuring possibility—the "independent and sovereign Republic of Mauritania"—by contrast to the disquieting and bleak "random American justice." These formulations capture the aspiration to rule of law and constitutionality, the presumed legacy of the transition from colonialism, and its disappointment, which has reached new intensity. Slahi's predicament captures the failure of the new world dispensation that followed the end of the Cold War and the "random" justice that holds up human rights but permits disappearance and torture.

Moreover, Slahi's biography of migration to Germany and Canada is typically postcolonial, and the logic of self-improvement that motivated him is evident when he describes with a sense of pained recognition what he saw from the plane as he returns to Mauritania, (now a captive under United States orders): "The suburbs of Nouakchott appeared more miserable than ever, crowded, poor, dirty, and free of any of life's crucial infrastructures" (2015, 87). Thus, *Guantánamo Diary* extends a standard postcolonial genre, the "been-to" narrative, or the story of the migrant returnee. Typically the return is either disastrous or is forced after a failure abroad, which is furthermore frequently associated with a violent experience.[7] In Slahi's version of this conventional story, the subject's movement across borders is not halted as a result of the return. It starts over under coercion and in conditions where there is a total loss of autonomy. As such, it illustrates in stark terms how the returnee's future is foreshortened, his aspirational life story belonging permanently to the past.

Time is tragically against Slahi. Detained indefinitely out of the public's view and with no imminent resolution of his case (the diary was written in 2005, published in redacted form in 2015, and he was released in 2016), Slahi speaks to his reader against a broken solidarity and from a failed recognition of the injustice done to him. Within this space of negation, which deepens even further through the depiction of his torture, Slahi develops a dialogue driven method of exposition that keeps alive his sense of self. His text constructs an articulate and cohesive subjectivity that suffers torture against the grain of Elaine Scarry's thesis that torture is an unmaking so profound that it threatens the future capacity of any (self)making, or as she puts this paradoxically, of the "'making making' itself, 'remaking making'"(1985, 279). Rather, as Darius Rejali argues "pain may in fact reinforce one's sense of self during torture" and "is not *sufficient* to destroy a prisoner's sense of reality" (2007, 442, emphasis in original). For some, pain coheres the self in resistance to the torturer, especially in the narrative reconstruction of the event. Thus, arguably, Slahi's sense of self deepens with his suffering, and more so through writing about his suffering. He admits having no shame expressing his pain: "I cry whenever I feel like it and it makes me stronger to admit my weakness" (Slahi 2015, 317). In the face of abandonment, Slahi's authorial voice succeeds in doing something more than answering back. He shifts the ground on which his reader stands, bringing the sealed off world of illegal rendition and detention to the fore, not as spectacle but as political argument. Reading immerses us in Slahi's point of view, which asserts itself against the policies that maintain the regime called "war on terror." Our terms of engagement pivot less on seeing and more on listening; we are intent on retrieving the voice of the text lying beyond the obstacles of redactions and editing.

Slahi is eager to convey to his lawyers the structure of the book in progress, which pivots on a breaking-point. He gives a date and writes: "you
may divide my time in two big steps: 1) Pre-torture (I mean that I couldn't
resist): I told them the truth about me having done nothing against your
country. It lasted until May 22, 2003. 2) Post-torture era: where my brake
broke loose. I yessed every accusation my interrogators made" (2015, xvii).
Since the text was written in 2005, we only have Slahi's voice from after his
breaking point. This voice displays a deep desire to establish the self as a
plain-talking, intelligent, rational subject who aims to reframe the discussion
of truth around the question left unanswered by the United States government: why has he been detained and why is he being kept in detention indefinitely? This question, the same as a *habeas corpus* petition, anchors his
claim of rights violations.

The question is also significant to the narrative structure of the torture
account. Interrogation is meant to elicit "intelligence," which, to be effective, must be closely guarded. However, the process also potentially surrenders the prerogative of narration to the victim: the intelligence gatherers
deny having him in their custody or torturing him, and they presume that
the victim will be in no position to tell the story of torture convincingly or
completely. Slahi manages to seize the ground from where to speak and
becomes the voice from inside Guantánamo. Although it takes a very long
time for his account to reach the public and does so initially in redacted
form, it remains one of the few accounts from inside, and, most importantly,
it resonates with the potential of the narratives of the other detainees.

Whereas Slahi's readers may be eager for the wealth of detail that he can
provide, his emphasis is on driving home the question of the illegality of his
detention. This does not diminish the importance of torture to the narrative,
but shows us that torture is essential to the setting. Torture becomes diffuse;
it is rendered as one and the same with the environment created by illegal
detention and rendition. The terror and stress are constant.

Consequently, torture is the environment in which Slahi's account unfolds, and once again Slahi insists on his perspective as a postcolonial
subject. He reminds us that he is already familiar with the culture of torture
regimes. "Coming from a third-world country," he anticipates that repressive governments make up reasons to detain you and if they detain you,
they usually interrogate and torture you (2015, 193). When he is detained by
the Mauritanians (under the instructions of the United States), he anxiously
anticipates torture, recognizing his circumstance as a common fate of detainees: "I wanted to sleep, lose my mind, and not wake up until every bad
thing was over. How much pain can I take? I asked myself. Can my family
intervene and save me? Do they use electricity?" (90). Even before this, in the
custody of the Senegalese, he anticipates mistreatment: "I started to have
nausea, my heart was a feather, and I shrank so small to hold myself together. I thought about all the kinds of torture I had heard of, and how
much I could take tonight" (77). Evidence of regimes of torture permeates

the text and unfolds in a continuum from one episode to another. As environmental and totalizing, torture's inevitability conditions the detainee's experience. Slahi refers to his constant state of terror and the physical impact it has: nausea, sweats, tremors, gastrointestinal and breathing difficulties, jumps in blood pressure, pounding heart. He tells us explicitly that he lived in a "constant state of terror and fear" (127). The cumulative effect of interrogation is itself a kind of education with a cognitive mapping. Slahi learns to predict his interrogators' questions and methods:

> But has there ever, in all of recorded human history, been an interrogation that has gone on, day in and day out, for more than six years? There is nothing an interrogator could say to me that would be new; I've heard every variation. Each new interrogator would come up with the most ridiculous theories and lies, but you could tell they were all graduates of the same school: before an interrogator's mouth opened I knew what he [redaction] was going to say and why he [redaction] was saying it. (310)

Repetition signals stalled time, but Slahi asserts his own sense of order on time. With experience, he demonstrates that it is possible to acquire a kind of mastery of the situation, which illustrates his tenacity as a subject facing off with his interrogators:

> ... instead of asking a direct question, they ask all kinds of questions around it. I took it as a challenge, and for the most part I would search the direct question and answer that. 'Your question is whether or not ...,' I would say. And [redaction] seemed to like that shortcut. (310)

Slahi strategizes and addresses questions tactically. Here he demonstrates that he took the prerogative of asking the question away from the interrogator. Even when he loses control under duress, revisiting his interrogation in his written account is an occasion to determine the meaning of the encounter. He confesses to the reader: "To be honest with you, I acted like every average person: I tried to make myself look as innocent as a baby. I tried to protect the identities of every single person I knew, unless he or she was too well-known to the Police" (94). Thus, Slahi indicates his awareness that he must present a persona to his interrogator and that his part in interrogation is also possibly performative. Denied his access to the law, and hence to an opportunity to come before a court as a legal person, denied also an explanation of the reasons for his detention, he must construct or improvise a "person" in front of his interrogator, fathoming as best he can an effective subject position.

Taking his performativity a step further in his invention of a writer's voice, Slahi clarifies his postcolonial critique. It locates the workings of colonial mimicry in the disingenuous posture of the colonizer toward the colonized and the doublespeak of the universality of human rights. In Homi Bhabha's terms, "The menace of mimicry is its double vision which in disclosing the ambivalence of colonial discourse also disrupts its authority" (1994, 88). Slahi's running ahead of his interrogator enacts such a disruption. He calls out the interrogator's "narcissistic demand of colonial authority" (Bhabha 1994, 88). The interrogator behaves like a brute but wants to be seen as more civilized than the presumed terrorist. Slahi's hybrid subjectivity as an educated postcolonial subject (again in Bhabha's sense of hybridity which is resistant and performative), enables him to expose the interrogators repeatedly to the reader. This is, furthermore, a textual operation, an essential dimension of Slahi's act of witness and a step beyond testimony where he recasts himself as an agent with the ability to respond to the harm done to him and reconstitute his subjectivity. Thus, what Slahi achieves is legible through Kelly Oliver's theory of witness as constitutive of resistant and ethical subjectivity: "Subjective agency is produced between knowledge and truth. The double meaning of witnessing can be exploited as the productive tension at the center of subjectivity, the tension between historically determined subject positions and infinitely response-able subjectivity" (2001, 105). As a writer, Slahi gives witness to his own experience—this is necessary and the key to moving beyond the dead end of Scarry's analysis of torture's effects. By positing himself as historically determined but also able to respond to his own predicament (give witness to it), Slahi remakes himself.

Thus, Slahi depicts the totalizing influence of the threat of torture in the dynamic between interrogators and detainees, which is both vertical and horizontal. A network of relationships builds out from the torture culture that connects the different spaces of Slahi's confinement: the prisons of dictatorial states such as Mauritania and Jordan, and the United States detention centers in Bagram and Guantánamo:

> Just as I was learning from other detainees how not to cooperate, the interrogators were learning from each other how to deal with non-cooperating detainees ... I now officially belonged to the majority, the non-cooperating detainees. I minded less being locked up unjustly for the rest of my life; what drove me crazy was to be expected to cooperate, too. You lock me up, I give you no information. And we both are cool. (64–65)

Horizontal interactions shape subject positions: interrogators learn from each other, whereas Slahi learns that he belongs to a group, the "non-cooperating detainees." These horizontal alliances become more fully formed as the exercise of vertical control intensifies.

We discover in Slahi's text the contiguous and transhistorical space of empire. Early in his ordeal, he holds on to the belief that the United States does not torture detainees and he is comparing oppressive regimes that he is familiar with in African and Arab countries. The logic linking detention to torture is evident to Slahi as a person who grew up in an African dictatorship. When he is being returned to a Mauritanian prison before his rendition, Slahi acknowledges his own familiarity with that space as a kind of belonging that he had tried to disavow by migrating to Germany: "I had been incarcerated a couple of times in the same illegal prison, and knowing it didn't make me like it. I hated the compound, I hated the dark, dirty room, I hated the filthy bathroom, and I hated everything about it, especially the constant state of terror and fear" (2015, 127). Detention is a waiting game in anticipation of interrogation. Under custody of the Mauritanian secret police, he thinks to himself: "Why don't they interrogate me right now, and do with me whatever they want, and everything will be over? I hate waiting on torture" (91). The constant anxiety and stress make him literally sick, which is evident even before the episodes of extreme interrogation. Continuity—the sameness of constant fear—and acceleration of his physical suffering mark the different conditions he enters as he comes under more direct control of the Americans. Going from one prison to another sets the conditions for a narrative of disillusion that shares elements with the sub-genre of dictator novels and its treatment of torture. Postcolonial disillusion with authoritarian regimes, such as we see in Nuruddin Farah's trilogy, *Variations on a Theme of an African Dictatorship* (discussed in Chapter 8), or the novels of Sony Labou Tansi, most notably *La Vie et demie* (1979), provides a rich backdrop against which to place *Guantánamo Diary*'s resistant narrative.

Thus, Slahi offers us a narrative that is deeply conditioned by the experiences that give rise to its occasion: it foregrounds a talking back and a constant contestation of the claims of the regime of torture, which he likens in an all-encompassing way to "dictatorship," his term for totalitarianism. Without rule of law to protect prisoners' rights and uphold prohibitions against illegal detention and torture ("That's how the civilized world works"), you are left with "dictatorship," he tells us (2015, 94).

The breakdown of legality that Slahi's narrative exposes does more than juxtapose democratic, rule of law-abiding states, and dictatorships. It transposes the discourse of rights disjunctively onto a global arena politically organized by empire. "Dictatorship is governed by chaos," he tells us, and it becomes clear that the operative dictatorship is that of US imperial reach, exposed by Slahi most effectively in his identification of empire's colonialist mimicry, its doublespeak about rights (2015, 94). As noted, this is a realization that he comes to in the process of writing a narrative that tracks his disillusionment with the United States. Suspending the rule of law creates conditions of extreme contingency where events unfold in an improvisational manner and in response to raw assertions of power. In physics, "chaos" denotes unpredictability and randomness. In its Greek etymology, it represents a space that is void and infinite, and hence impossible to know and utterly disorienting. It becomes destructive to the self. Slahi, in the grips of "dictatorship," is sucked into "chaos," but his resistance is evidence of that dictatorship's incomplete hold.

The book is a defiant bucking of such disintegrating forces. However, we cannot read the text only from a premise that it makes the case for Slahi's release through his compelling self-portrayal. That would position it too close to the sentimental logic of slave narratives, even though Slahi evokes the comparison himself: "Slaves were taken forcibly from Africa, and so was I. Slaves were sold a couple of times on their way to their final destination, and so was I. Slaves suddenly were assigned to somebody they didn't choose, and so was I. And when I looked at the history of slaves, I noticed that slaves sometimes ended up *an integral part of their master's house"* (314, emphasis added). Instead of emphasizing how Slahi's circumstances align with those depicted in slave narratives, as Goyal does, it is more apt to note that the analogy breaks down. In what sense would it be possible to claim that Slahi becomes an "integral part of [his] master's house"? He is cast out under the presumption that it is necessary to ban him in order to avoid the collapse of his master's house. Slahi instead is drawing attention here to how the sentimental appeal is not available to him. In another reference to slavery in the text, he uses it to talk back to his interrogator: "You are holding me because your country is strong enough to be unjust. And it's not the first time you have kidnapped Africans and enslaved them" (212). Once again he locates himself as an African subjected to the arbitrary assertion of power by empire. The historical reminder of culpability in the slave trade places it as a counternarrative to the Enlightenment and its ideas of liberty, individual freedom, and rights at the core of the issue of the illegality of Slahi's detention. Thus, much of Slahi's narrative documents his talking back, both in instances where he recounts conversations he had and when he elaborates his responses as part of his narrative reflection. Talking back returns us constantly to his demand for an explanation of why he was detained in the first place.

Left critiques of the "War on Terror"

Slahi's location of himself as a postcolonial subject acquires added valence when placed in the context of critiques by the left of the United States "war on terror." Slahi's account disrupts key assumptions about the subjectivity of the detained and demands we decenter the account of the war on terror as constructed by such influential thinkers as Judith Butler. As we will see, the critical difference between these accounts pertains to the vexed problem of temporality. In the extended chapter on "Indefinite Detention" in *Precarious Life: the Powers of Mourning and Violence* (which was written before the news of Abu Ghraib and the revelations about torture), Butler evokes the detained as specters, persons who have suffered "desubjectification" through the violation of their human rights (2004, 98). The near contemporaneity of the writing of Slahi's account and Butler's reflections accentuates his geographical/spatial position in relation to her at a vanishing point. Focusing all her attention on speaking against the power responsible for the abuse, Butler describes an extra legal action by a "prerogative power" that is evidence of a "resurgent sovereignty" that "deems" the detainees "too dangerous" to be treated within the system of law (54). She repeats this formulation with the stress on the verb *to deem* throughout the essay: in the United States, we have "government officials who simply deem" (58); the "act of 'deeming'" can only happen in a "state of emergency" (59); "deeming" someone "dangerous" (59, 71); deeming someone dangerous is not the same as finding them "guilty" as it does not require evidence (75–76); and finally "officials 'deem' a given prisoner to deserve indefinite detention" (93–94). In all these instances, "deeming" is an exercise of "prerogative power" (54) that uses the law only as a "tactic" (62). The analysis is exclusively of the source of this "prerogative power" and the forms it takes, both in how it expresses itself in concrete actions and how it reshapes the relationship between governmentality, legality, and a "resurgent sovereignty" (54).

Moreover, Butler puzzles over the contradiction between her sense that she is witnessing a new turn in history and is thus tasked to find the language to describe an emergent type of power, and her recognition of the old, an anachronistic resurgence of a type of sovereignty displaced historically by the evolution of the state into a form of governmentality (97). This tug between the old and the new is evident when Butler discusses a sovereignty that "might emerge as a reanimated anachronism within the political field unmoored from its traditional anchors," which leads her to "call into question, as Foucault surely also did, the notion of history as a continuum" (53). She elaborates further: "This inverse relation to law produces the 'unaccountability' of this operation of sovereign power, as well as its illegitimacy," yet she characterizes this breach (that which is produced against expected practice) as a "reanimation of sovereignty," whereby sovereignty seems necessarily to evoke a past stage of history (66).

Butler pushes against Michel Foucault's assertion of a clean historical break between sovereignty and governmentality and his contention that "governmentality cannot be derived from sovereignty" to argue that "governmentality might become the site for the reanimation of that lost ground, the reconstellation of sovereignty in new form" (97). Positing that the program of indefinite detention is a resurgence in these terms, Butler highlights its exceptionality. Indefinite detention exceeds the frame of established theory and its implied historical model, and presents as new. Putting it a little differently, we can say that although the theory of governmentality had a chronology, now things seem to Butler out of sequence; what makes indefinite detention possible (a sovereignty that emerges unexpectedly out of the bureaucratic practices of governmentality) throws us out of sequence, importantly exposing the "racial frame" that permits such a shift (57).

As noted, Slahi's assertion that he was betrayed by his own country, whose weak sovereignty allowed for the breach of legality and his rights, establishes a temporality that links the aftermath of colonialism to the "war on terror." Moreover, his narrative emerges as powerful proof that he was not effectively "desubjectified." And this is not because the power exerted against him did not have "desubjectification" as its goal. The literary endeavor, the effort of writing, intervenes critically, as Harlow has shown it does for detainees throughout history. It provides the means for the detainee to assert a presence within the prison and to bring forth his subjectivity as a point of view that contests his dehumanization. Slahi, in fact, asks the same question as Butler: How is a policy of indefinite detention possible and what does it tell us about the conception of sovereign power that underwrites it? By calling this a new type of sovereignty, operating from a "lawless and prerogatory power, a rogue sovereignty" (56), Butler misses its continuity with its antecedent ideologies of empire, and hence cannot respond adequately to the workings of mimicry. Furthermore, she risks exposing her own thinking as symptomatic of this dynamic. It is empire as context and temporality (as long durée) that holds the greater explanatory power and links the dots of history in such a way as to make Slahi's account legible. Butler's chronology places the events of her present moment beyond the history of European imperialism in Africa and locates itself instead in United States, post-Cold War history. Her "new" moment comes after universal human rights have achieved hegemonic status as political ideals. But this "new" will not hold if there is no willingness to uphold these ideals: *"Whether or not we continue to enforce a universal conception of human rights at moments of outrage and incomprehension, precisely when we think that others have taken themselves out of the human community as we know it, is a test of our very humanity"* (Butler 2004, 89–90, italics in original). Butler thus distills the crisis into a crisis of "our" humanity: the humanity of United States citizens whose passivity in the face of (and also active complicity with) this resurgent, "rogue" sovereignty allows it to assert itself.

Slahi too asks repeatedly what the meaning of human rights is. Yet, posing the question of universal humanity from his point of view carries with it the resonance of a long history of colonized peoples unmasking colonial mimicry, whose enduring remnants Butler does not confront head on. Her insistence that the "reanimation of sovereignty" only occurs during "national emergency" or "states of emergency" might evoke the theoretical language of biopolitics, but these are terms with strong historical resonance for postcolonial societies that frequently passed through states of emergency and extreme repression before achieving independence.

Butler's emphasis on the valence of *deeming* (the determination made to cast a person as "too dangerous" and hence to be detained indefinitely) is perhaps also an important point where the incompatibility of her account and Slahi's becomes palpable. To "deem" someone not worthy of rights and relegate them to a contiguous but separate space that renders them invisible is a familiar gesture to students of empire. Butler distances herself from this action through her analytical prose. However, "to deem," as a unilateral and arbitrary gesture without legal recourse, creates mystification and distances us too neatly, obscuring the precise mechanism of "rogue sovereignty." From a postcolonial perspective, we are aware of the subjectivity of those cast out, and spoken for, and become invested in bringing forth their subjectivity.

The necessary critical intervention here, therefore, is to put pressure on Butler's theory to be more responsive to history. What is elided in her reflections is a tradition of imperialist thinking and practice immediately accessible to Slahi for whom the connections between his present moment and the colonial history that has marked him as a political subject come into sharp focus during his ordeal.[8] Butler locates the contest between the ethical and political within the center, calling on the broader citizenry of the United States to wrestle with the implications of its silent participation in the "war on terror." But Slahi has a location as a subject beyond his status as a Guantánamo detainee: he has a nationality (he is Mauritanian); he was an African migrant to Germany and Canada; he has a trade that locates him in our technological age; he has a politics, which as he explains to us over and over made him an ally of the United States against communism in Afghanistan (a key chapter in his life that, like other African stories from the Cold War era, places him precariously in the cross winds of the superpowers' changing alliances); he speaks several languages and the English he uses to write this text is a language he picks up from popular culture and from his interactions and reading during detention. He is a reader who can comment on the Bible as well as the Koran, Ben Franklin, and *Catcher in the Rye*, and he listens to 2Pac. He draws on Mauritanian folktales as deftly as Chinua Achebe used Ibo proverbs to convey the moral universe of his culture.[9] The challenge for Butler is how to articulate her necessary critique to a United States public without erasing the subjectivity and historical particularity of the detainees all over again by placing them in a sphere that is necessarily, for the force of her critique, beyond the vanishing point, evoking horror from its darkness.

Thus, *Guantánamo Diary* does not only shed light on what went on in Guantánamo: it shatters its premise of a bifurcated world. Butler's theory does not have space to accommodate this subjectivity. *Guantánamo Diary* has come into existence as a published text, redactions and all, miraculously against the odds of Butler's description of the zone of exception. It is also crucially important that it was published through the efforts of lawyers and other activists who exemplify a practice of solidarity that complements the literary in Harlow's sense. The text does not give us information that we can put to use somewhere. It performs a recalibration of our sense of what realities we have access to, decentering the critique of the war on terror.

Whereas Slahi's circumstances during his detention are despairing, his world, in the sense of his understanding of himself as a subject in relation to political power, is not destroyed or rendered incoherent, or inaccessible to him. His compass remains intact; he writes (*reconstructs* his experiences) soon after the period of detention during which he was tortured. Consequently, in some important measure and without diminishing the impact of the physical pain inflicted upon Slahi, torture has failed to achieve its aims, and the book, by decentering the narrative of the war on terror, disrupts the premise of absolute sovereignty that Butler describes. In his examination of the problem of voice, Rejali concludes: "the inexpressibility that matters in torture is the gap between speakers and their communities, not the gap between the brain and the tongue" (2007, 442–443). The critical issue is one of audience and, in this case, it is exacerbated by the daunting gap of nearly ten years that it took for the book to be published. After publication, the text points to a different crisis, a potential failure of reading, especially in the way that some audiences persist in their preoccupation with Slahi's guilt or innocence despite the fact that even the United States admitted there was no evidence of his involvement in terrorism. Slahi's text ends up centering less on the question of whether or not he was tortured—we come to the text already knowing that he must have been—and the redactions do not even try to hide torture. Yet, his account should return us insistently to the illegality of his detention and torture.

Conclusion

There is a surprising and unsettling conciliatory postscript in the book that takes the author's voice we have come to know intimately and places it behind his lawyers. Here we learn that Slahi has told his lawyers that "he holds no grudge against any of the people he mentions in this book" and invites them "to read [the book] and correct it" if they see errors. Finally, he expresses a hope "to one day sit with all of them around a cup of tea, after having learned so much from one another." Slahi makes it clear that although the main objective is his release, the violence done to him compounded by his continued indefinite detention without trial constitutes a history that must urgently be reckoned with, reflected upon, and witnessed. Even with his release and the publication of the restored text, such a reckoning is still incomplete. In this postscript, he invites a collective reflection by all participants, showing his understanding that what happened to him is not just an individual story, or even a story about a few hundred detainees, but a story that exposes the logic of power undergirding our world order. "Around a cup of tea" is also a unifying and reconciliatory expression where "around" appropriately evokes a circle. By identifying himself as a Mauritanian citizen shaped by Africa's colonial history and linking his present circumstances directly to that history, Slahi urges us to reframe our understanding of the "war on terror" much more historically.

Notes

1 Slahi's compelling interiority has been the focus of critical attention. He shows evidence of it by repeatedly addressing his reader and consistently refusing to fall into the binary logic of the Bush administration's us vs. them logic. Moreover, Slahi uses "elements of dialogic structure" in order to "underscore human dignity and its subject positions as relational and mutually constitutive" (Moore 2016, 28).

2 Harlow makes another literary allusion that applies to *Guantánamo Diary*. She emphasizes "reconstruction" in her analysis of Gramsci's *Prison Notebooks*, which "testify to the continued if reconstructed importance of writing and the written to Gramsci in prison" (1992, 20).

3 Siems "Notes on the Text" only appears in Slahi (2017), the Restored edition.

4 Thus, Coetzee warns: "there is something tawdry about *following* the state in this way, making its vile mysteries the occasion of fantasy." He sees a further challenge in the task of representing the torturer, concluding that "The approaches to the torture chamber are thus riddled with pitfalls, and more than one writer has fallen into them" (1992, 364).

5 Moreover, there is additional slippage between "diary" and "memoir," a term used by Siems in his explanatory material. "Memoir" assumes a degree of closure and distance from the narrated experiences that does not apply to Slahi's text either.

6 Slahi refers to "7 years" because he was first questioned by Canadian authorities in 2000 regarding the Millennium Plot. This line of inquiry was eventually dropped by the interrogators as there was no evidence to support that Slahi had any connection at all to the Millennium Plot (2015, ix).

7 For example, Chimamanda Ngozi Adichie's *Americanah* (2014) develops the been-to plot, but there are many precursors including Chinua Achebe's *No Longer at Ease* (1960) and, more controversially, Tayeb Salih's *Season of Migration to the North* (1970).

8 Alternatively, Slahi conveys this through a process of "subjectification" that is part of the creation of "political dissensus" (in Jacques Rancière's sense) and plays out in the process of reconstructing his experience in writing (Moore 2016, 32–33). Thus the "subjectification" taking place during the writing process can be opposed to the "desubjectification" that Butler claims is the result of illegal disappearance and torture.

9 Through Mauritanian proverbs, Slahi drives home the ironies of his experiences. For example, for more than four years the interrogators were fixated on his use of the words "tea" and "sugar" in his emails, convinced that they were code: "'What do you mean by tea and sugar?'/ 'I mean tea and sugar.'" To explain this, he elaborates: "Another Mauritanian folktale recounts about a man who was born blind and who had one chance to get a glimpse of the world. All he saw was a rat. After that, whenever anybody tried to explain anything to the guy, he always asked, "'Compare it with the rat: Is it bigger? Smaller?'" (95–96).

Works cited

Achebe, Chinua. *No Longer at Ease*. New York: Ballantine, 1960.

Adichie, Chimamanda Ngozi. *Americanah*. New York: Anchor, 2014.

Bhabha, Homi. *The Location of Culture*. London, UK: Routledge, 1994. DOI (2d ed): 10.4324/9780203820551.

Butler, Judith. *Precarious Life: The Powers of Mourning and Violence*. London: Verso, 2004.

Coetzee, J. M. *Doubling the Point: Essays and Interviews*. Edited by David Atwell. Cambridge, MA: Harvard University Press, 1992.

Coundouriotis, Eleni. *The People's Right to the Novel: War Fiction in the Postcolony*. New York: Fordham University Press, 2014.

Goyal, Yogita. "The Genres of *Guantánamo Diary*: Postcolonial Reading and the War on Terror." *The Cambridge Journal of Postcolonial Literary Inquiry* 4, no. 1 (January 2017): 68–87. DOI: 10.1017/pli.2016.32.

Harlow, Barbara. *Barred: Women, Writing, and Political Detention*. Hanover, NH: Wesleyan University Press, 1992.

Laqueur, Thomas W. "Bodies, Details, and the Humanitarian Narrative." In *The New Cultural History*, edited by Lynn Hunt, 176–204. Berkeley: University of California Press, 1989. www.jstor.org/stable/10.1525/j.ctt1ppfh6.

Moore, Alexandra Schultheis. "Teaching Mohamedou Ould Slahi's *Guantánamo Diary* in the Human Rights and Literature Classroom." *Radical Teacher* 104 (February 2016): 27–38. DOI: 10.5195/rt.2016.263.

Ngũgĩ wa Thiong'o. *Detained: A Writer's Prison Diary*. Nairobi: Heinemann, 1981, 1981.

Oliver, Kelly. *Witnessing: Beyond Recognition*. Minneapolis: University of Minnesota Press, 2001.

Rejali, Darius. *Torture and Democracy*. Princeton: Princeton University Press, 2007. DOI: 10.2307/j.ctt7rwf8.

Salih, Tayeb. *Season of Migration to the North*. London, UK: Heinemann, 1970.

Scarry, Elaine. *The Body in Pain: The Making and Unmaking of the World*. New York: Oxford University Press, 1985.

Siems, Larry. "Introduction." In *Mahamedou Ould Slahi, Guantánamo Diary*, edited by Larry Siems. New York: Little, Brown and Company, 2015.

Slahi, Mohamedou Ould. *Guantánamo Diary*. Edited by Larry Siems. New York: Little, Brown and Company, 2015.

Slahi, Mohamedou Ould. *Guantánamo Diary: Restored Edition*. Edited by Larry Siems. New York: Little, Brown and Company, 2017.

Slaughter, Joseph R. "A Question of Narration: The Voice in International Human Rights Law." *Human Rights Quarterly* 19, no. 2 (May 1997): 406–430. Project MUSE. DOI: 10.1353/hrq.1997.0019.

Soyinka, Wole. *The Man Died: Prison Notebooks of Wole Soyinka*. London: Rex Collins, 1972.

Tansi, Labou. *La vie et demie*. Paris: Seuil, 1979.

Taub, Ben. "Guantánamo's Darkest Secret." *The New Yorker*, 15 April 2019 (22 April 2019 issue). Web. newyorker.com/magazine/2019/04/22/guantanamos-darkest-secret.

8   Evoking the disappeared in Assia Djebar and Nuruddin Farah

> What a comfort now that the voice had returned, the voice which kept him company when he was lonely, the voice of angels, of his saint protector, of his articulated reason.
>
> *Sweet and Sour Milk*, Nuruddin Farah

In dark times, writers evoke the words of other writers. They turn to their reading, the texts that have shaped their minds and conscience, for direction. Even more poignantly, they retrieve the words of dissenting writers who have gone ahead of them into the dark: arrested, disappeared, tortured, assassinated. This reclamation has multiple valences. It is defiant. Repeating the words that the regime attempts to stamp out, the writers resurrect the disappeared by speaking in their voice. The reclamation is also suppliant, seeking courage in the clear-eyed vision of those who went before them. Written as private thought, it rehearses a speech apart, in some protected space that exceeds the now and its narrowing possibilities. Following the vein of this internal, imaginary conversation, writers moreover discover their own creativity, producing works that extend what came before by positing a solidarity with their readers that will keep alive the hope of freedom from state oppression.

This chapter focuses on a particular type of text that explicitly reclaims and builds on the writings or words of disappeared and censored persons. By evoking the disappeared through their words, the two authors under examination here, Assia Djebar and Nuruddin Farah, forge their own political statement to address the state's violation of civil and political rights. Most importantly, their reference to disappeared writers illustrates how speech retains its oppositional force, defying silence after disappearance. Writers amplify the condition of the disappeared who "exist as a present absence. *Exist*, and not *are*, because disappearance entails a permanence in an impossible state" (Gatti 2014, 30). Their works animate a palpable presence of missing persons into the future. Djebar and Farah, noted for their individualism and trenchant critiques of tradition, are dissenting figures who were driven into exile. In their works, they explore the implications of dissent specifically as a problem for writers and of writing. Djebar's memoir, *Algerian White* (2000, *Blanc de l'Algérie*, 1995) and two novels, Farah's *Sweet and Sour Milk* (1979) and Djebar's *La femme sans sépulture* (2002, "Woman Without a Tomb"), shape a self-reflexive literary project focusing on how dissent sustains human rights struggle into the future. Although bleak, the realities they portray encompass a world of the mind nurtured by the words of those who came before. By depicting the effort to hold on to such voices, their works take-up ongoing resistance in their contemporary circumstance.

Algerian White creates a delicate balance between Djebar's anxiety over the waning influence of past literary works (including those by giants of Algerian literature such as Kateb Yacine) and her own powerful testimony of their enduring significance as guides in dark times. She assembles portraits of journalists, novelists, and poets whose deaths ruptured normality, forcing her to assess their lives and answer the question, what kind of person was this writer? *Algerian White*, in turn, informs my approach to *Sweet and Sour Milk*, the first novel of Farah's trilogy, *Variations on the Theme of an African Dictatorship*. We can read Soyaan as the figure of the assassinated writer, and thus a fictional surrogate for Djebar's historical examples. In the novel, Soyaan leaves behind secret memoranda exposing the regime, which his twin brother, Loyaan, uses to search for truth. Distrustful of how others construe Soyaan, Loyaan sticks to Soyaan's words. His close reading, in a manner of speaking, immerses him in his brother's world to the point that he takes on his role and is in turn targeted by the regime. The third example, Djebar's novel *La femme sans sépulture*, posits Djebar herself as the artist under assessment. In the novel, she revisits material from her film for Algerian television, *La Nouba des femmes du Mont-Chenoua* (1977). By twinning her persona as author and filmmaker, Djebar echoes Farah's treatment of the twin brothers in *Sweet and Sour Milk*, where the memory of one becomes the secret interlocutor of the other, constituting his interiority. Moreover, Djebar's fictive rendition of the torture of a historical figure and her claims to documentation despite the fictional status of the text intervene in the constraints that limit the evocation of the disappeared.

Farah and Djebar treat documentation and narration as intertwined, not opposed as realist aesthetics has sometimes posited (Lukács 1971, 111). Their stylistic innovation is not for aesthetics' sake, but dedicated to the real and historical. Each stubbornly wrestles with the events of human rights violations as they are embedded in the complexity of human motivation and historical contingency. Delineating what is at stake for human rights in their work entails understanding their complex metapoetics, construed broadly as writing that crosses genres and forms and reflects on its own methods.

A liturgy for dead writers

To characterize her project in *Algerian White*, Djebar uses "liturgy" in its ancient Greek sense of the performance of a public office (2000, 13). The book documents what happened at funerals, directly recounting the gathering around the body of the dead writer. But, more importantly, Djebar sees the funeral as spawning a figurative gathering, "materializing through the pen" (2000, 13). Many of her readers thus interpret "liturgy" as Djebar's desire to invent a literary, funerary ritual to compensate for what was denied in life (Fallaize 2005, 58–59; Talbayev 2018, 212). Arguably, however, ritual puts the emphasis in the wrong place, and Djebar's use of "materializing" is more apt: her procession of writers is a making real of those whom Algeria subjected to a "double death"—loss of life and a "falling out of memory" (Erikson 1999, 97). The dead writers and their oeuvre function as a metonymy for an unstable, fragmented Algeria that cannot cohere even with historical retrospection and hence needs to be held in trust for a period, suspended as a narrative of the literary imagination.[1] This lack of cohesion and Djebar's effort to create an adequate literary surrogate for the absence of a viable Algeria create a difficulty of form. She warns that her text is not elegy, not "lament," but neither is it a polemic ("I do not wish to polemicize," [2000, 13]). Instead, she sticks to the effort to convey detailed facts she finds compelling. The book, thus, combines meticulous documentation with the elaboration of an extended and polyvalent metaphor of "Algerian white," which evokes the blank page, the erasure of history, the white of Algeria's veiled women, and the topographical features typical in visual representations of Algeria (Fallaize 2005, 56, 60–61). Presenting her subjects in a symbolic "procession" for the reader, she creates a retrospective of each individual case: "As simply as possible … I re-establish an account of the days—with sometimes innocent signs, presages—the days leading up to the death" (2000, 13). Her attentiveness to "signs, presages" that stand out retrospectively establishes a pattern of narration she then applies to a historical Algeria in crisis during the Black Decade of the 1990s civil war, and with particular reference to the years 1992–1993. Ironically, for Djebar, Algeria is inflicting the signature violence of the colonial era anew in the 1990s: disappearance, assassination, torture. This repetition throws the nation's revolutionary legacy in crisis and poses the question, what is left of Algeria after such an ironic return? To answer, *Algerian White* shuttles back and forth between the Algerian War of Independence and the civil war of the 1990s.

Djebar's strong sense of a literary, or more broadly a writerly, milieu—a solidarity of the pen, acts as the bulwark against oppression and the repeated assaults of the state on civil and political rights. Moreover, the writer's "search for a scrupulously faithful account" of the circumstances surrounding the deaths of other writers reveals their bodies as "propitiatory," or having the power to atone (Djebar 2000, 14). The atonement takes the form of a corrected narrative, one which needs to be revised to respond to unfolding events, which give a new understanding of the past. To capture the truth in its complexity, one must drill down to the facts surrounding each death, and pare down to the essence of each writer's story so that it can emerge uniquely.

Djebar distrusts the homogenizing effect of large sweeping historical theses. The goal, therefore, is not to cohere a single Algeria ("several different Algerias are being sketched out") but to come to grips with a complex history (2000, 14). Remembered in varied and contradictory ways even among Djebar's intimate friends and associates, Algeria is a collage of languages, religions, ethnicities, classes, and topographies, all of which Djebar is intent on keeping in flux. Offering this multiplicity of the national idea makes it harder to silence and is a potential source of renewal.

Critics have noted the fragmented structure of the text and its confusing transitions between different temporalities (Fallaize 2005, 57). The structure, however, might come from a different idea. Although Djebar assembles 19 individual profiles, she organizes them in carefully configured groups. The starting point is three persons assassinated in close succession in 1993. These are "close friends" to whom she dedicates the book: Mahfoud Boucebci, M'Hamed Boukhobza, and Abdelkader Alloula. They are counterpoised to other clusters, most notably a group of four who died before independence and whom she invites to come with her *"on the edge of the quagmire ... [to] look deep into it, let us together question the other absent ones, so many disturbing shadows!"*. These figures are Albert Camus, Frantz Fanon, Mouloud Feraoun, and Jean Amrouche (2000, 105). Each cluster of deaths, therefore, creates a peer group that stands for a particular historical passage, and Djebar establishes a genealogical approach undermining the finality of the writers' abrupt demise. Death as an event yields to the observant attendant a clarifying assessment of the past, a judgment akin to "what it all came to," which Djebar rehearses repeatedly with each death she recounts. The living writer's task is to keep the conversation about the meaning of these lives open. Thinking in this deeply associative manner, Djebar is susceptible to flows of emotion and insight that help her construe continuities towards a larger synthesis. History is always pressing, and adumbrations of what is to come create the impression of a recursive pattern of events that she stubbornly tries to break through her reasoned history.

Because she focuses on writers, Djebar examines texts, not just lives. Literature, like history, is also recursive, appearing as the "circle of words from before" (2000, 47). The works she alludes to in *Algerian White* exhibit a rich intertextuality whereby they include references, sometimes silent, to other literary works, making palpable for the reader a polyglot Algerian literary tradition. More provocatively, the layering of texts demonstrates how literature functions as an ethical enterprise, sustained through an active practice of writing. Thus, Djebar brings to life a concert of voices that visit her imagination and resurrect the presence of her lost associates.

Intertextuality attains dramatic dimensions, for example, when she imagines hearing the assassinated, Arabic playwright Abdelkader Alloula—"with no theatrical effects, in an even tone"— recite verses by francophone Kateb Yacine. Before his death Alloula had been translating a play by Kateb and also visiting pediatric cancer patients at a hospital in Oran. To entertain the children, he told Djebar, he would share lines from the play. Djebar had not witnessed this but now evokes the recitation, showing how writers live on in their works when read by those other writers who have endured like them furtively "in the shadows." She repeats the recitation for the reader:

> Thus to die is to live
> War and cancer of the blood
> Slow or violent, to each his death
> And it always is the same
> For those who have learned
> To read in the shadows
> And who, eyes closed
> Have not stopped writing
> Thus to die is to live. (Kateb quoted in Djebar 2000, 80)

The full significance of this evocation, however, is more complex. Djebar adds the relevant details that tie her to this imagined scene: attending Alloula's deathbed, she heard his last words to her, "eyes closed" (2000, 80). Djebar suggests that "eyes closed" functioned as a coded message between her and the dying Alloula. Because the full import of this communication is not felt until Djebar writes retrospectively about Alloula's assassination, Djebar shows how literary language works over extended time against the political forces that rewrite history into official accounts marked by erasures and distortions. Literary language has a capacity to hold meaning in reserve for the appropriate moment or the right reader. Moreover, this long wait does not suggest that the poem remains silent until rediscovered or reread "in the shadows." The writer (in this case Djebar) occupies a meantime immersed in the language of other writers, citing each other in a concert of voices. Connecting the dots between what she remembers as Alloula's last words and Kateb's poem is possible only from within this literary world. This is important for the narrative of human rights because it shows how a set of literary associations keeps the memory of repressed events accessible till a moment when the full import of their truth can be felt.

In a metapoetic manner, Djebar asks where a writer's voice comes from. She describes it as "*that strange voice for the self alone*" and wonders "*from where does it rise, whose voice is it in truth?*" (2000, 131, italics in original). Similarly, Farah's Loyaan discovers his brother's voice in his own mind as his "articulated reason" (1979, 215). When the voice is absent, the loneliness is crushing. Djebar also wonders, however, how such voices fall silent, why writers stop writing. She speculates that to be temperamentally attracted to silence (not writing, not speaking) is in fact a writer's trait because of how it turns one into a listener, into someone responsive to the environment: "*Do not write, let the emptiness spread out, weigh it in your hands, let it calm you. Let yourself live. Let yourself be lulled by the anthem of time, everyday phrases, drown in the chit-chat—children cry in the night, outside the bustling crowd ...*" (2000, 131, italics in original). These thoughts at the bedside of Malek Haddad, a novelist dying too young of cancer, capture Djebar as she practices an intense form of presence. She surrenders to the sounds and sights of ordinary life reaching her from the hospital window while attending to the extraordinary moment of her friend's imminent passing.

Djebar explores the possibility of "what might have been" in addition to the assessment of "what it all came to" stirred by a life just ended. In a chapter called "The Spectre of Post Independence," Djebar looks back at the period preceding the height of the war in 1956–1957. She recalls Camus's call for a truce in January 1956 as a brief moment when Algerians thought they could see a resolution to the conflict (2000, 110). It matters less that Camus was wrong than that he left an impression of how things could have been otherwise and, for Djebar, writers who help us see how things might be different are important in their moment and later. Camus's vision put the worst that followed into perspective. His death before Algeria's independence—like that of the others (Fanon, Feraoun, and Amrouche) clustered with him—makes his faith in Algeria and its betrayal by history all the more poignant for Djebar. The "reversed form of inclusion" of a *pied noir* in this pantheon, moreover, speaks to the ethical imperatives of her vision (Fallaize 2005, 60).

The memory of Camus guides Djebar's account of the darkest period of the War of Independence. A few months after Camus's call for a truce, the escalation of the war brought mass executions of detainees. Djebar recounts the executions through the testimony of the women from the imprisoned men's families who mourned at the prison gate. In yet another powerful although silent intertextual allusion, Djebar situates these women at the gates of the Barberousse prison similarly to Anna Akhmatova's women in "Requiem," who wait at the gates of Nevsky prison during Stalin's purges (Akhmatova 1973, 101).[2] Akhamatova's archetypal scene positions the women as witnesses against the state who, although blocked from seeing by the gates of the prison, counter its effort to erase the lives of the detainees by providing an intimate perspective on the announcement of the sentences. Djebar's women at the gate likewise approach to read the names announcing who was executed. The "white notices" terrorize with their suggestiveness as it is the only communication the women receive about their loved ones. However, by drawing the women close to the prison, the notices, meant to underscore the inaccessibility of the prison, expose its workings. Djamila Briki thus remembers: "*And the water! ... When there was lots of water in front of the gate it was because they'd cleaned up the blood by squirting it with great jets of water from a hose*" (111, italics and ellipses in original). These specific details create an image of the action (pouring water from a hose to clean a mess) which is almost domestic and ordinary except, of course, for its purpose. The sense of discovery, of having found out or even seen what was supposed to be hidden, functions as accusation. The water overruns the boundary of the gate, spills out of the prison, and creates an unexpected encounter between the women and the state that endures as testimony. Comparing 1956–1957 to 1993–1994, Djebar underscores the absence of a voice similar to Camus's: "*there is no one to stand up, as did the Camus of '56 [...] no one today able to pronounce once more, in the midst of struggle, those words of an impotence not quite powerless, those words of suffering that one last time continues to live in hope ....*" (2000, 114, italics in original). Camus could imagine solidarity at a bleak moment and, moreover, had the opportunity to express it. By contrast, Djebar notes "*if I were to say 'you,' I would be speaking only to the dead, to my friends, my brothers of the pen*" (Camus quoted in Djebar 2000, 114, italics in original). She acknowledges the "impotence" of Camus's words, which changed nothing and made the wrong assessment of the moment. But it is "an impotence not quite powerless." Although speaking for his moment, Camus bequeathed his words to other writers in the future and thus Djebar can turn to them in her dark moment. He sought to break the loneliness that afflicts us during conflict and to posit the possibility of coming together through a shared recognition of suffering. And he expressed himself conditionally: "If I had the power to give a voice to the solitude and anxiety which lies within each of us, it would be with that voice that I address myself to you" (Camus quoted in Djebar 2000, 110). This tentativeness, not daring to presume for others, invites a collective awareness without imposing it. The violence of 1993–1994 is bleaker for not producing a voice analogous to Camus's.

Thus Djebar uses the occasion of Camus's speech to draw a parallel to her own situation as a writer. In fact, she uses this passage as the epigraph to the book and wonders who would be the "you" that she might address the way Camus did. Her answer takes us back to the role writers play for each other, her "*brothers of the pen*" (2000, 114, italics in original). Collectively, this transhistorical brotherhood holds the truth of Algeria, yet Djebar is anxious about the ability for it to survive the current destruction. She is alarmed by the appropriation of Algeria's revolutionary history to legitimate the counterrevolutionary repression by the post-independence National Liberation Front (Daoudi 2016, 33–34). The state was actively recasting history as "a caricature of the past in which sublimated heroes and fratricidal murderers were to be mingled in a hazy blur" (2000, 128). Not only was this a way to lie about the present but it makes it impossible to retrieve Algeria's Independence War in its complexity.

Djebar does not want to remember the anticolonial struggle through "sublimated heroes." She calls urgently for writers to take up the challenge for a nuanced and complex history but feels that the only writers who have addressed this have already passed and are figures relegated to the past.[3] The dilemma is a "mire," and the way out a search for the right "language" and "aesthetic" to "give an account of these changes" (2000, 128). Djebar explicitly sees this as a task for literature, rather than journalism or history. We might say then that literature's contribution to narrating human rights is to be a portal that allows entry into an imagination receptive to a human rights narrative. Literature does not necessarily offer the full narrative but holds onto the past to suggest how one might navigate it for the purpose of truth telling.

Remembered as a writer

Sweet and Sour Milk is an example of such a work that opens up the possibility of human rights narration. The novel does not offer a political solution but captures and preserves truths it promises to mobilize at some later date. Farah begins with a scene that is structurally parallel to *Algerian White*: a witness sits at the deathbed of the person who will be remembered as a writer.[4] Similarly to Djebar's Algeria of 1992–1994, the regime of the "General" (Somalia's dictator Siyad Barre) is intent on rewriting the country's revolutionary history. It hijacks the memory of the dissident Soyaan and recasts him as hero for the regime. To do so effectively, the regime must also eradicate the traces of his dissenting speech, attribute different words to him, coopt those willing to go along, and terrorize everyone else. Thus, the reader is confronted with another "mire" of complexity. In the case of Farah's Somalia, an outwardly disciplined society transforms into a morass of secret alliances and deception conveying an extreme instability of the real. The truth struggles to surface through Farah's conversational form, organized in charged exchanges between individuals, or as interiority, a character's conversations in his head. Interrogative locutions proliferate, leaving the reader to surmise answers without knowing enough.

In addition to portraying Soyaan as a writer read by his brother, Loyaan, the novel gets at the problem of how to represent the disappeared. Farah creates a paradox as Soyaan dies in plain sight at home, but has been disappeared all the same: the state engineers his poisoning so that the death is impossible to explain and then manipulates Soyaan's memory so his real history vanishes. "An economic adviser to the Presidency," Soyaan had joined an underground effort led by "intellectuals and professionals" to expose the regime's use of disappearance and torture (1979, 36–37, 150). His political engagement turned him into a writer who sought to disrupt the official representation of Somalia by exposing the state's creation of a Stalinist gulag in Africa (the General is the "Grand Warden of a Gulag," 11). Not only is the focus on persecuted intellectuals similar to *Algerian White* but Farah, like Djebar, sees the return of colonial violence: "Africa is again a torture-chamber" (1979, 134). Soyaan left behind his accusatory memoranda, but Loyaan also relies on Soyaan's spoken words, remembered by his close associates. Thus Soyaan's voice, like the writers who visit Djebar's mind, pervades the novel.

Critics have repeatedly read the novel as detective fiction, or the story of Loyaan's efforts to solve the mystery of his brother's death (Adam 2002,

331; Masterson 2013, 34; Moolla 2014, 118). But this reading sidelines the human rights concerns with forced disappearance and torture, which not only are incidents in the plot but determine the formal features of the text: its exploration of the capacity for language to hold onto that which the state wants to destroy. Soyaan's death by poison is a battle of physical, embodied life and expression, words struggling to override the effort to stamp out his person. Soyaan hiccups uncontrollably in his last breaths and the hiccups make language material, like objects dropping out of his mouth that we can hold and examine (Moolla 2014, 120).

The defiant words that Soyaan leaves behind become Loyaan's indispensable guide, revealing his brother to him but also providing a code to follow. At his deathbed, Soyaan tasks his brother with the "demystifica-*hic*-tion of in-*hic*-formation. Tell the *hic* masses in the simplest *hic* of terms what is happening" (1979, 16). These instructions pertain to language: they explain how one talks about the regime. Soyaan's aim to expose the fate of the disappeared and tortured can only be fulfilled in a linguistic style of straight talk. Moreover, the dissident group to which he belonged held that "'the written word, more powerful than the gun, will frighten them [the regime]'" (152). In his writings, Soyaan described "the top civil service" as "Clowns. Cowards" (1979, 36). Implying that they are acting a charade of loyalty to the regime in order to stay out of danger, he explains: "To survive, you must clown" (1979, 37). Soyaan's dictum (demystification of information), therefore, calls for the unmasking of false appearances and the imperative to tell the people in the "simplest" terms what is happening.

Communication, however, is anything but simple in this novel. Language exchanged between characters is coded and facts are only guessed at. The proposition that Soyaan died "of complications" typifies the novel's struggle to convey events: it is undoubtedly true, but explains little (1979, 32–33). Similarly, Loyaan does not know how much to trust the accounts of torture that he hears. A friend of the family is an important witness to the regime's torture because, as a doctor, he has been called to treat its victims (1979, 40–41). Yet Loyaan does not trust him. He is certain that torture is happening but does not know whether Ahmed-Wellie's narrative is bait to draw him out and snare him somehow (1979, 175). In this paranoid environment, truth emerges gradually after rehearsing conversations and interactions repeatedly in the memory to identify tonal variations and inconsistencies that might be revelatory. By contrast, the words left behind by Soyaan are direct and explicit. In a letter to Loyaan, he described Mogadishu after independence, guiding Loyaan on his return from abroad. After Soyaan's death, this same letter with its careful description of the new architecture, roads, and billboards praising the president and "heroes of his own choosing" (1979, 78) holds clues that suggest how the regime will spin Soyaan's death, remaking him as a hero of its "choosing." The letter's directness acquires layers of irony. It is worth coming back to, and hence the reader starts to understand the cumulative force of Soyaan's words.

Although Loyaan is initially motivated by the imperative to find out how and why his brother died, this quest becomes more than an act of filial loyalty to his twin. Loyaan adopts his brother's mission to speak the truth, which proves transformative. Soyaan's manner of speaking, emphasizing candor and transparency, is also a way of life. The two cannot be separated: one lives through a relationship to language. Consequently, however, Loyaan must also confront a crisis of representation caused by his brother's death. By exploring Soyaan and Loyaan's relationship to language, Farah identifies a key problem of forced disappearance. Because it brings the representation of facts into crisis, human rights scholars address disappearance as a problem of language. A "catastrophe for identity and meaning" (Gatti 2014, 15), disappearance requires a response that evokes the person and events without having recourse to facts. Thus, disappearance effects "the disarticulation of words from things, of meanings from facts, a disarticulation turned into structure" (Gatti 2014, 16). Although forensics might yield answers by identifying victims, the "biological approach" does not account fully for the damage done, the "identity-breaks" of disappearance (Capdepón 2017, 479).

The paradox of a visible victim of disappearance in Farah's novel addresses the gap of such "identity-breaks." It moves past the first order question of biological identity and seeks answers by evoking the person's expression, their manner of speaking, their articulation ("articulated reason" as Farah puts it) instead. The state's authority to determine biological identity comes into force but is ambiguous. The official obituary for Soyaan confuses the twins' identities by publishing a photograph of Loyaan instead of Soyaan. It is unclear whether this is an error or a warning to Loyaan, but the mix-up points at the imperative for Loyaan to think beyond biological identity. Loyaan resolves his quest to repair the "identity-break" of disappearance. In the end, he answers the question about his brother's identity by slipping into Soyaan's role and adopting his manner of speaking: Soyaan's underground organization invites Loyaan to take his brother's place and presumably take up the task of documenting the regime's crimes. He will, therefore, inhabit Soyaan's "political" voice.

Extensive violations of civil and political rights epitomize the state's betrayal of the promise of modernity held out by independence. Samuel Moyn has made the contentious claim that decolonization was a struggle for self-determination rather than human rights. By opposing self-determination and human rights, Moyn ignores the status of "self-determination" as the "premier human right," according to postcolonial theorists (Slaughter 2018, 770). For Moyn, economic development instead of "classical liberties or even 'social rights'" was the end goal of "anticolonialism," which he sees, moreover, as "its own distinctive tradition" competing with human rights for space in international institutions such as the United Nations. Thus, he avers anticolonialism was an alternative project, which "human rights in their more contemporary sense would have to displace" (Moyn 2010, 85–86).[5]

Moyn blurs the distinction between anticolonialism and decolonization; he does not parse these terms. Yet, in countries like Somalia that were independent by 1960, decolonization, not anticolonialism, would be opposite human rights during the period discussed by Moyn. Decolonization was an ongoing struggle of the people for self-determination against increasingly oppressive states whose new independence was far from complete. This continuing decolonization struggle reflected a realization that African leaders retrenched from rights language in comparison to the anticolonial era when it was "wielded vigorously and effectively by independence activists to challenge colonial subjugation and negotiate independence" (Ibhawoh 2018, 175). Farah shows the efforts to attain the full citizenship and rights promised by independence while the Cold War made a charade of national sovereignty, deeply compromising self-determination. The state maintained the appearance of sovereignty through repressive measures, violating human rights and spawning dissident voices. Opposing these violations is part of the human rights struggle of decolonization during the Cold War, which resisted the interference of the super powers detrimental to rights and freedoms.

The breach of national sovereignty is a source of shame, or "embarrassment," for Soyaan and later Loyaan. Moreover, the patriarchal family is likewise a source of shame: violent, regressive, and owing its loyalty to the state more so than to kin. State, nation, patriarchy, clan pull Somalis in different directions, creating breakdowns of meaning. Loyaan's disorientation is quite profound, especially when he tries to map contemporary Somalia onto what he thought he knew: "He felt embarrassed by all this ... *What am I? Who am I? Whom am I dealing with? What century is this? Of what era must I partake fully, actively?*" (1979, 162, italics in original). Not having an anchor in history is the difficulty. Loyaan confronts a perplexing overlay of old and new that undermines his confidence in his modernity as an educated, previously apolitical, medical professional.

Confusions of identity stem from the hold of patriarchal patterns of authority that flow from family to state and back to family, maintaining a seamless hold on public and private life. Keynaan, the twins' father, exemplifies the state's reach into the family. A torturer for the state who was purged after the death of one of his victims, Keynaan reinstated himself by lying for the regime and betraying his familial ties to his son. But he also emerges as torturer in his personal life. He beats the twins' mother, Qumman, who appears after Soyaan's death with "bruises" on her face, "her forehead had bled and dried" (1979, 26). He also beats viciously Beydan, his pregnant second wife and the widow of his torture victim, who does not survive the birth of her child (1979, 167). Keynaan was ordered to marry Beydan in a judgment of mock reparative justice, which made Beydan an antagonist to Qumman. As Keynaan's surrogate (despite or perhaps because of being abused by him), Qumman creates a negative dynamic that is aggravated by the twins' empathy for Beydan whom they see as a victim of the regime.[6] Beydan's humiliating circumstance—being married to her deceased husband's torturer—suggests an allegory of the people tethered without power to an abusive state.

This family circumstance contributes to the shame the twins feel as their father's sons but also as representatives of the elite to whom the leadership of the nation was supposed to devolve after independence. The General is a patriarch ("The father of the nation. The carrier of wisdom," 1979, 11) who refuses political power to the sons of independence and their modernizing influence. The sons, in turn, resist the patriarch in the name of the nation and hence in defiance of the state that has breached the integrity of the nation by coming under Soviet influence. As one of Soyaan's associates, Ibrahim, explains, the dissidents vowed "to serve not the interests of any superpower but this nation's" (150–151). Therefore, the twins feel a national humiliation being Somalis under Barre's, Soviet-backed dictatorship. Soyaan told his father: "But I feel humiliated, I feel abused, daily, minutely. A friend of mine is in for anti-Soviet activities. But where are we? What era is this? Is this Africa or is this Stalin's Russia?" (Farah 1979, 11). As we saw, Loyaan echoed a similar dislocation referring to another clash—that of tradition, patriarchy, and modernity. Thus, both brothers suffer a historical confusion: they do not recognize the "era" they are in. In an interview that reflects back on the Cold War, Farah has spoken about "the Soviet-managed ideological climate in Somalia" and described the country as "a puppet of the Soviet bloc" in the 1970s (Farah 2019, 5). Somalia's compromised sovereignty makes writing about it or in its name difficult.

Timothy Bewes identifies "postcolonial shame" as "an event of writing" where the "incommensurability" between form and reality opens a "gap" (a gap "felt as an event of the text") that is a provocation to the reader (Bewes 2011, 15, 26). Farah's interrogatives constitute such a gap and create the feeling of coming up short. As a writer, he tries to convey a sense of historical instability, the in-the-moment uncertainty of how to perceive the historical event. Bewes sees this "discomfort with form" as "a historical proposition," emanating from our proximity to catastrophic historical events that we cannot fully assess (2011, 18). The "mire" that Djebar alerts us to and that we find again in Farah's novel is indeed a "historical proposition," and for both writers historical failure is palpable. The eras are historical reversals, betrayals of aspirations to freedom of the independence era (Taoua 2018, 147).

Soyaan grappled with the extent of torture on the continent. The injuries of torture, moreover, are intimate, exacerbating his shame. As his lover, Margaritta, reports: "'Africa,' Soyaan used to say, 'embarrasses me'" (1979, 134). Ahmed-Wellie's testimony regarding torture victims reflects the embarrassingly intimate nature of the injuries: he is asked to examine the genitals of a victim whose face is covered and the badly beaten breasts of a female victim (1979, 40, 174). Moreover, he is frustrated in his attempt to identify these victims as they are among the disappeared. As noted, Farah sees Africa's torture regimes as a "re-creation of the same methods and things these career-soldiers learned from their colonial masters" (1979, 135). In the novel's climactic moment when the entire neighborhood has been ordered to sweep the streets for the visit of foreign dignitaries and Loyaan talks back to the officials, he loses his connection to his brother: "He was lonely. The voice which until recently had helped him with suggestions wouldn't come any more. He was alone" (1979, 213). This abandonment reflects his shame at being forced to sweep despite talking back. His resistance is futile and reckless, endangering his sister alongside him. He feels diminished and embarrassed, bereft of his brother's courage. Yet, alone in prison, Loyaan finds the voice again as he steels himself for renewed defiance (1979, 215). The isolation of the cell resolves the problem of shame but also situates him precariously in the gap of disappearance.

Clawing one's way out of the mire involves reasserting control over meaning. Words are a legacy the dead leave behind, and Soyaan's last words become particularly politicized. The contest to claim them pits the regime, but also the twins' parents, against Loyaan. The gap created by the "disarticulation" of disappearance is permanent; there is no possibility of a return to redress the finality of the loss. Within the space of the gap, "the falling apart" as Gatti puts it, "a battle is waged" for "meaning" (2014, 29). As a first-hand witness, Loyaan heard his brother call out his name ("Loyaan") repeatedly as he was dying. Rather than the affective scene of fraternal love one might expect, this is Soyaan's urgent plea to his twin that he take-up the cause. The regime understands this and moves aggressively to stamp out the words, creating a false story that Soyaan died uttering "Labour is Honour," or state propaganda (1979, 81). As a result, they create a myth of Soyaan's rectitude that only his brother sees as problematic. Even their mother accepts the regime's praise as fitting ("the honour due to him") and contrasts her view of things as they should be to Loyaan's "random choices," undercutting her son.

To steady himself when arguing with their father over Soyaan's memory, Loyaan recalls Soyaan's words once more. Soyaan had described their differences from their father as:

"Not so much generational as they are qualitative—the differences between us twins and our father. My father grew up with the idea that the universe is flat; we, that it is round. We believe we have a perspective of an inclusive nature—more global; our views are 'rounder.' We believe that his are exclusive, that they are flat (and therefore uninteresting) as the universe his insularity ties him to." (1979, 90)

Although on the surface this addresses the binary between a modern and a traditional Somalia, Soyaan insists the clash is not generational. The language of generational clash belongs instead to the patriarch. Keynaan, dismisses his sons' generation as spoiled and selfish beneficiaries of independence whose loyalty is to "the countries in which you received your academic training" (1979, 99). Soyaan's disavowal of this logic exposes it as an attack on world view and culture, coming back to the regime's targeting of intellectuals. The flat world view is insular but ironically has accepted Soviet interference. The global, round world view acknowledges cosmopolitan cultural influences but rejects the violation of national sovereignty. When Soyaan says these are qualitative rather than generational differences, he is positing them as conflicting and incompatible world views. Loyaan assimilates this point of view and wonders in his own turn:

> This was not so much a question of generation, linking or dividing persons on this continent. No, it was a question of cultural trends, what strands of cultural affinities hung down and reached one. In short, it was a question of how cultural discontinuities had woven Solomonic arabesques of difference between any two given persons. (1979, 163)

Loyaan articulates an urgent a question about futurity and hope. He wonders, given the degree of dissonance, "What future was there for the unborn?" (1979, 163). Holding on to Soyaan's diagnosis of his times renews his dissent, but the outlook for the future is bleak. Loyaan, by novel's end, is forced into exile to Serbia and must wait out his era on the sidelines. Farah has unambiguously put the emphasis on the meantime, which is the realm of the literary, of writers and intellectuals.

What measure of the real in the "place" of the disappeared?

Dissenting speech, as found throughout Djebar's oeuvre, takes the form of reading the present through the lens of the past. Although the emphasis usually falls on Djebar's feminist intervention, she sees history in broadly political terms, aiming to ignite debate and revision that cuts across paradigms. Her capture of historical material through interviews and oral histories in documentary film and fiction provokes both a reconsideration of the facts of history and a reflection on the challenges of making repressed histories consequential and transformative. *Algerian White*, as we saw, exhibits a degree of reflexivity by examining how writers sustain each other as resistant voices. Djebar's late novel, *La femme sans sépulture* (2002, "Woman without a Tomb"), revisits material from her film, *La Nouba des femmes du Mont-Chenoua* (1977). Together, the two works allow us to investigate how similar historical material travels from one medium to another (documentary film to historical novel), demonstrating, moreover, how Djebar builds a narrative method on revision, or telling and retelling. Consequently, the writer situates herself as a commentator on her own work, extending the types of exploration from *Algerian White* to herself. Words captured in the past resurface, functioning as a guide for reexamining the deeper past (the momentous events of Algeria's struggles against colonialism) whereas they are also ground from which to pivot to the troubled history of the 1990s. Moreover, the civil war of the 1990s, Algeria's "Black Decade," is the urgent point of reference held in common by *Algerian White* and *La femme sans sépulture*.

La femme sans sépulture incorporates the filming of the documentary as an event in the characters' past, establishing it as a historical layer that merits reexamination. Both the novel and *La Nouba* address the disappearance of Zoulikha, a female revolutionary in the Algerian War of Independence, although the film grapples more directly with how the masculine, heroic idiom of the War of Independence instrumentalizes her memory. The song with which the film closes exemplifies this established narrative, reminding the listeners that even in freedom "Zoulikha still lives in the mountains" as the revolutionary spirit of the people.[7] Coming at the end of an intensely feminized exploration of memory that seeks to disrupt such erasure of women's historical materiality, the song's masculinity is jarring. Djebar hopes to have unsettled us sufficiently to understand that she has offered us instead "the difference of a feminine political reason in decolonization" (Khanna 2008, 122). The novel then takes up the task of making Zoulikha a concrete, individualized historical subject, which became imperative for Djebar as a response to the violence of the 1990s. Although Djebar began writing the novel in the early 1980s, she did not complete it for almost 20 years, which indicates her shifting orientation to the material in response to historical events (Hitchcock 2010, 207). Moreover, revising a widely known history is the ongoing project that situates Djebar as a reader of her own work.

La Nouba skirts around the issue of how to represent Zoulikha's torture by evoking it allusively through the memories of other women who lived through the war. Djebar, moreover, structures the film in parts, imitating the "nouba," a symphonic form in Andalusian music (Khannous 2013, 5). The musical motif complicates the narrative structure by superimposing musical time over narrative time and slowing down the exposition of the film by making the viewer pass through the exact architecture of the musical form. Moreover, in Arabic, "nouba" means to take a turn or "get an opportunity," which declares Djebar's intent to give the women of Cherchell a chance to speak about the war, thereby multiplying the voices and perspectives in the film (Bentahar 2016, 415).

As is the case generally with disappearance, Zoulikha's history creates a crisis of language and challenges us to think of the disappeared in *"their place"* of disappearance (Gatti 2014, 31). Djebar's film and novel delineate different strategies around this problem of an inaccessible place. The novel's title alludes to the lack of burial and, by giving an account of the torture, the narration brings back the body in a sense.[8] *La Nouba*, on the other hand, tackles the place of the disappeared indirectly, offering a dense, visual meditation on setting with images of the coast, the mountains, the fields, the road, the town, the caves, but also of structures: white walls, windows, arches, watch towers, homes, barns, the wine barrels' factory, an elegant villa, and the fanciful suggestion of a counter-architecture, glass houses. Leila, the protagonist, is on a quest to find out details about her brother's disappearance. She lost most of her family in the war when she was 15, but her brother's unresolved disappearance haunts her. Her restless driving through the villages of Mont-Chenoua symbolizes her search. She interviews women survivors who remember different events of the war in the mountains, including the arrest and disappearance of Zoulikha. Leila's exploration of memory comes at another moment of crisis in her life. A western educated architect, she has returned to Cherchell to be with her husband, a veterinary doctor recently injured in a riding accident and confined to a wheelchair. Ali's silence and withdrawal are more debilitating than his lack of mobility (he is able to walk on crutches later in the film). An injured and contained masculinity, therefore, provides the opening for a woman's perspective on memory. The masculine gaze, rendered impotent in the husband's debility, allows Leila to break free.

Dressed in white and facing a white wall, she turns inward to her "fond" memories. She then slowly approaches a window to look out and her mind returns to childhood memories of the war. The visual emphasis on topography frequently framed through windows (of a building or a car), the slits of the watchtower, or the opening of a cave suggests that this kind of looking is a form of listening that makes the women (from children to grandmothers) and their activity come to the foreground. The topographic realism is counterpoised by the fantastic captured in the film's visualization of Leila's grandmother's storytelling to the young Leila. The storytelling scene then becomes collective as the screen fills with story circles, and the role of the women as holders of memory becomes apparent.

Yet, the lacuna from the absence of a causal narrative of her brother's loss remains, illustrating how forced disappearance represses the story of torture. Typically, in the Algerian War of Independence the disappeared were torture victims who either succumbed to their injuries or whose visible scars made them dangerous witnesses, and hence they were killed. Disclaiming responsibility, the state would invariably announce that they released the prisoner and that they disappeared thereafter (Klose and Geyer 2013, 186). Leila's wanderings create a web of associations that takes the place of her brother's absent story. Zoulikha's disappearance, on the other hand, witnessed and remembered by many, stands in as a collective symbol of those lost, although Djebar both acknowledges and resists this symbolic function.

Evoking the disappeared inevitably draws attention to the limits of what we know. Thinking of the experience as situated, as a place, challenges us to imagine. As Ranjana Khanna notes, Djebar understands fictionalization as a necessary part of documentary: "the documentary, then, becomes very planned and can be crafted almost fictionally, as if to make a political intervention, articulating hope through fictionalized documentation." Representation must be disrupted and resituated because the place from where women can speak and be heard cannot simply be assumed (Khanna 2008, 127–128). Despite the film's fictional premise of Leila's quest for her brother's story, *La Nouba*'s groundbreaking feminist aesthetics have elided the other challenge of representation: grappling with the place of disappearance.

La femme sans sépulture follows the filmmaker of *La Nouba* (a fictionalized stand-in for Djebar) who returns to the area of Mont-Chenoua 20 years after making the film, seeking to complete her investigation of Zoulikha's torture and disappearance. Yet instead of documentary, the reader encounters a disjuncture between the real and the improbable that recalls the fantastic scenes in *La Nouba*: Zoulikha's voice, speaking from the dead, interrupts the narrative four times in chapters addressed to her daughter Mina, who had visited her in the mountains shortly before her arrest. The fictionalized details of what happened to Zoulikha suggest a different measure of the real, necessary for the historical reopening of the narrative of torture. This type of realism was not essential to the making of *La Nouba*, which focused on the collective experience of women (hence, the *nouba* motif) accessed via the memorialization of Zoulikha.

In *La femme sans sépulture*, Djebar imagines Zoulikha's experience of torture, giving the reader an entry into that difficult emotional space skirted in the film where disappearance remains opaque as a sister's unresolved and unresolvable mourning for a brother. Moreover, the altered historical context of "cette nouvelle saignée" ("this new bloodbath") of the 1990s gives Zoulikha's resistance a different resonance, relaunching her as a historical figure for a new purpose: shaming the Front de libération nationale (FLN), former revolutionaries who are currently oppressors. The wave of disappearances, of history repeating itself and even accelerating in 1990s Algeria, creates new urgency around disappearance: "des milliers d'innocents sont portés disparus, à leur tour, parfois sans sépulture" ("millions of innocents have been disappeared, now in their turn, sometimes left without a tomb") (2002, 218). Seeing the present as an ironic repetition of colonial violence, Djebar finds the reason why it is appropriate to give Zoulikha a fictionalized voice and sensitize contemporary Algerians to the betrayal of their postcolonial state. Djebar unmasks the regime's appropriation of the heroic narrative of the War of Independence for its propaganda (a target of her critique in *Algerian White* as well) whereas her attention to Zoulikha's historicity underscores the materiality of those being disappeared in the "new bloodbath."

In the "Avertissement," Djebar announces the imperative to document: "Dans ce roman, tous les faits et détails de la vie et de la mort de Zoulikha ... sont rapportés avec un souci de fidélité historique, ou, dirais-je, selon une approche documentaire" (2002, n.p., "In this novel, all the facts and details of the life and death of Zoulikha are presented with historical fidelity, in what I would describe as a documentary approach.") Through the use of personal pronouns, Djebar asserts her prerogative and authority as a creative artist to tell Zoulikha's story in the manner in which she deems most effective. At the same time, this artistic prerogative follows a model and precedent, the images of the ancient mosaics in Cherchell: "J'ai usé à volonté de ma liberté romanesque, justement pour que la vérité de Zoulikha soit éclairée davantage, au centre même d'une large fresque féminine—selon le modèle des mosaïques si anciennes de Césarée de Maurétanie (Cherchell)" (2002, n.p., "I used the artistic license of a novelist precisely so that Zoulikha's truth will be revealed to advantage, as if she were the center of a depiction of women in a fresco, such as we see in the ancient mosaics of Cherchell.").

The mosaics portray the Sirens episode from Book 12 of the *Odyssey*, and hence they are also a literary allusion, situating one text in relation to another. At a time of political despair, when Djebar is revisiting a painful history for its lessons, she turns to Homer via these ancient mosaics that locate the Homeric tradition in her geography. Emphasizing these cultural links across the Mediterranean, Djebar creates a deeper resonance for her challenges as a writer. The filmmaker/narrator of the novel visits these mosaics and is struck by the parallel in storytelling circumstances. Circe warns Odysseus about the content of the Sirens' song ("woe to the innocent who hears that sound" [XII: 50]) without specifying what the songs are about. In Odysseus's account of what he heard, the sirens call their song "our song of Troy" (XII: 234) and claim that the men returning from war "goeth more learned" (XII: 236) after listening because: "No life on earth can be/Hid from our dreaming" (XII: 244–245). Inspired by the mosaics, Djebar uses the allusion to the *Odyssey* to comment on the impossible dimensions of stories of suffering. But she also signals her capacity for "dreaming" like the Sirens, and thus for imaginative rendering. The Sirens' song, seductive and for Odysseus, necessary, gives witness to war through dream. Like the sirens, Djebar wants to hold her readers captive to the details of Zoulikha's suffering, the how of her torture and death, despite their resistance to it. The reception of a torture narrative faces a pull and tug dynamic that opposes "a demand for a collective and political public accounting" to the resistance or refusal of such narratives because of the details they convey (Harlow 1992, 252).[9]

The image of the tied-up Odysseus listening to the Sirens's song suggests the reader's capture by the narrative. Reading brings on an immobilization, a voluntary involuntariness. Djebar evokes powerfully the attraction/repulsion dynamics of such stories, but also the reader's courage in risking some loss of autonomy to surrender to the story. Alternatively, to refuse the details of such stories is to be complicit in a historical forgetting that allows atrocities to repeat—an urgent lesson at the moment of the novel's composition. Djebar urges us to accept her mediated, artistic account of Zoulikha's torture for its truth and seize the moment to take stock of the last decade ("ces derniers dix ans au moins," 218).

From within this Homeric idiom and despite its allusive prose, *La femme sans sépulture* conveys with precision French practices of torture, and repeats the particular euphemisms used to name these. Zoulikha anticipates "le supplice de l'hélicoptère" where she would be interrogated under threat of being thrown out of a helicopter so that she would land "comme une figue trop mûre, abandonée sur un versant de notre montagne" ("like an overripe fig, abandoned on a slope of our mountain" [2002: 65]). Electroshock in the vagina is layered with references to birth and sexual passion. This confusion of discourses reflects the code words used during torture where the prisoner was expected to "labor" until she has *produced the information*" (Lazreg 2007, 133). The "pregnancy metaphor" supports the justification that torture saves lives by gaining information (Lazreg 2007, 133). Sexual torture, referred to as a "séance," had a "stagelike quality" that underscored elements which lend it an episodic wholeness (Lazreg 2007, 131). In the novel, Zoulikha emphasizes her sexual history as wife to three different men and mother to four children in a deeply patriarchal society. The interchangeable "Torture ou volupté," makes her sexual history bear on her experience of torture (2002, 198). Speaking as one destroyed by the violence targeting her gender and sex in particular, Zoulikha dissociates from her body and speaks from beyond it, a premise possible by the narrative's fictionalization.[10] Zoulikha's memory of pain muddles bodily sensations. Torture, birth, and intercourse converge with immense destructive power against the self. Hanging onto life if only barely and as if suspended beyond time ("hors du temps," 2002, 198), Zoulikha speaks of her body as possibly awaiting a metamorphosis. Yet, the insistence on the materiality of the body is hard to miss. We do not slide from references to the body in pain to a metaphor of birds in flight, for example, a common motif in torture of male resistance fighters, but from torture to birth or intercourse, both decidedly embodied experiences. And, moreover, these references are anchored in the lived life, the historical subject's biography posited through fiction.

Djebar's revision of her own work becomes apparent in her effort to explain her output as a filmmaker and address the skepticism of her critics who saw her language practices in *La Nouba* as problematic (Bentahar 2016, 426). In the novel, she discusses the importance of respecting communal attitudes that both demand exposure of the facts and insist on dignity. The "filmmaker" asks the women who remember Zoulikha what is more important in telling her story, "le respect ou la fidélité?" ("respect or verisimilitude?" 51). Their answer is that treating Zoulikha in a dignified manner and not showing images of her body is more important than absolute fidelity to the facts. However, the interviewees also tell her that she is different from the sensation seeking journalists. She is one of their own to whom they are willing to narrate Zoulikha's story so that they can be rid of the bitterness ("l'amertume") in their mouths (2002, 48). The community's recognition of the filmmaker, therefore, opens up the story of the individual once more to the collective, not through symbolization this time but by exposing the historical entanglements of that community. Zoulikha's history is also the women's history as it is their memory of her that brings her story to life.

Djebar's narrator notes how the women's stories fit into each other as "une histoire dans l'histoire" (2002, 129). In French, where history and story are both the same word ("histoire"), the statement is ambiguous: is it a story within a story, a story within a history, or a history within a story? More provocatively, the narrator explains that we follow the narrative thread of the women's testimonies in order to find our [contemporary Algerian women's] liberation at the end: "pour, à la fin, nous découvrir ... liberées" ("so that in the end, we can discover ourselves liberated" [2002, 129]). What is the meaning of this liberation, this purging of bitterness? Liberation is entangled in exposure, recognition, a surfacing in narrative, and thus a breaking through to visibility. It is not accidental that Djebar envisions liberation at the moment when she returns explicitly her earlier text, in this case *La Nouba*, and reexamines its premise. A conversation in her own head, in the writer's voice, posits that which remains unrealized but needs to remain a possibility.

Both Djebar and Farah confront disappearance as a crisis that requires "building a language suitable for that which is not easy to talk about" (Gatti 2014, 118). Their narratives of disappearance experiment with the human rights mode of "narrated lives," which appear in testimony, memoir, NGO websites, human rights reports, and many more formats (Schaffer and Smith 2004). Capturing the arc of a life interrupted by catastrophe offers a measure of reality that can potentially bring public recognition to victims. But literature also occupies a long meanwhile during dark times when the only space for dignity, recognition, and truth is held by words. Writers not only produce new works but their practices of intertextuality and allusion keep accessible a literary corpus addressing disappearance.

Notes

1 Peter Hitchcock offers the idea of the "long space" to capture how the novel as postcolonial form posits an extended time to create (or keep alive) the possibility of historical transformation (2010, 10). His study focuses on examples of trilogies and tetralogies by postcolonial writers and, in this context, he reads Farah and Djebar side by side.
2 Farah also makes allusion to "Requiem" stanza I: "At dawn they came and took you away" (Akhmatova 1973, 103). For example, Soyaan anticipates his arrest as a similar scene: "When they finally come, having broken the pride of dawn, they will find me prepared" (1979: 8). In his memorandum, he warns, "Listen to the knock on your neighbour's door at dawn. Harken: the army boots have crunched grains of sand on the pavement by your window. Listen to them hasten" (1979, 37).
3 Djebar is referring to Kateb Yacine and Abdelkader Alloula, whom I mentioned earlier. The question of how to talk about history "remain[s] a gaping hole, a dead eye" with the exception of the work left by these two (2000, 128).
4 John Masterson, drawing a parallel between Farah's *Variations* trilogy and Djebar, describes Farah's labyrinthine narrative that records a "pervasive sense of disintegration." This sense of disintegration reflects a similarity between both authors' effort to speculate about what happens behind the state's veil of secrecy (2013, 33).

5 In a postcolonial critique of Moyn's thesis, Joseph R. Slaughter situates the opposition between sovereignty, or self-determination, and human rights within a wider discourse of the period: "In the 1960s, the insistence that self-determination was not a human right and that anticolonial struggles were not human rights struggles was a partisan political claim that rejected countervailing third wordlist arguments like those articulated at Bandung in 1955" (2018, 759).

6 In the fierce competition for honour and social standing, Qumman wants to diminish Beydan and hence blames her for Soyaan's death. Loyaan does not believe this but Beydan cannot speak for herself from her subaltern position.

7 Fabian Klose and Dona Geyer stress the extent to which the women of the rebel areas suffered the consequences of French repression and their practices of collective punishment (2013, 147–148). The wilderness of the mountains was prized for being free of French surveillance. As the war continued, however, the French practiced a "scorched earth strategy" which included napalm bombings (Klose and Geyer 2013, 150). Djebar includes historical footage showing the bombings in her film.

8 According to the women's testimony in *La Nouba*, Zoulikha's body was left on the streets of her village and the people were forbidden from burying her. On the second day, however, the body disappeared and what happened to it remained a mystery. Zoulikha disappeared in 1957. In 1982, a man claimed to have buried her remains, which were eventually identified (Mortimer 2016, 139).

9 Harlow discusses Simone de Beauvoir's intervention on behalf of Djamila Boupacha, a victim of torture by the French. Beauvoir insisted on "'a complete account'" of Boupacha's ordeal to overcome the French public's self-perception as human rights respecting guardian of the Enlightnment (1992, 252). To push past these attitudes of denial, the narrative of torture had to be unambiguous and matter of fact.

10 Djebar echoes other African writers, such as Yvonne Vera, who felt it was imperative to render full accounts of women's experience of sexual violence in war and but did so in a very layered, symbolic prose, as we find in *Without a Name* (1994) and *Stone Virgins* (2002).

Works cited

Adam, Ian. "The Murder of Soyaan Keynaan." In *Emerging Perspectives on Nuruddin Farah*, edited by Derek Wright, 331–344. Trenton, NJ: Africa World Press, 2002.

Akhmatova, Anna. "Requiem."In *Poems of Akhmatova*, translated by Stanley Kunitz, Max Hayward. Boston: Little, Brown and Company, 1973.

Bentahar, Ziad. "A Voice with an Elusive Sound: Aphasia, Diglossia, and Arabophone Algeria in Assia Djebar's *The Nouba of the Women of Mount Chenoua*." *Journal of North African Studies* 21, no. 3 (March 2016): 411–432. DOI: 10.1080/13629387.2016.1150183.

Bewes, Timothy. *The Event of Postcolonial Shame*. Princeton: Princeton University Press, 2011, www.jstor.org/stable/26287348.

Capdepón, Ulrike. "Review of *Surviving Forced Disappearance in Argentina and Uruguay: Identity and Meaning*." *Human Rights Quarterly* 39, no. 2 (May 2017): 478–480. Project MUSE. DOI: 10.1353/hrq.2017.0028 by Gabriel Gatti.

Daoudi, Anissa. "Algerian Women and the Traumatic Decade: Literary Interventions."*Journal of Literature and Trauma Studies* 5, no. 1 (Spring 2016): 41–63. Project MUSE. no. 1. DOI: 10.1353/jlt.2016.0014.

Djebar, Assia. 1977. Directed by Djebar Assia. *La Nouba des femmes du Mont-Chenoua.* Film, Women Make Movies.

Djebar, Assia. *Le Blanc de L'Algerie.* Paris: A. Michel, 1995.

Djebar, Assia. *Algerian White,* translated by David Kelley, Marjolijn de Yager. New York: Seven Stories Press, 2000.

Djebar, Assia. *La femme sans sépulture.* Paris: Albin Michel, 2002.

Erikson, John. "Translating the Untranslated: Djebar's *Le blanc de l'Algérie.*" *Research in African Literatures* 30, no. 3 (Autumn 1999): 95–107, www.jstor.org/stable/3821019.

Fallaize, Elizabeth. "In Search of a Liturgy: Assia Djebar's *Le blanc de l'Algérie.*" *French Studies* 59, no. 1 (January 2005): 55–62. DOI: 10.1093/fs/kni069.

Farah, Nuruddin. *Sweet and Sour Milk.* Saint Paul, MN: Greywolf Press, 1979.

Gatti, Gabriel. *Surviving Forced Disappearance in Argentina and Uruguay: Identity and Meaning.* Translated by Laura Perez Carrara. New York: Palgrave Macmillan. DOI: 10.1057/9781137394156.

Harlow, Barbara. *Barred: Women, Writing and Political Detention.* Hanover, NH: Wesleyan University Press, 1992.

Hitchcock, Peter. *The Long Space: Transnationalism and Postcolonial Form.* Stanford: Stanford University Press, 2010.

Homer. *The Odyssey.* Translated by Robert Fitzgerald. New York: Vintage, 1990.

Ibhawoh, Bonny. *Human Rights in Africa.* Cambridge, UK: Cambridge University Press, 2018. DOI: 10.1017/9781139060950.

Khanna, Ranjana. *Algeria Cuts.* Stanford: Stanford University Press, 2008.

Khannous, Touria. *African Pastsand Futures: Generational Shifts in African Women's Literature, Film, and Internet Discourse, Presents.* Lanham, MD: Lexington Books, 2013.

Klose, Fabian, Geyer, Dona. *Human Rights in the Shadow of Colonial Violence: The Wars of Independence in Kenya and Algeria.* Philadelphia: University of Pennsylvania Press, 2013, www.jstor.org/stable/j.ctt3fhw4p.

Lazreg, Marnia. *Torture and the Twilight of Empire.* Princeton: Princeton University Press, 2007. DOI: 10.2307/j.ctt1bmzmz7.

Lukács, Georg. "Narrate or Describe." In *Writer and Critic and Other Essays,* 110–148. New York: Grosset and Dunlap, 1971.

Masterson, John. *The Disorder of Things: A Foucauldian Approach to the Work of Nuruddin Farah.* Johannesburg: Wits University Press, 2013, www.jstor.org/stable/10.18772/12013045706.

Moolla, F. Fiona. *Reading Nuruddin Farah: The Individual, the Novel and the Idea of Home.* Woodbridge, Suffolk, UK: Boydell & Brewer, 2014. DOI: 10.7722/j.ctt4cg5w2.

Mortimer, Mildred. "Zoulikha, the Martyr of Cherchell, in Film and Fiction." *PMLA* 131, no. 1 (January 2016): 134–139. DOI: 10.1632/pmla.2016.131.1.134.

Moyn, Samuel. *The Last Utopia: Human Rights in History.* Cambridge: Belknap Press of Harvard University Press, 2010. DOI: 10.2307/j.ctvjk2vkf.

Schaffer, Kay, Smith, Sidonie. *Human Rights and Narrated Lives: The Ethics of Recognition.* New York: Palgrave Macmillan, 2004. DOI: 10.1057/9781403973665.

Shringarpure, Bhakti. "Nuruddin Farah and the Cold War in Somalia. Interview with Bhakti Shringarpure." *Research in African Literatures* 50, no. 3 (Fall 2019): 4–6. DOI: 10.2979/reseafrilite.50.3.03.

Slaughter, Joseph R. "Hijacking Human Rights: Neoliberalism, the New Historiography, and the End of the Third World." *Human Rights Quarterly* 40, no. 4 (November 2018): 735–775. DOI: 10.1353/hrq.2018.0044.

Talbayev, Edwidge Tamalet. "Whiting Out Algeria: On the Limits of Assia Djebar's *Le blanc de l'Algérie* as Post-Traumatic Liturgy." *CounterText* 4, no. 2 (August 2018): 212–235. DOI: 10.3366/count.2018.0128.

Taoua, Phyllis. *African Freedom: How Africa Responded to Independence.* Cambridge, UK: Cambridge University Press, 2018. DOI: 10.1017/9781108551700.

Index

Abani, Chris 54, 68, 69, 72
Abrahams, Peter 24–5, 29, 38n2, 38n4
Abrams, Kathryn 141
Achebe, Chinua 19, 45, 60n5, 172, 174n7
Adichie, Chimamanda Ngozi 72–3, 174n7
Aduaka, Newton 68, 78–9, 81, 82n9
Afghanistan 167, 172
Africa: as absent object 4; Africanist
  approaches to human rights and 8;
  Africans' individuality in literature 24;
  child as identity in 82n8; children as
  allegory for nationhood in 74;
  children as allegory for poverty in 110;
  as dark continent 3; demise of
  publishing houses in 64; dignity versus
  rights in 38n2; exclusion from
  humanity and 8; ICC's standing in 10;
  oral tradition in 35; Pan-Africanism
  and 21; postcolonial narrative of 57;
  realist accounts of 98; statelessness
  and 133n11; traditional family in 38
African Charter on Human and Peoples'
  Rights 18, 20
Afshari, Reza 60n1
Agamben, Giorgio 117–18
Agier, Michel 118, 124–27, 129
AIDS 107, 141
Akayesu, Jean-Paul 137, 139, 143–44,
  152n4
Akhmatova, Anna 181, 195n2
Akpan, Uwem 86, 94, 107–9, 110,
  111–12n17
Alcoholic Anonymous 65
Algeria 9, 177–83, 189–95, 195nn3–4,
  196nn7–8
Alloula, Abdelkader 179–80, 195n3
Amrouche, Jean 179, 181
apartheid 21–9
Apocalypse Now (film) 44, 80

Arango, Tim 87, 111n4
Arendt, Hannah 121, 127
Argentine National Commission on the
  Disappeared 158–59
Armenia 60n2
assemblage theory 10
Attah, Abraham 80
Azoulay, Ariella 6, 55, 138, 143–45

Bakhtin, Mikhail 87–8, 111n9
Balakian, Peter 60n3
Balzac, Honoré de 87
Bandung Conference (1955) 196n5
Barlet, Olivier 82n9
Barnard, Rita 97
Barre, Siad 99, 111n10, 183, 187
Barthes, Roland 117
Beah, Ishmael 54, 61n12, 65–6, 67
Beasts of No Nation (film) 68, 78–81,
  81n2, 82n5
Beauvoir, Simone de 196n9
Belgium 46, 50, 150
Beti, Mongo 19
Bewes, Timothy 187
Bhabha, Homi 167
Bloch, Ernst 38n4
Boltanski, Luc 89–90, 96
Botswana 20, 21, 22–3
Boucebci, Mahfoud 179
Boukhobza, M'Hamed 179
Boupacha, Djamila 196n9
Briki, Djamila 181
Brison, Susan 142–43, 154n11
Burundi 131
Bush, George W 174n1
Butler, Judith 158, 169–72, 173, 174n8

Cabral, Amilcar 56, 59, 60
Calhoun, Craig 89–90

Printed in the USA
CPSIA information can be obtained
at www.ICGtesting.com
LVHW011546290823
756637LV00005B/484